Facing Tomorrow

Facing Tomorrow

A Guide for Living after Loss

Phyllis McElwain, PhD, CADC

Library of Congress Control Number: 2010910652
ISBN: Hardcover   978-1-4535-4180-7
                 Softcover   978-1-4535-4179-1
                 Ebook   978-1-4535-4181-4

This book was printed in the United States of America.

To order additional copies of this book, contact:
Xlibris Corporation
1-888-795-4274
www.Xlibris.com
Orders@Xlibris.com
81780

Contents

The Meaning of Grief
     Defining the Grieving Process
          Conscious Reactions
          Unconscious Reactions
          Cultural/Societal Reactions
The Uniqueness of Grief
     Individual Grief Patterns
     Reasons We Grieve
     Reasons We Are Unprepared

The Meaning of Grief Work
     Factors Influencing Grief Work
          Age and Gender
          Personality Process
          Coping Efficacy
          Social Support and Cognitive Appraisal
     Purpose of Grief Work
     Goals of Grief Work

Preface

Death is an experience shared by all mankind. Yet it is a subject we do not like to contemplate or discuss. Without open discussion about loss and death, one is surprised, anxious, and fearful when the myriad of emotions surface during and after the loss of a loved one. This book discusses how one is affected by death, how to deal with the pain and loss, and how to go on living when in the beginning of the grieving process survival seems an impossible feat.

I chose to write this book because of my personal experiences with loss. After suffering a serious work-related injury, my husband survived against tremendous odds, learned to walk again, and lived twelve additional years from the initial accident. During this period he suffered numerous medical problems and endured fifty-five surgeries before developing a heart condition. He died at the age of forty-three of a massive heart attack.

I learned during this time there are many losses to grieve besides death itself. I also found I was woefully unprepared for dealing with any of these losses. Unfortunately, there were few resources in our area to assist me in processing my grief. I began gathering information and journaling about my feelings. This helped me through the difficult transitional times and gave me direction in restructuring my life after the loss.

I believe humans cope with crisis, trauma, and loss better if we understand what is happening to us and if we know what to expect. Having been an educator for a major part of my life, I view education as a valuable coping tool. The idea for my book, *Facing Tomorrow*, was conceived as I worked through my grieving process. I changed careers several years after the death of my husband and entered the field of mental health counseling. After starting private practice, I developed a grief education program of the same name as this book, which I have used in practice for the past fourteen years. When clients and participants in my seminars on grief asked if I had the program in book or tape form, I decided to formalize the information into a book.

While many of the feelings and views expressed in the book are my own, I also want to give readers information from some of the leading experts in the field of loss and reconstruction of life after death. This is not just a book for clinicians, but also a book for the survivors of a death experience. It is a resource for navigating the confusing and frustrating process of grief. It is not a how-to guide, but simply a description of the process of moving from the moment of loss toward healing and restructuring one's life.

While I have been a therapist for many years, I do not profess to have all the answers about grief. My goal is to share with you, the reader, information that may be helpful to you in your journey of grief. You will be able to identify with some of the information in this book. There also will be some information, which will have no meaning to your particular situation. One thing I learned on my grief journey is to choose those things, which helped me the most. It is my hope you will find some nugget of information that will prove useful in your life.

I would like to acknowledge the professional assistance of Dr. RonSonLyn Clark and Dr. Stephen Daniel for their advice, guidance, encouragement, and expertise. Rev. John Conn, a wonderful pastoral counselor and friend, gave me much-needed help in the early days of my loss. He also was instrumental in assisting me in my career change to mental health therapy. I want to acknowledge the wisdom I gained from my late husband, Gary "Jock" Steward, whose life and death inspired me to write about the life lessons we both learned. My present husband, James McElwain, encouraged me to persevere in the completion of this work and gave me his unwavering support. My support network of my late parents, Norma and Tommy Nichols; my sister, Freida Campbell, and her husband, David; and my son and daughter-in-law, Scott and Dawn Steward, continually encouraged me when times were difficult. I owe them as well as a host of friends a great debt of gratitude. Lastly, I want to thank my clients of the past years for allowing me to enter your private world of grief, which broadened my understanding of the grieving process.

Chapter 1

THE BEGINNING OF A JOURNEY

Isaiah 53:3 of the New International Version of the Holy Bible, in speaking of the suffering servant, says "A man of sorrows, and familiar with suffering." This verse aptly describes all of us who have experienced the loss of someone we loved. We definitely are filled with sorrow and well acquainted with suffering. Losing a loved one leaves a hole in our heart the size of the person lost.

Nothing in life prepares us for the journey, which is begun when a loved one dies. The death is a profound experience. The old life is lost forever. Things will never be the same again. The beginning of this journey through major life change is bewildering. Adding to the trauma is the overall lack of life skills necessary to deal with a change of this magnitude.

I should have expected my husband's death since he was hospitalized numerous times with life-threatening complications requiring fifty-five surgeries during the twelve years following his injury. But when death finally came, it was a shock to me. The last moment was so *final* and of such importance. I was shaken to my core by the realization eternity is truly a breath away. It made me realize it doesn't matter whether or not a death is anticipated. When the moment finally comes, it is sudden in its impact on those left behind.

Death is a major life-changing event. Yet we face this event with no preparation. Dr. Alan Wolfelt was one of the first experts in the field of bereavement to note the poor preparation most people have for dealing with loss. Our society strives to prepare us for every major event in our lives. We prepare for our careers by years of education and/or training in our chosen field. Graduation events are planned in great detail with many activities celebrating the completion of a milestone. In our modern society, weddings are planned far in advance with attention given to every detail. Usually, there is a period of being engaged to give the couple time to plan for the coming nuptials and to have time to become acquainted with each other's habits, personalities, values, and customs in order to build a more successful marriage. Births are looked forward to for months. Prospective parents are educated about the coming birth as well as impending parenthood. Divorce, another major life-changing event, has a period of distancing from each other before the final break.

Even smaller events, such as family vacations, receive time and attention from various family members in order to meet the expectations of the vacationers. There are christenings, baptisms, retirement preparations, and planning for many other milestones in life actively encouraged by society. Yet death, a major life event, usually comes totally unplanned and unexpected, leaving the survivors facing a disrupted life filled with disorienting and emotionally confusing feelings.

The bereaved survivors are thrust into this grief journey, totally clueless as to how to proceed with the process of grieving. Unprepared for the intensity of the emotions following the loss of a loved one, the survivors struggle to gain a foothold in the suddenly foreign world of bereavement. Is it any wonder many survivors feel as though they are going crazy?

In the beginning of the journey of grief, you say and do things that are very unlike your normal behaviors. Sometimes you do not know the person you've become, and the people around you often do not know this different person in their midst either! There seems to be no end to the stream of feelings, not just from day to day, but from minute to minute. The unpredictability of your reactions brings the realization that you do not understand grief at all. Surrendering to your grief takes great courage. It is admitting you are in pain, and you fear the task ahead. No matter how frightened you are, you must rise to meet the challenge of this journey. Judy Tatelbaum, in her book *The Courage to Grieve*, says,

> Having the courage to grieve leads to having the courage to live,
> to love, to risk, and to enjoy all the fruits of life without fear or

inhibition. For many of us it is our fear of loss, and the grief implicit in loss, that prevents us from fully living our lives.

In order to develop the courage to grieve, it is important to fully understand the grieving process.

What is grief?

Dr. Alla Renee Bozarth describes it in the following way:

Grief is a passion, something that happens to us, something to endure. We can be stricken with it, we can be victims of it, we can be stuck in it. Or, we can meet it, get through it and become quiet victors through the honest and courageous process of grieving.

In the writings of Dr. Alan Wolfelt, he says,

Grief is the constellation of internal thoughts and feelings we have when someone loved dies.

Grief is the deep pain felt when something or someone of great value is lost to us. Grief is an array of intense emotions flooding your life when it is shattered by the loss of someone. During grief, your very soul takes a direct hit, bringing a total loss of peace, harmony, and contentment in your life. Sympathy and kind words cannot begin to stem the flow of emotions spewing forth from the pain.

In the grief process, there are three types of reactions: (a) conscious reactions, (b) unconscious reactions, and (c) cultural reactions. Understanding each of these reactions impacts your grieving process. Knowledge helps you to successfully reconcile your loss. Lack of understanding can seriously impede your ability to reach a state of reconciliation.

Conscious Reactions

Conscious reactions are those of which you are aware in the initial phases of loss. Feelings of hurt, sadness, emptiness, and pain begin immediately upon experiencing the death of your loved one. Many survivors openly cry and show great emotional distress as part of the conscious reactions.

Tasks to be completed at the time of loss are actions, which represent conscious reactions to the loss. For example, there are legal and business formalities to perform. Arrangements must be made for disposition of the body. The funeral service must be arranged. Depending on where the loved one died, there can be numerous details to attend to during the initial hours following the death, such as dealing with hospice, the hospital, or law enforcement. Attending and participating in the visitation and funeral service, arranging for the burial and the committal service, contending with the numerous phone calls, and arranging for someone to take care of the arrival of food, flowers, and out-of-town visitors can be exhausting tasks. These will produce emotional conscious reactions.

Behaviors of wanting everyone to go away and leave you alone are common. Not being able to eat, feeling disoriented, being irritable, feeling needy, and being fearful are just a few of the conscious reactions a mourner may experience. In other words, you know you are doing and feeling these things. You are aware of your behaviors.

After the initial days pass, other actions such as visiting the gravesite, making arrangements for the marker, deciding about the loved one's belongings, changing financial affairs, securing death certificates, and taking over the responsibilities your loved one previously shouldered produce more conscious reactions such as "I don't want to do this!" "This is too much for me to bear!" "Please take my pain away."

Dealing with the expenses generated by the loss and tackling the massive number of thank-you notes, which must be sent after the death, are two additional activities mandating conscious decisions on the part of the mourner. Emotional reactions at this time may be wishing things were different, wishing you could wake up and have your old life back, and simply missing the daily presence of the one you loved. Missing the little things, the conversations, the jokes, and even the quarrels are reactions of which you are aware as you begin to process what happened.

Unconscious Reactions

Unconscious reactions are those feelings and actions that occur but of which you are unaware. These reactions can greatly affect your grief journey. One such action is the denial of the loss. This is not the logical knowledge that the loved one is dead. Of course, you know the loved one is dead because in most cases, you have seen the body. Denial is the sensation that the situation is not a real experience. It is feeling you will get back to normal when these first few days of activity are over. It is the sense of unreality you have about the whole event. It is the feeling that this is a temporary situation.

For me, it was as though I did everything I needed to do in automatic pilot. I kept thinking there would soon be an end to the whole unpleasant experience. I knew my husband was not coming back, but I had definitely not accepted the fact that he was not coming home again. Dr. Alan Wolfelt put it best when he said,

> You will first acknowledge the reality of the loss with your head. Only over time will you come to acknowledge it with your heart.

Adding to this sense of unreality is the unconscious thought that death is not possible in your own life. You know death is out there in the world, but you do not truly believe it will come to you and yours. Dr. Elisabeth Kubler-Ross, in her book *On Death and Dying*, discusses how we deny that we are mortal and will die someday. She says deep down inside, we have great unconscious fear of our own mortality. When death strikes so closely to us, that fear is intensified. We may not be fully aware of that fear, but it adds to our feelings of unease and anxiety.

Another unconscious reaction is the association of death with punishment for some perceived or undetermined bad behavior or thoughts by the deceased or surviving family members. Unconsciously not being able to distinguish from thoughts and deeds thus creates guilt in some survivors. This is often seen in the "if onlys" voiced by the survivors, producing further self-torture. Mourners often express dismay at the fact bad things do (and did) happen to those who did not deserve such a fate.

Unconsciously, the survivor may have an entitlement belief. This belief is "If I am a good person, I am entitled to a good life." When death comes, unconsciously, you feel deprived of the good life, which was expected because the loss so tremendously diminishes your life.

This entitlement belief led me to feel at times during my husband's long physical battle and subsequent death that fate had handed me a dirty deal. God was not listening to me. I had the task of resolving issues, not only with my faith but also with my resentment of other people who appeared to be untouched by difficult times and who seemed to have the perfect family life. These people still had their family circles intact. They could go on vacations. They could have more children. They were not struggling financially. It was easy to focus on all the good others had while I was dealing with harsh realities of life. I was resentful because to me, it seemed the difficult times came only to my family. Logical? No. But my unconscious sense of entitlement, which precluded bad things happening to us, allowed me to develop some resentment. It did not matter that this was not logical thinking.

Cultural/Societal Reactions

The cultural/societal environment in which you live dictates a large portion of your grief patterns. Different cultures, religions, and value systems provide a frame of reference for what is acceptable grief and what is not. Each family has traditions passed down through generations, and these traditions guide the grief patterns. These traditions and rituals prescribe not only the behaviors considered acceptable for the bereaved, but also include the customs pertaining to the visitation, services, hospitality, and numerous other customs of the community in which the bereaved person lives.

The service held for the deceased varies from culture to culture as to the form of mourning seen as acceptable—including length of time for the service, mourning period, and which particular rituals will be performed. The purpose of the traditions and rituals is to give the loved ones a sense of closure for the loved one's life in this world. These traditions and rituals signal the beginning of life for the survivors without the physical presence of the loved one in their daily lives. The funeral is a gift to the deceased from those who loved him. It is a celebration ritual commemorating his life in this world. It is saying, "We loved you. We cared about you. You were important to us."

The reality of the separation of the deceased from the mourners begins with the funeral in most cultures. This ritual provides an acceptable outlet for displaying the emotions felt by the survivors and to share their love for the deceased publicly with friends. It is also a forum for sharing the memories of the life lived by the deceased. Extended family and friends are united at this time as a support network for the bereaved.

It is important, however, for bereaved people to understand that this network of support is temporary. As those less close to the loved one return to their normal routines, the devastated mourners often find life a lonely cold place because there is no normal routine for the mourner after the funeral ritual.

One of the most influential cultural reactions affecting the survivor is one's spiritual or religious background. What you believe as a person has great impact on your grief. You may question your value system at this time. You may have doubts about where you are heading in life, what you want out of your life, and what exactly is your purpose now you have suffered this terrible loss. You may even question your faith.

Your faith may deepen. You may feel closer to God or to your higher power. You may realign your beliefs. One thing is certain: There will be a change. Death brings your core beliefs and truths to front and center. You examine them in minute detail as you walk your journey of grief. This does not mean your faith and beliefs lessen or weaken. It simply means you have a different view of life—what you believe and what you need to be fulfilled. You adjust some views because you learn more or, perhaps, because they must be adjusted to meet the needs of your new life. You become more aware of the importance of rituals and traditions, friendships and loved ones. You become in tune with the spirit of your soul. You learn the things that most soothe your soul and bring you inner peace as you move toward healing from the deep wound of loss.

The Uniqueness of Grief

Because you are a unique creature with different personalities, abilities, and viewpoints from others, you act and react to life experiences in a different way than others around you. Grief affects people differently, and therefore, each person will not grieve in the same manner.

> At the bottom every man (or woman) knows well enough that he (or she) is a unique human being, only once on this earth; and by no extraordinary chance will such a marvelously picturesque piece of diversity in unity as he (or she) is, ever be put together a second time.
>
> —Nietzsche

I have experienced great losses in my life. My husband died, as well as my beloved grandparents and parents. I have also lost some very dear friends. I know a great deal about how grief feels. I know how I dealt with it. However, I cannot say I know how you feel. This is because you are a different individual, and I am not you. I am not in your shoes. I did not have the relationship you had with your loved one. I do not have the thoughts and personality you have nor do I have exactly the same coping skills you possess. Each of us, who has experienced loss, share some common feelings and reactions; but our grief is *not* the same.

Just as grief varies among different mourners, it is important to understand that it also varies within families. Not understanding the uniqueness of each person's grief can compound the difficulty of the grieving process. It can even lead to problems between family members.

I counseled a couple whose child died. Each parent grieved in different ways. One parent was more emotional and cried a great deal. This parent also wanted to go to the cemetery every day. The other parent, coming from a family background of more stoic people, was more hesitant to show grieving behaviors. This parent also felt going to the cemetery was unnecessary. This parent did not feel the child was there nor was it a comforting activity. Each parent thought the other parent was not grieving in the "right way" and began to question the love each had for the child. Through counseling, this couple began to see there was no right or wrong way to grieve. Eventually, they were able to support each other instead of letting the death put a wedge between them.

So it is with all mourners. Some mourners are very emotional with their grief and will openly cry, wail, or show distraught behaviors. Others may be more reserved and not show the deep hurt they feel. Neither one is the wrong way to grieve, but each mourner must grieve in the way that helps him the most.

Author Ted Menten uses the illustration of putting on your shoes and socks to illustrate this difference in grieving patterns. Two children in his camp for kids undergoing chemotherapy were arguing about the correct way to put on their shoes and socks. One boy said that it was sock, sock, then shoe, shoe. The other boy was indignant with this process and steadfastly held to the idea that the correct way to do it was to put on a sock and a shoe, then the other sock and a shoe. Mr. Menten broke up the argument by suggesting they both wear sandals that day. However, he says that it reminded him one must be careful about giving absolute answers to questions because "a wise person knows there are many paths through a forest." So it is with the journey of grief. There are many paths through the forest of grief.

Another difference in the pattern of grief is the amount of time it takes for the journey. There is no time limit! It takes what it takes. Some people will process the grief faster than others. Some people move very slowly through their grieving process. There are so many variables to consider in determining the length of time. The age of the deceased, the relationship with the mourner, the coping skills of the mourner, and the circumstances of the death are just a few of the things impacting the length of time for grieving.

Length of the grieving period has absolutely nothing to do with how much you loved the person who died. The difference in the length of each person's grieving period is quite often greatly misunderstood by our society. This is most difficult for the mourner when others put a time constraint on the process. Others often blame widows and widowers if they start another relationship or marry too soon. I stress to clients, who ask how long their grief will last, the lack of a prescribed time limit to grief. Many mourners fear they are taking too long. It will take you as long as it takes you. Let no one dictate your grief.

Your relationship with the deceased loved one is like no other. Therefore, your grief will be different from the grief of others, no matter what their relationship was with the deceased. This is not to say others are not grieving. It simply means your grief, like your fingerprint, is unique only to you.

Your journey through grief is a journey through the seasons of healing. Dr. Bozarth calls this the "seasons of the soul." She calls this a journey through death and loss into renewal and life. You have fall (the death); winter (the mourning period); spring (the planting of new seeds, new life choices); and finally, summer (new blooms once more), which is a time of renewal of your life. The time of renewal means you are successfully living a different life without the physical presence of your loved one.

Dr. Alan Wolfelt says the journey through death and loss into renewal and life exemplifies grief is a process. It is not an event with a beginning and end. There is no such thing as one and done when you are grieving. The process of grief is an ebbing and flowing of emotions. One experiences ups and downs, along with constant changes, which slowly move one forward with the new life created by the loss. It also means you are on a journey with no time deadline. You are mapping your own course and following your own timetable. This understanding gives you permission to grieve the way you personally need to grieve. It allows you to have your own personal grief and enables you to allow others the same opportunity. Just as no two snowflakes are the same, no mourners grieve in exactly the same grief pattern.

Why do you grieve for loved ones who have died? Basically, you grieve because you lost something you loved very much. Grief is the flip side of the coin of love. Because you loved and loved deeply, you hurt to your core when the object of that love is taken away. Actually, you are grieving for yourself and your own sense of loss. The loved one who died no longer has physical feelings, but you are left behind—alive and capable of feeling—therefore, you are experiencing great emotional pain.

Grieving is a necessary and important process for your physical and mental well-being. It is a job, which must be done. Understanding the process is the major key to coping with loss. Doug Manning, in his writings on grief, says it is a natural reaction. He says that just as you rest when you are tired, drink when you are thirsty, cry out when you have pain, you grieve when you suffer loss. Grieving is a healing process for deep hurt.

The more intense the love, the more intense the hurt is when the loved one dies. The only way to avoid the pain of loss is to avoid loving or investing in anyone in your life. What an apathetic, hollow existence that would be! I do not believe anyone would give up a moment of happiness with the loved one in order to avoid the pain of loss. Loving makes a person vulnerable to hurt. But avoidance of loving in order to avoid pain makes a person live in the shadow of life—not fully participating, not committing, and not receiving the joy of fully living.

Since death and loss are such a part of the life cycle and will touch each of us numerous times in our lifetime before it actually comes for us, why are we so unprepared for grief? Part of that answer is that we live in a death-defying society. People do not want to dwell on the unpleasant subject of death. It is not a popular topic to discuss. Our society becomes uncomfortable when people show great distress or emotion. C. S. Lewis, in his book *A Grief Observed*, said the following in discussing his experiences after the loss of his wife:

> An odd by-product of my loss is that I'm aware of being an embarrassment to everyone I meet . . . perhaps the bereaved ought to be isolated in special settlements like lepers.

This was the first time in his life he felt so vulnerable. He felt he presented people with a problem of what to do with him. This is an excellent example of the fact that people do not know what to do or say to the person who is bereft. This reluctance to discuss death causes problems for not only the bereaved, but also for those people who would like to be able to help the mourner.

Acceptance of death is hard for our society. Talking about death often is seen as a negative attitude. No one wants to mention the *d* word. Since it is an uncomfortable topic for most people, when a death occurs, the survivor is unprepared to grieve. Those who could be of the most help don't know what to do or say. So living in this death-defying society, you find yourself rushing to get back to normal, not knowing how to deal with death as a natural experience of the life cycle.

Another reason for being unprepared to grieve has to do with the medical and technological advances made in the world today. Before modern technology, it was a common part of life for births and deaths to take place in the family home environment. Death often happened due to the lack of medical expertise in treating many common illnesses. The death toll among the young and elderly was very high. So death was a life event, which happened often and was a less formalized process than it is in our modern world. In early centuries most people died in the family environment surrounded by their loved ones. Compare that process to today where over 60% die in institutions such as hospitals and nursing homes.

With the advances in medical treatments, many procedures can be done to sustain life. Medical technology has contributed greatly to the decline of the death rate and increase of life expectancy. Hope that something can be done beats in the hearts of everyone when a loved one grows ill. There are many medical miracles performed today to save people who would have perished in previous years. Death is kept at bay, and life is sustained.

In order for life to be sustained, it requires the loved one to be in a facility with constant medical monitoring and care beyond what the family can do. This is not necessarily a bad thing, but it does remove families a step from the dying process. Removing death from the routine experience in family life leaves you less prepared to grieve.

Dr. Nancy O'Connor agrees in her writings about grief that the removal of the family from the deathbed has depersonalized death in modern society. This goes hand in hand with the advances in technology. Loved ones are cloistered in intensive care units or hospital rooms where family cannot be with them around the clock, and children are certainly not permitted to be in the rooms. The recent increase in palliative care and hospice care has done a great deal to return one of the great life-changing events—death—to a family-oriented experience.

My late husband always feared he would die in an intensive care unit in the hospital away from home. Fortunately, he was home from the hospital the last time for one week and died at home, the way he wanted. Dying in a hospital was a very real fear for him, and I quite understood why he felt the way he did about it. A momentous event, such as departing this world, should be in a place you love and, if possible, attended by those you love the most. You should be allowed to be, if at all possible, where you want to be when you make the transition from this life to the next.

Depersonalizing death has taken an important experience away from families. I was fortunate to be with several loved ones at this transitional time. It is truly an emotional and moving experience. It is an opportunity to be on holy ground with the ones who are most important to you. For me, it gave great peace of mind and lessened the fear of death when I was able to participate in the last moments my loved ones lived on this earth. We were able to say all that needed to be said, and my loved ones knew it was okay for them to go on ahead. We were able to assure them that those who were being left behind would be okay and be able to carry on with life. To be allowed to personally be a part of that process was very important in helping me to grieve my losses. It allowed me to feel, as writer Barbara Johnson put it, that they are "not gone . . . just gone on a head."

The journey of grief, once begun, begins a lengthy and time-consuming process. It is a journey, which is overwhelming, frightening, and often lonely. The road is long to reach the point where life is good, and joy can once again be felt.

In the early part of this journey of grief, the tasks seem impossible. The hurt is so intense and pain so deep that it does not seem possible to ever experience joy again. The Bible promises this is possible when in John 16:20 it says, "And you will be sorrowful, but your sorrow will be turned to joy." It is hard at the time of such devastating loss to see how this could ever be.

You are journeying through one of the most intense experiences of your life. You cannot be an idle bystander. You cannot withdraw from the world. Yes, at the beginning of this journey, you will be very sorrowful. With commitment and dedication to the healing work before you, someday joy will return; and through the process of grief, you will have learned to savor those precious moments to the fullest.

Chapter 1 References

1. Aiken, Lewis, R. 2001. *Dying, Death and Bereavement.*
2. Bozarth, Alla Renee, PhD. 1990. *A Journey through Grief.* Center City, MO: Hazelton.
3. Grollman, Earl A. 1974. *Concerning Death: A Practical Guide for the Living.* Boston, MA: Beacon Press.
4. Johnson, Barbara. 2004. *Laughter from Heaven. P. 30, Nashville,* TN: W Publishing Group.
5. Kubler-Ross, Elisabeth, MD. 1969. *On Death and Dying.* New York, NY: Macmillan
6. Manning, Doug. 1979. *Don't Take My Grief Away: What to Do When You Lose a Loved One.* San Francisco: CA: HarperCollins Publishers.
7. Menten, Ted. 1994. *After Goodbye: How to Begin Again after the Death of Someone You Love.* Philadelphia, PA: Running Press.
8. O'Connor, Nancy, PhD. 1984. *Letting Go with Love: The Grieving Process.* Tucson, AZ: La Mariposa Press.
9. Staudacher, Carol. 1987. *Beyond Grief: A Guide for Recovering from the Death of a Loved One.* Oakland, CA: New Harbinger Publications.
10. Tatelbaum, Judy. 1980. *The Courage to Grieve: Creative Living, Recovery, and Growth through Grief.* New York, New York: Harper Row.
11. Wolfelt, Alan D., PhD. 1992. *Understanding Grief: Helping Yourself Heal.* Muncie: IN: Accelerated Development Inc. p.3, p.17
12. Yancy, Philip. 1990. *Where Is God When It Hurts?* Grand Rapids, MI: Zondervan Publications.

Chapter 2

GRIEF WORK

Over two million people die in the United States each year. Most of these people leave behind someone to mourn their passing. Untold thousands of people experience grief from other major life-changing events. Sadly, few of these people know how to do grief work.*

Every mourner has before him the tremendous job of grief work. This job involves the mourner in many tasks over a period of months, perhaps even years, to attain healing from loss. The biggest step in beginning grief work is to be proactive and to commit to the healing process. You must set your intention on taking control of an out-of-control situation. To heal, you must refuse to remain a victim. Author Doug Manning says, "You must constantly remind yourself that you truly want to heal."

Facing adversity of any kind takes strength and courage. What is courage? It is doing what has to be done even though you may not feel like doing it. You may not want to do it, or you may even fear to do it, but you do it anyway. That is courage. We have an inner core of strength and courage that sometimes is not tapped until a major adversity arises. Former prisoner of war (POW) of the Vietnam War Bruce Laingen said it best when he said, "We're like tea bags. We don't know our own strength until we get into hot water."

Having the courage and strength to commit to healing is of utmost importance to the mourner. People ask me how my family and I had the strength to survive over twelve years of the health problems experienced by my husband. I think Mr. Laingen's quote sums it up rather well. Looking back on those times does make them appear overwhelming, but when you are in the midst of the suffering, you find the strength to take it moment by moment. In the beginning of the journey, we did not see the whole trip. We dealt with the journey one step at a time.

Christian author Stormie Omartian, in her book *Just Enough Light for the Step I'm On*, verifies this in her writings about life and God's grace. She says we pray for grace and light to find our way. Usually, we want the whole way lighted, and we want a mountain of grace. Not only do we want those two huge requests, we want it all at once! In reality, all we actually need is just enough for the step we are on at the time. That is how my family and I made it through those difficult years. That is how the strength to do the grief work comes to you. Calling forth just enough strength for the step you are on is sufficient.*

Dr. Alan Wolfelt, in *Understanding Your Grief*, emphasizes grief is not a disease. Therefore, you cannot be cured from it. In other words, you do not ever get over it or get finished with it. Grief is a deep emotional wound. Like any wound, grief can be healed, but a scar will always remain. Reaching healing, which is the purpose of grief work, simply means you are able to reconcile this drastic life-changing event of loss into your life and once again experience the joy of living.

Why Grief Work?

We refer to this chaotic process as grief work because it is the hardest work you will ever do. It is a job you did not apply for and for which you were not trained. It is a job foisted on you and which you must do alone. However, it is a labor of love. It is difficult to do because we invested so much of ourselves in loving someone else. That person died, and we face the huge job of reconciling the loss. It is because we loved in great measure that we find this labor so difficult.

A study by Henderson, Hayslip, and King analyzed the relationship between adjustment and bereavement-related distress. One approach the researchers cited in referencing the importance of grief work and

---

* Statistics from: O'Connor, Nancy, PhD. *Letting Go with Love: The Grieving Process.* Tuscon, AZ: La Mariposa Press.

adjustment to changes was the dual process model of coping with bereavement proposed by Stroebe and Schut (1999). This model explores the idea of grief work as the act of contemplating and processing the events, relationships, changes, and emotions associated with the loss. Coping within this system is described as a relationship between the dual processes of grief work and the initiation of new roles, life changes, and methods for avoiding the processing of bereavement experiences.

Factors Influencing Grief Work

The dual process model of coping with bereavement calls attention to our generalized adjustment processes, which we use to navigate through many stressful life events even before we encountered an experience with death. When we consider how we cope with other life difficulties, we find our general adjustment process has a great deal to do with how successfully we will complete the adjustment to our losses. This is substantiated by the information collected in this longitudinal study.

The research group of Henderson, Hayslip, and King found that there are several factors influencing bereavement distress. Age and gender were two factors. The age of the mourner and the age of the deceased had a clear impact. There are different stressors on survivors at different ages in life.

For example, when my husband died, I was a young widow with a child to rear. The stress of earning a living and single parenting was a different kind of stress than the stress an older person faces upon the death of a spouse. At an older age, the loneliness seems to be a bigger stressor. Younger widows and widowers with young children never seem to have enough time to be alone with their grief. Older ones seem to have too much alone time.

The age of the deceased person impacts the grief process greatly. While we loathe losing our loved ones at any age, it is easier to reconcile the death if the survivor feels the deceased led a full life, had a quality life, and/or was able to accomplish his goals in life. The death of a child or younger person leaves the mourner to feel that the life was cut short. The death ends the promise that life held. It leaves future accomplishments unachieved. The milestones that will never be celebrated are additional stressors.

The gender of the mourner is another influence on the grief process. Women generally have a larger support network of friends who are familiar and comfortable with emotionally charged conversations. Men do not. Although men have good friends, as a rule, they do not share emotions with each other as women do in friendships. When a death occurs, men are often left with no outlet to express feelings and, quite often, do not know how to express what they feel.

Moreover, research indicates it is not unusual for men to enter into romantic relationships more rapidly after the death and to demonstrate more significant struggles accepting the loss. Women typically report greater emotional distress, admit to feeling helpless, and express more significant changes in identity and social role than men.

In this longitudinal study, personality processes were another factor found to impact the grief work of survivors. It was noted that individuals with depression, anxiety, or other psychological conditions before the loss had more difficulty in adjusting to the loss of the loved one. This finding supports the notion that problems with adjustment and adaptation prior to the death will intensify with the death, strongly influencing the course of bereavement and coping during the months and years following the loss. People with a more optimistic personality generally fare better when faced with hard times than the ones with a more pessimistic view on life.

Furthermore, the degree of self-confidence the survivor has prior to the loss has an impact on the manner in which the survivor approaches the adjustment to the death. A perceived level of control of one's life and the belief in one's competency were found to be personality processes, which positively impacted the adjustment to loss.

The third influence on the grief work found in this study was the coping efficacy of the bereaved. Coping responses affect both the physical health and the psychological well-being during grief. Poor coping skills before the death will cause great difficulty after the loss. Coping skills such as being able to set problem-focused goals, using spiritual beliefs and resources, and being able to draw positive meaning from the series of events are all found to be efficacious when adjusting to bereavement. While men showed more active approaches to conquering bereavement, helpful in demonstrating coping utility, women found it more helpful to use social and emotion-based strategies.

The fourth important factor found to be an influence on the survivors' grief work was social support and cognitive appraisal. This is not a surprising finding. Survivors who have a strong social support system are found to have less depressed mood, greater planning and goal-oriented behavior, and suffer less negative functioning than those who do not possess that network. Greater family cohesion or a network of close friends gives the survivor needed support in adjusting to the loss. When a survivor has a positive cognitive appraisal of his ability to cope and deal with the loss, more positive behaviors are demonstrated.

I was fortunate through all my losses to have an excellent support system of family, extended family, in-law family, and a host of friends who stayed the course with me and helped me keep my equilibrium. One's religious community is also a great provider of support for those mourners who have a strong connection to a church base.

In my practice, I see examples of difficulty in coping when the survivor has no family left or the family does not live near enough to the bereaved to lend support. This leaves the survivor adrift and feeling truly alone. Among the older population, the intense loneliness and isolation felt has a serious impact on their physical and mental health. Having unity within families, community within social groups, and actively participating in the affairs of everyday life are important ways to positively influence the process of grief work and help relieve the distress. Providing these long-term support networks, especially for the elderly or those with little family, is an excellent program for communities and religious organizations to undertake.

Grief work is a time of convalescence. It is a time to take active steps to assure the outcome of healing. Just as we have convalescence from illness or surgery, we need convalescence from the wound of loss. It is helpful for the survivor to understand some of the influences that will affect the grief work he does and to understand the importance of actively building a good support network to aid in this work. The support network is only half the battle.

As the study points out, cognitive self-appraisal is the other half. We have to feel we can make a positive choice to participate in our own healing process. We cannot expect others to do the work for us. Neither can we fall into self-pity nor can we stick our heads in the sand, hoping the whole unpleasant situation will go away. We have to be positive that we can take actions to restructure the pieces of our lives. We have work to do, and we must believe we are up to the task.

Former President Jimmy Carter said,

> Faith, either in God or in ourselves, will permit us to take a chance on a new path, perhaps different from the one we now follow. It may be surprising where it leads.

This is true during all the times in life when we must revamp our plans and change our course whether it is due to death, separation, relocation, or any of the other changes, which come throughout a lifetime.

Goals of Grief Work

There are two major goals for the mourner to accomplish with grief work. One is to acknowledge and truly accept that the death has occurred. This means accepting the physical relationship is now over. The second goal is to experience and deal with all the emotions and problems this loss creates for the mourner.

Tasks of Grief Work

With these two goals in mind, there are several tasks for the mourner to do in order to successfully complete the grief work.

1. Stay in the pain.

You cannot run away from grief. It is important to process the grief, not to weaken life but to strengthen it. The first task of grief work is to immerse your whole being in the pain. You cannot go around the pain. You cannot deny it. Denying it impedes your healing. Feeling the pain and working through it gives great insight into the pain of others. It is important to do this in order to live again.

People who get better after the death of a loved one complete the grief work and accept the pain. Putting the pain on hold by not dealing with it will not make it go away permanently. Barbara Johnson, a leading Christian author, compares grief work to a life raft. She says to deny the pain is like jumping off the raft into a school of hungry sharks. "If you don't face your grief and work through it, it will eat you alive."

Staying in the pain means allowing yourself to fully experience all the emotions you feel after a loss. If you fail to do this, delayed grief can occur. You either grieve now, or you will grieve later. At some point, the grief will rear its ugly head. The grief must be processed because it is life's way of giving us closure.

A lady who came to one of my support groups several years ago is a good example. She was in her early sixties and came to the group because her husband died. A year passed, and she was still unable to reconcile her life. It was to the point where her adult children and grandchildren were exasperated with her. Her friends lost patience with her, and she felt isolated and alone.

One day, in a group discussion, she began crying and shared with the group that she was the lone survivor of a house fire when she was sixteen years old. She lost her parents and her only sister in the fire. She had never fully grieved the loss. She added she always felt guilty for being the one who lived. She never communicated this to anyone during all the years since the fire until she spoke about it in the group.

Shortly after the tragic fire, she met and married her husband. They were married for forty-five years when he died of a sudden heart attack. She confided, after his death, that she began to have nightmares about the fire. She was unable to stay alone at night because she was fearful of going to sleep alone in the house. She knew her family was at the end of patience with her, but she didn't know what to do. Her children and grandchildren could not understand why she was so fearful. The necessity of providing someone to stay with her every night created a complication for everyone, and she feared having to leave her home.

This case exemplifies postponed grief can resurface years later. When it does, complications arise. In individual counseling, this client was helped to grieve both losses. She addressed her survivor's guilt from the fire. She also explored the feelings of anger she harbored about the earlier deaths and the more recent death of her husband. Gradually, she began to heal. She began to reconcile to her new life and adjust to the changes brought by grief. It was not until she faced the pain of the losses in her life that she was able to restructure her life and take positive steps.

2.   Mourn as well as grieve.

The second task in grief work is to mourn as well as grieve. Dr. Alan Wolfelt distinguishes these two actions in many of his writings. Grieving is internally feeling the pain of the loss. Mourning is taking the grief outside you and expressing it publicly. Many activities make up the mourning process. Some of them are going to the cemetery, talking about the loss, crying, commemorating special dates, and taking time off from usual social functions. Our society encourages us to grieve, but it does not encourage us to mourn.

After my husband died, I found after a period of time that I made people uncomfortable if I cried. It was okay to cry during the initial days of loss. The visitation, funeral, and committal service were approved situations for tears. After that period of time, the mourner is made to feel embarrassed if he becomes emotional publicly. This puts a tremendous strain on the mourner to hold inside the hurt and sorrow.

This is especially so for bereaved men. Our society teaches males to be strong and to be in control of stressful situations. Men are not supposed to cry according to these social rules. Unfortunately, we teach young boys that crying shows weakness. Society's unspoken rule says if you are suffering emotional distress, and you are male, you are supposed to hang tough and keep a stiff upper lip. Society's refusal to fully allow the mourning process puts mourners at a disadvantage in accomplishing the task of grieving and mourning.

Not wanting to participate in social activities is another form of mourning. Decades ago, our society allowed the bereaved a full year to mourn the loss and did not expect the bereaved to be a social person during this time. I found this definitely is not the case in today's world. If the mourner is not back into the swing of things in six months, many friends and acquaintances begin to shake their heads and think you are taking too long to mourn. My heart was not into doing very much socially for some time. I was not ready to get on with my life as though everything was normal. I needed some alone time to sort my feelings and deal with my emotions.

For many bereaved people, visiting the cemetery is an important form of mourning. They feel better after a visit. It was not a form of mourning helpful to me, so I did not do it. However, it is surprising the number of my clients censured by others for spending time at the cemetery. I do not advocate pitching a tent and spending inordinate amounts of time daily at the cemetery. This could fall into the category of unhealthy grief, which will be discussed in a later chapter. However, if it is helpful to a client to do this form of mourning, I encourage it as long as it is done in moderation *and* is comforting.

Commemorating the loved one is another form of mourning. It is a positive form. It not only expresses your loss, but it entails doing things, which celebrate the life your loved one lived. The commemoration I did for my husband and in-laws was to purchase a brick in memory of them, inscribed with their name to put in the family garden at the local hospital in their community. There was also a scholarship fund established in memory of my husband, which, for several years, gave a small scholarship to a young person in need. When the hospital in my parents' community built a family prayer garden, I also purchased an inscribed brick in their memory. None of these mourning tasks was done at the initial time of the death, but were forms of mourning I was able to do as time passed, and I continued to process my loss.

3. Cry when you need to cry.

Discussion of the different forms of mourning brings forth the importance of this task of grief work. Crying is a human need. Sooner or later, everyone cries. The Bible is full of examples of people who cried when experiencing pain and loss. David cried on several occasions. When Jesus heard about the death of Lazarus, John 11:35 says simply: "Jesus wept." The followers of Jesus cried upon hearing of his crucifixion. There was great crying and wailing in Egypt when the angel of death passed over the homes.

Crying is an important task of grief work and externalizes the pain we feel on the inside when we suffer devastating loss. American writer Washington Irving wrote,

> There is a sacredness in tears. They are not the mark of weakness, but of power. They speak more eloquently than ten thousand tongues. They are messengers of overwhelming grief . . . and unspeakable love.

Tears are a wonderful natural resource and are therapeutic. Crying gives physical release from the stress of grief. In *Oliver Twist*, Mr. Bumble declared that crying "opens the lungs, washes the countenance, exercises the eyes, and softens the temper."

Many scientists believe tears remove toxic waste from the body. This is one explanation for the feeling of release we feel after a good cry. Years ago, Loretta Young, the actress who acted in many emotionally-moving movies, said, "Tears will melt the heart that is frozen in grief." Personal experience leads me to agree with the validity of the importance of tears in processing deep hurt.

People worry crying too much will make them ill. Grief-stricken clients say, "I cry all the time." In reality, this is not true. When we are doing grief work, we may cry many times during the day, but we do not cry *all* the time. As we process our grief, the crying periods lessen in intensity or reduce in the number of times we cry during the day.

One of the biggest impediments to mourners in accomplishing the crying grief task is others thinking this behavior should be discouraged. We make people uncomfortable when we cry. They do not know what to do with us. It makes them feel helpless. What do they need to do for us? In reality, people do not need to do anything but let us cry. Tears are allowed! If there ever was a time tears are called for, it is when suffering great pain and loss. Empathetic friends and family merely need to stand by and allow the mourner this expression of pain. Simply pass the tissues!

It is important for the mourner to know there are different kinds of crying. Some of the forms of crying depend on the mourner's cultural background. While some mourners cry, others may sob. Some of us cry and sob. Eastern cultures encourage a form of crying called wailing. In Jerusalem, there is the Wailing Wall where mourners express their deep pain.

Crying is a visible sign of pain. If the crying deepens, it becomes sobbing. Sobbing expresses deep emotional hurt. As the sobbing deepens, we may begin to wail. If we were to list these forms of crying on an intensity scale from less intense to the most intense, we would start with crying, go to sobbing, then to wailing. Wailing is quite loud and expressive.

Ted Menten, author of *Gentle Closings*, says of crying:

> I believe in grief and sorrow and wailing; and tears flowing
> like Niagara Falls. Tears mean something. They mean we're
> alive and feeling.

This indicates this grief task overrides the sense of numbness we initially feel.

Dr. Alan Wolfelt coined the phrase *borrowed tears*. This form of crying takes place when we have processed our grief further from the time of initial loss. These tears often come when least expected and usually come from some other person's pain or sorrow. Borrowed tears may occur when we are touched by something in our environment. It could be something we see, something we hear, or something we read. These tears are not triggered by anything that reminds us of our deceased loved one, but they occur because our emotions are tender from our losses. Events, which would not ordinarily affect our sensitivities, touch our heartstrings; and we become emotional.

I love to read fiction. About ten months after the death of my husband, I was reading a novel. As I became caught up in the story line, the life of the main character touched me deeply. I began to cry as I read. It became more and more difficult for me to read this book. I put it down several times because I cried so hard it was impossible to continue reading. Finally, I finished the book along with a box of tissues. I was perplexed as to why this was a difficult book for me since it was not a story of death or loss. What was wrong with me? When I read how Dr. Wolfelt described borrowed tears, I felt that the mystery was solved. My reaction to the heroine's struggle with adversity struck a chord in me, which produced sympathetic tears for her pain and suffering.

4.   Talk about the person who died.

Talking about the person who died is paramount for us when we do grief work. Terry Kettering, whose wife died, penned the following poem, which illustrates our frustration when people around us do not understand the importance of this task.

The Elephant in the Room

There's an elephant in the room.
It is large and squatting, so it is hard to get around it.
Yet, we squeeze by with "How are you?" and, "I'm fine,"
And a thousand other forms of trivial chatter.
We talk about the weather; we talk about work; we talk about everything else—
Except the elephant in the room!

There's an elephant in the room.
We all know it is there.
We are thinking about the elephant as we talk.
It is constantly on our minds, for you see, it s a very big elephant.
But we do not talk about the elephant in the room.
Oh, please, say her name.
Oh, please, say "Barbara" again.
Oh, please let's talk about the elephant in the room.

For, if we talk about her death, perhaps, we can talk about her life.
Can I say "Barbara and not have you look away?
For, if I cannot, you are leaving me
Alone . . . in a room . . . with an elephant.

—Terry Kettering

It is indeed maddening to be treated like Mr. Kettering in the poem "The Elephant in the Room." Talking about our loved one, his life as well as the death, is therapeutic for us.

Unfortunately, our need to talk exceeds the amount of time our family and friends are willing to listen. It helps us to talk repeatedly about the loss. This is part of making the death real. It also provides us with the opportunity to sort through our memories. However, as we become more repetitious with our talking, others try harder and harder to deflect the conversation. In reality, people get tired of our same old conversation and rightly so. We do not mean to be boring, but we do need so much to talk about it.

Many people will not allow us to mention the deceased because of the mistaken fear it will "bring it all back to us." As though we could ever forget it! The loss is in our mind constantly. This reluctance on the part of people to allow us to talk about the loss goes back again to the discomfort people have with what to do or what to say. In reality, all we need is a listening ear. We are not seeking advice. We are not seeking a magic fix. Nothing will make it better. What we yearn for is empathetic support and the security of knowing that someone is there for us as we sort through these new feelings.

Once, in a meeting, as we talked about the need to have a good listener, a woman said that she thought the best advice to give people who want to help the mourner is to remember the three h's: hang around, hug, and hush. We all laughed, but we agreed that this is putting it very succinctly. As a person doing grief work, we need someone we can count on being there for us. We need hugs, either physical hugs or emotional ones. We do not need endless suggestions, stories, or chatter. We just need a silent presence to accompany us through a difficult time. We do not need more advice from well-meaning friends. We need more listening.

Putting our thoughts and feelings about the deceased into words is a healing experience. When we wear out the listening patience of our family and friends, a support group can be helpful in accomplishing this grief task. Not only does this supply us with listening ears, it also helps us to recognize the existence of others who face similar problems. It allows us to find others who are managing to survive the unsurvivable. The discovery in the group discussions that we are not unique in suffering a loss gives us hope that there is a way through the pain.

Shakespeare's *Macbeth* says, "Give sorrow words; the grief that does not speak whispers the o'erfraught heart and bids it break." The importance of talking about the loss cannot be understated. The feelings, the anger, the disappointment, the sadness, and the pain must be voiced. Even the feelings of relief, which may come from the release of our loved one from the pain and suffering of a long illness, must be expressed. Mourners must find someone who will listen. When you are processing grief, remember:

"You alone can do it, but you can't do it alone."

—Barbara Johnson

Support group discussions enable us to communicate about our loved one and about our reactions to this loss. Through this communication, we learn that our reactions are not unusual or unnatural. It gives validity to our mourning. Many times, we fear we are not mourning in the correct way. Sometimes we fear going crazy. There is no plan for mourning. There is no *Grieving for Dummies* book we can purchase to show us the way. We cannot purchase grieving blueprints. We are suddenly blinded in our normally lighted world and are feeling our way along the corridor of grief. We have lost our compass and our way. We need a flashlight. A support group can be the flashlight! A support group validates we are normal. We are, to put it simply, grief-stricken.

Early in my journey of grief, I was given a poem written by Eloise Cole. I read it many times because it certainly zeroed in on how I felt. It is named "Falling Apart."

Falling Apart
I seem to be falling apart.
My attention span can be measured in seconds;
My patience in minutes.
I cry at the drop of a hat.
I forget things constantly.
The morning toast burns daily.
I forget to sign the checks.

Half of everything in the house is misplaced.

Feeling of anxiety and restlessness are my constant companions.
Rainy days seem extra dreary.
Sunny days seem an outrage.
Other people's pain and frustration seem insignificant.
Laughing, happy people seem out of place in my world.
It has become routine to feel half crazy.
I am normal, I am told.
I am a newly grieving person.

—Eloise Cole

The opportunity to talk to others about reactions, like the ones described in the poem, helps us to relieve the stress that fills our lives after a death. Dr. Bowlby points out how important it is to spend time with a person who is comfortable in letting us talk about our loss. It has a positive impact on our grieving process. In the book *Seven Choices: Finding Daylight after Loss Shatters Your World*, Dr. Neeld also recommends talking about your loved one and your loss. It is not that we are expecting someone to give us answers, but it is in the dialogue that we find out what is really true for us. When we put our words into conversation, it allows us to hear our own voice.

I find when I talk through my thoughts, it often turns on a light of understanding I did not see when only thinking the thoughts. Putting voice to the thoughts can help in resolving difficult feelings. Why? It enables one to put a feeling into a concrete word. It puts a name to our fear and/or anxiety.

Bereaved individuals participating in a bereavement study by Muller emphasized the importance of having others listen to them empathetically as they talked about their loved ones and their feelings of loss. They emphasized there was no expectation of finding out what to do, and in fact, the mourners did not want to be told that information. Just knowing they could talk about the loss and have someone accompany them through this dialogue time was extremely helpful in coping with the loss. Sharing memories and stories of the deceased was seen as a way to come to terms with the death.

5. Do a life review.

A fifth task in grief work is a life review. The life review has four purposes. First is integrating the loss into your life and reframing your relationship with the deceased. He is no longer with you physically, yet you feel his presence every day. Second is finding a space for the deceased in your psychological life. The new position of the deceased person must be secured in order for you to allow new relationships to form. The third purpose of the review is reconciliation of the ambivalent feelings toward maintaining a relationship with the deceased. The fourth purpose is sorting and storing memories of life with the deceased.

The relationship with our loved one is as alive in our hearts and minds as it ever was. Mitch Albom, in *Tuesdays with Morrie*, described his relationship with Morrie by using a quote from Jack Lemmon, which is of great comfort to all who suffer the loss of a person they love: "Death ends a life. It does not end a relationship." The task is to be able to separate the physical relationship from the psychological one. You must reframe the relationship in the reality of your new life. Just as the deceased began a new life with the last breath they took here, you began a new life too. Securing a place for the relationship with them in this new life is very important.

Another task to be accomplished with the life review is to reconcile the ambivalent feelings the survivor may have toward maintaining a continuing relationship. On the one hand, the memories of the relationship are a joy to you. On the other hand, they can also be the source of great pain because they bring back the enormity of what was lost.

I wanted to think about my husband and the times we had together, but it also was a reminder of the times that were gone forever. The memories were bittersweet. This gave me mixed emotions as I thought about my past life with him. I found this same ambivalence in sorting through memories when my parents died. There are wonderful memories to keep of loved ones, but they do emphasize in early grief phases the tremendous impact of the loss.

The fourth life review task is the storing of memories of life with the deceased. During this task, talking about the individual and the things you did with him is important. Looking at photographs, rereading letters and cards, looking over scrapbooks, and going through the belongings of the deceased are parts of the storing process. Objects, which link you to the person you lost, are of great importance. These may be items of clothing, jewelry, photos, souvenirs, and a myriad number of other things we associate with the deceased.

Because these linking items are of such importance to the grief work, disposing of the loved one's belongings is a deeply personal task. It is important for the mourner to avoid letting others rush you into doing this chore. You will know when you are able and ready to complete this grief task. It is an emotional time for you, but it is also very therapeutic. Unless you want help with this task, let others know you will take care of this by yourself. Unless circumstances make it necessary to do it quickly, this task is best left until you are in an improved emotional state.

It took me a while to accomplish this task once I started on the process. Why? First, I would sit and slowly go through a drawer. If there was anything to read, I read it. It took me forever to look at the many pictures. I sorted and resorted items. Some possessions I wanted for a keepsake. Some, I wanted to save for our son. I wanted to select special items for family members and good friends. Then there was the junk! Everyone has junk. However, it was my loved one's junk, and I wanted to be the one to decide what to give away and what to throw away. A lot of tears were shed as I worked through this chore. A lot of memories were reviewed, and a lot of smiles came upon my face as I remembered funny times. Was this an easy task to complete? No. Did it help my grief process to do it? Yes!

A widow in one of my support groups shared she was very upset because her adult children cheated her out of processing her grief in this way. Three months after her husband's death, she went out of town to visit her sister. Her well-meaning children thought it would be much easier for her to come home to a place without all those reminders of their father. While she was away, they packed all his personal belongings. They chose what to keep and what to eliminate. When their mother came home, the children were stunned by her emotional outburst over what they did in her absence. This is a good example of misplaced good intentions taking away a person's grief process.

One of the most common mistakes others make is to rush the mourner through this process. Allow the grief-stricken mourner time to build the physical energy and to develop the emotional stability to make these decisions. This is not saying a shrine should be kept. If no progress is made in disposing of the loved one's things after a year, there may be a problem. Again, the mourner needs time to accomplish this task.

This last purpose of the life review, sorting and storing memories, is a daunting task. The memories retain the images of our loved one and allow us to keep the relationship. Memories give us a feeling of having a piece of the loved one with us. Memories can be helpful, or they can be sources of pain. The bereaved person experiences several types of memories: comfort memories, triggered memories, blocked memories, fading memories, and idealized memories.

Comfort memories are those that bring great solace. The further you get in your grief process, the more the memories become comfort memories. Former President Jimmy Carter said,

"A joyous occasion is never quite as wonderful as when it becomes a memory."

The memories of happy occasions warm your heart during the winter of your grief. A client once asked me how she could tell when her grief was getting better. I told her I knew I was better when the memories brought more smiles than tears.

Triggered memories are those memories springing forth unintentionally, which are painful to us. These are more commonly closer to the time of the loss. When our feelings are still new and our nerves raw, someone or something may trigger a memory of our loved one that renews the grief. The memory is a burden at this time. It is a carrier of acute pain. An example of this for me was being in a crowd and catching a whiff of my husband's favorite cologne. This always triggered overwhelming sadness. Another one was hearing our favorite song on the radio.

Blocked memories are those that we cannot bring forth. These usually occur in the early days of grief. In the beginning, we may only recall rudimentary memories. We are still numb and in such disbelief our minds are not functioning well. This is the mind's way of protecting the vulnerable survivor from being overwhelmed by the emotions. You can only deal with the memories in small amounts; therefore, many are blocked from your conscious thought.

As time passes and the mourner moves on in the grieving process, some memories fade. Fading memories are distressing because you fear this is a sign of forgetting the loved one. However, do not worry because not all memories fade. Only some fade, and the reason is a diminishing need on the part of the bereaved mourner to keep that particular memory alive.

Many of my memories have faded but not the most important ones. Sometimes, others will remind me of a memory I had forgotten. Usually, this is a memory that meant more to those family members and friends than it did to me. The strength of the importance of the memory to my relationship with my husband seems to be the determining factor for me in storing the memories.

As you sort and store your memories, you must be vigilant to avoid keeping idealized memories. Human beings have a way of being very selective about what they hear and what they remember. We tend to hear and remember what best suits us. Idealizing the deceased is a serious mistake. When you do that, you lose them twice. You lose them once to the death of their body, and the second loss is the loss of the true memory of them.

There is an old hymn beginning with the words "Precious memories, how they linger," and this is true when a loved one dies. The memories of that person become the most precious legacy left to the survivors. Material things left by the deceased may be valuable. Some objects have sentimental value. But the most prized possessions cherished by the survivors are the many memories of the deceased, which live on in the hearts and minds of the survivors.

Some memories bring a smile or a chuckle as you remember humorous times spent together. Other memories bring a tear to your eye and an ache to your heart as you remember sad times, hard times, courageous times, and painful times. If you are totally honest, there are even memories that bring forth anger, aggravation, or irritation. This is because you remember things the deceased did, which were not kind, forgiving, or generous. However, this is all right. The person you are remembering was *human*. To remember a perfect person is to deny the person's human qualities. That is to deny his true existence.

Realistic memories of the loved one pay them the greatest honor. It is remembering the deceased realistically that gives the person continuing life. The real person is alive in your heart and mind, not a false, perfect person. The tendency to idealize the dead is natural, but it often keeps the survivor from progressing through grief toward reconciling the loss. As the deceased person becomes more perfect in your mind, the living people around you fall further behind in measuring up to your expectations. This is unfair to others in your life. This action contributes to the feeling of guilt because the more perfect the deceased person becomes, the more you remember your own shortcomings.

It is painful to remember, but losing the memory of someone you loved is more painful. Forgetting them is a frightening thought. The purpose of your grief work is not to erase memories and forget, but to reach the point where your thoughts are not controlled by the pain of memories. Preserving the memories is part of your sacred trust. You are the gatekeeper of this legacy. Memories assure you of the continued presence of your loved one. No one knows better than the survivor.

> You do not have to see what you love in order to know it is safe in your heart.
>
> —Elizabeth Stalling

Memories are to be cherished. We must keep *all* the memories of our loved one—the good, the kind, the just, the unjust, the generous, the selfish, and the humorous. It is this kaleidoscope of memories that comprises the unique personality of your loved one. That unique person was the one you loved. Yes, precious memories—how they linger. Memories supply the glue for a broken heart.

6. Live in the present.

When you think you cannot cope with the days, weeks, and months that lie ahead, stop and listen to yourself. You do not have to take on a mountain. All you have to do is cope for one day and one day only. Follow the Alcoholics Anonymous's (AA) twenty-four-hour plan! This means doing your grief work one step at a time. In order to be able to handle this task, you must crawl before you walk, so to speak. Just as a baby walks in the beginning with small unsteady steps, the mourner deals with the grief in tiny steps. It may seem it is one step forward and two steps back, but staying in the present and taking your time makes you navigate this path of grief successfully.

One of the hardest parts of the day is the hours of night. It seems just as children get sick at night when the doctor's office is closed, you become the most panicky and afraid when the long lonely hours of night arrive. Author Lynn Caine talks about the hour of the wolf, which she dreaded when she first became a widow. She said,

> This is the time of night when our greatest fears come up from the unconscious to haunt us like a ghostly wolf stalking its prey.

Her hour of the wolf came at three in the morning. However, she emphasized your hour of the wolf might come at different times of the day. Whatever time it does come, you begin to worry and become anxious.

You may play the what-if game. You know the one to which she refers, "What if this happens?" or "What if that happens?" "What will I do?"

Living on the twenty-four hour plan makes it impossible to worry about yesterday, tomorrow, next week, or next month. If you live day by day or hour by hour, you take those baby steps needed to get you through the grief work. The first fifteen minutes of the day are so important. If you can get your feet on the floor, get out of bed, and make it to the kitchen for your coffee, you have accomplished something. Making it the first fifteen minutes leads you to trying for another fifteen, and so it goes. Before you know it, you have made it to noon. Breaking the day into segments was very helpful for me in keeping away the panicky thoughts of additional responsibility and the fear of not being up to the task. It also keeps the wolf away from the door!

As you stay in the twenty-four hour plan, try to accomplish one thing. It may be returning a phone call. It could be fixing lunch. It may be writing one note. You might choose a myriad of small tasks such as washing your hair, taking a shower, or washing the dishes. The importance of accomplishing some tasks, no matter how small, is it reminds you there are still some things in your life you can control. Operating in the twenty-four hour plan is choosing to take the mountain of grief one step at a time, one day at a time.

Not adding the burden of past mistakes and worries to the fear and anxiety about the future reduces the enormity of the task you face. The essay used in Alcoholics Anonymous, advocating the twenty-four hour plan, says you should not worry about two days of the week. These days are yesterday and tomorrow. Yesterday is gone forever and cannot be replayed. Tomorrow has yet to be born. This leaves only *today*. You can fight the battle of just one day.

Eckhart Tolle, in his book *The Power of Now*, discusses at length the importance of accepting the *now* as a way of gaining inner peace. Inner peace is the solace the distressed mourner struggles to achieve. Inner peace is not to be confused with happiness. To be happy, you must have positive conditions in your life. With the death of a loved, one this is not possible. However, your soul cries out for inner peace at this time. A step toward that peace is to allow the present to be as it is. When you do not accept the present as it is, you create drama and intense stress within yourself because you are struggling against reality.

Although it is impossible to be happy when a loved one dies, you can be at peace. Inner peace goes deeper than surface happiness. It comes from acceptance of what happened in the present moment. It comes when you stop wasting your energy railing over something that occurred in the past and is beyond your control. When you accept the present for what it is, you can achieve, under the sadness, serenity. You become open to the presence of a supportive being. Serenity is being able to be quiet in the midst of chaos. The scriptures put it well by saying,

> Be still and know that I am God.
>
> —Psalm 46:10

For me, it was taking the question, Why did this happen to me? and turning it into Now this has happened, help me, Lord, to handle it. It was when I quit resisting against reality that I could feel peace flow over me.

This analogy was given by Eckhart Tolle, illustrating what it means to stay in the now:

> You are walking along a path at night, surrounded by thick fog. But, you have a powerful flashlight that cuts through the fog and creates a narrow, clear space in front of you. The fog is your life situation, which includes the past and future. The flashlight is your conscious presence. The clear space is the NOW.

You know what it is like to be in the *fog*. This is your struggle. The *flashlight* is your conscious choice to stay in the presence of the light because the light is the only place you can see where you are going. The light is the only place where you can take a sure step. As you move the light forward step by step, you slowly move forward. To stay in the present is to stay in the *clear space*.

Spencer Johnson, in his simple-but-eloquent book *The Precious Present*, captures the essence of what the mourner must learn to do. Live in the moment. The present is truly a gift. When you stay in the present time, you discover your own humanity. You savor the blessings of the moment as well as deal more effectively with the sorrows. Staying in the present and accepting the now, is where you find God.

7. Redefine your identity.

The task of redefining your identity takes a great deal of time. It was previously emphasized that there is no time constraint to your grief. As columnist Ellen Goodman wrote, "There may be one minute managers, but there are no one minute mourners." Redefining self-identity is a major undertaking for the mourner, and this process will be a work in progress for many months, perhaps years after the loss.

What makes this task so difficult is the death shakes you to your core. You are so invested in the person who died that to exist without him in the same way is impossible. "If I am not a spouse, who am I?" "If I am not a child to anyone anymore, who am I?" "If I am not a parent, who am I?" These are only a few of the questions you ask as you struggle with the identity crisis in your life after loss.

The goal of redefining your self-identity is threefold. First, you have to reclaim yourself. Second you have to find completeness. Third, you have to reinvest the time the relationship required. This does not happen quickly nor does it happen without a great deal of soul-searching. Since your thinking processes are so muddled at the beginning of the grief journey, it is easy to see why this is one of the grief tasks that is not consciously undertaken until later in the journey. Of course, the death immediately brings some changes in your identity, but it is only after considerable time has passed that you are able to consciously think about these goals.

One of the first losses the mourner is aware of feeling is the loss of who you are. Since you define yourself by your relationships, when a relationship is lost, you are at sea as to where you fit in the scheme of things now that things have changed. Your spouse, for example, is often the mirror you use to validate your thoughts and feelings about everyday events and the world in general. You bounce ideas off your spouse, and his opinions and views can affect your own opinions and beliefs. When your spouse dies, the mirror is gone; and the survivor may miss the mirror function of the spouse, which contributed to the survivor's sense of self.

Catholic nun Sister Marla Reilly answered this question of "Who am I?" in this way:

> I am the person I always was. I am the person who began my life, but I have been shaped by my life experiences. All the experiences, good or bad, are accidentals that do not change my identity. Yet, they do figure as contributors to it. Grief has caused me to consider this question of who I am. It has shaken me from complacency to find the theme that has existed since my birth.

Her answer is a good one for the mourner who is seeking identity. As we search for that identity, we find we are the same as we were at birth.

Self-identity can be lost due to the layers of life experiences covering it. With introspection comes the understanding of self-identity. It is usually only after a life-altering event such as the loss of a loved one that we take the time to explore, self-evaluate, and rediscover who we really are.

An analogy illustrating this is,

> There was a piece of furniture made from excellent wood. For various reasons, it was painted over numerous times throughout the years. To restore the natural beauty of this piece, required the removal of the many layers of paint. As the paint disappeared the beauty of the grain once again appeared. The wood's beauty was there all the time, but it had been hidden by the layers of paint.

This describes the process of finding the self-identity. Our self-identity may have slowly changed throughout the years as the layers of life covered it. The life problems, demands, and sorrows slowly obliterated the original identity. As the mourner processes the grief redefining his role, the true self-identity emerges again. Just as the wood's beauty was there all the time, your self-identity was there, but hidden. Your job in this grief task is to rediscover it.

This is what is meant by reclaiming yourself. You must not only reclaim your physical self, mental self, and emotional self; but you must reclaim your abilities, skills, and talents, which you may have covered over as you met the demands of the life you lived. Now is the time to rediscover these things about you.

Survivor Changes

One of the first changes noticed by the survivor is the change in your role. The role you play in life is not as noticeable to you before the death as it is after the death. When I was widowed, I felt like half a person. I felt married for the previous eighteen years of my life. This married role affected how I looked at the world around me and how I operated in the world. I was part of a twosome and operated as part of a couple. Suddenly, I was single. The world looks quite different from the vantage point of a single person. Not only that. I found it changed how others view you too.

When your spouse dies, there are subtle changes in how you fit into all kinds of situations, including social gatherings. There is a different perception of you by others, which you pick up rather quickly. I truly felt like a fifth wheel and found I no longer fit into couple gatherings. Our friends were very good to include me, but I could not get past feeling I did not belong. When everyone is paired in couples, an odd number makes for awkwardness all around.

Again, when my parents died, my role changed. I suddenly felt like an orphan. Even though I was a mature adult familiar with grief, when my parents died, I was unprepared for the lost feeling I experienced. My parents were always there for me. Since they knew me from the moment I took my first breath, they knew me best. I enjoyed my role as their daughter and invested a great deal of myself into that relationship. When they died, it left a huge void. A lot of time and energy was spent performing my daughter role. Now, that time and energy had to be reinvested.

The role change after loss may require the survivor to take on additional responsibilities. Depending on who died, the survivor's role may have to be expanded to cover the many things the deceased person took charge of doing.

If the person who died required a great deal of care, the responsibilities of the survivor may take a drastic drop. This is also a big adjustment when you are not responsible for as many things as you were before the death. You feel you are not busy enough, or you have too much time on your hands.

A second change the survivor must make is in self-image. Much of our self-image comes from the relationships we have with other people. Many times, we get our sense of completeness from these relationships. It is important to feel complete in your own right in order to successfully change your self-image. Self-confidence comes into play in this change. When you are not complete within yourself, you often lack the confidence to tackle new things, to problem-solve, and to adjust to changes.

To successfully live as the different person you are now after the loss, you must have a positive self-image and self-confidence. Facing yourself is the task of building a new life. Author Lynn Caine says that it is when you decide the life urge is stronger than the death urge that you are able to make this change. This is when you struggle to embrace this new identity.

You cannot just wait to return to your old self. That is not going to happen. It is unrealistic to expect to eventually get back to your old life, although in the beginning that seems to be what we think will happen. This is impossible because a key component of your life—your loved one—is gone. I can never live the life I lived before the death of my loved ones. They were too much a part of that life, and they are no longer in this world.

When the loved one draws his last breath in this world, you, the survivor, draw your first breath in a new world. I am not the same person I was. I cannot be. Part of what made me what I was is no longer alive, so I had to change. This is not to say life is better or worse. It is different. Because it is different, it takes a different me to live that life. This requires a change in my self-image.

The third change the survivor must make is in worldview. When the loved one dies, many plans and hopes change. Things you thought you would do or accomplish may not be possible now. Depending on how you accept the loss and deal with it, your outlook on life changes. Some survivors become bitter and angry. Others become more compassionate and kind. Some see the world as a cold, cruel place. Others see it as a compassionate, caring place.

Beliefs may go through a change. Some become stronger and some weaker. Some beliefs change because they no longer fit the new life. In this change of worldview, there can be a loss of direction. Sometimes, it takes a while to discover what the new direction may be. Either for the positive or the negative, the worldview of the survivor goes through a change.

As you go through these changes in the journey, you slowly come out of your cocoon of grief, which has been, up to this point, your self-protection. You are ready to emerge from the cocoon, much like a butterfly, and take your place in the mainstream of life to renew and form new relationships, to find new focus, and to attain peace in the new life as the different person you have become.

Phases of Grief

In 1969, Dr. Kubler-Ross identified five stages of grief associated with death and dying. Since that time, many studies of the subject have been completed. Her initial stages have been tweaked, changed, reworded, and reinterpreted. However, her findings have been the basis for most of the work on how to help survivors navigate through the grieving process. Her stages were (1) denial/isolation, (2) anger, (3) bargaining, (4) depression, and (5) acceptance.

While many of the terms Kubler-Ross used to describe the stages have prevailed today, discussion has taken place by professionals in the field of bereavement as to the use of the word *stage* to describe the process. The idea of stages implies there is an orderly progression to complete during grief work. This sounds too organized. Professionals agree grief work is anything but orderly. It is messy, complicated, and totally unorganized. Therefore, a more apt description of the process would be to call these *phases* rather than *stages*.

In speaking of the disorganization of the process, professional grief therapists verify some mourners go though all the phases, but others do not. There is not an order to follow, and some mourners go in and out of a phase numerous times as they process the grief. For example, there is one type of denial at the very beginning of the loss, yet it will often surface again months later in actions by the mourner that illustrate there is again denial of the loss.

Shock and denial are most common when the loss first happens. This is when the mourner says things like "I just can't believe this" or "There must be a mistake."

In the case of a diagnosis of a terminal illness, the shock and denial may come when the diagnosis is given. Along with the shock and denial comes a sense of numbing. It is as though you hear things from a long way off, and your feelings shut down.

There is a sense of unreality to what you hear, and it seems to be more than your mind is capable of absorbing. Perhaps you go into clinical shock. Clinical shock lasts approximately seventy-two hours. This is usually the amount of time needed to get through the arrangements and funeral. It is not uncommon to hear mourners say they do not remember a great deal about the visitation or funeral. It seems like a dream to them. They are in shock, or numb, during this process. This sense of unreality does help in coping with the unthinkable in small amounts as you are capable of absorbing the shock.

Another phase is anger and guilt. Many survivors told me they were never angry, while others were still so angry they could hardly speak during the sessions. It is important to express anger, if that is an emotion you feel. Sometimes, anger is with the medical establishment. "They save people all the time! Why couldn't they save my loved one?" The anger may be with the person who died. This is not logical, but grief emotions often are not logical. Anger can be directed toward other people who seem to be happy. You are angry at the world. You are angry with God. You are angry and often have no place to direct your anger. Anger is a very frustrating emotion and can be damaging to your mental health if not expressed in an appropriate way.

Intense anger can bring with it guilt. Guilt can slowly spiral into depression. Guilt robs you of the privilege of dealing with the problems and mires you down in the if onlys. If only I had sent them to the doctor sooner. If only they had stayed home that night. If only I made them eat healthier. You cannot be hopeful if you feel guilty. Guilt places you in the past where you can take no action and keeps you from the present where you need to be.

Suffering is another phase covering a large range of grief tasks. When the shock wears off, the suffering begins. The disorganization in your life brings the fear you will not be able to endure it. This is the acute mourning stage. You hurt to your soul, and there seems to be no help. During this stage, there may be deep yearning for the presence of the loved one. Obsessive preoccupation with the deceased is common. Barbara Johnson, a Christian writer, calls it "yearning, churning, and burning."

Questioning is a phase all my clients experienced. The most common question clients ask me is, Why did this happen? Mourners seem to feel if that question could be answered, they would feel better in some way. I do not think there is an answer to that question, and I do not think it would make anyone feel one bit better if there were. You hurt because it happened. You miss the loved one's presence. You are feeling deprived.

Questioning can create spiritual crisis for many mourners. The anger they feel toward God does not fit with their idea of a loving god. Why would He let this happen? The spiritual crisis will be discussed in a later chapter.

Acceptance is the phase reached when you accept the loss happened. It is accepting the finality of death. This does not come for some time after the death. For me, it was several months after the death of my husband. It hit me one day: "This is it. He isn't coming back." Up until that point, I felt as though I was living in a temporary state. I knew he was dead, but psychologically, I had not fully accepted it. I had buried him physically but not psychologically. I knew at that moment of acceptance, this was my new life. Things were not going to go back to the way they used to be. Everything had changed. My task, I realized at this point, was, "What am I going to do with this different life?"

A person must get to this place in the grief process before reconciliation can take place. Until the death is fully accepted, you cannot rebuild, you cannot integrate the loss into your present life, you cannot progress forward. This is probably one of the lowest points for the mourner, but it is a necessary low. From these ashes, the phoenix arises.

A final phase for discussion is the restructuring phase. This begins to happen in small ways from the day of the loss but cannot reach full restructure until acceptance has been achieved. Dr. Bernstein calls it the "integration of loss" phase. She describes a loose progression of phases ranging from initial shock and numbness to acute grieving, then gradual adaptation to the final integration of the loss. Judy Tatelbaum refers to it as "reorganization." She describes the phases of emotions after the period of shock as suffering and disorganization. She sees the purpose of the tasks of grief work to be for the bereaved is to reach a state of reorganization.

There is no quick way to work through the phases of grief. There is no time line for the phases. As stated previously, you will go through these phases at your own pace. Some people flow back and forth through several phases. Some hit them all. Some skip phases. You may find yourself going through a phase early on in your grief and coming back to that phase later in the grief process. It is a long and painful process. There is no shortcut. There is no way to circumvent the pain. As Alan Wolfelt said in his book, "It hurts MORE, before it hurts LESS."

Chapter 2 References

1. Albom, Mitch. 1997. *Tuesdays with Morrie, p. 174*, New York, New York: Random House, Inc.

2. Bartocci, Barbara. 2000. *Nobody's Child Anymore: Grieving, Caring, and Comforting When Parents Die. P. 68*, Notre Dame, IN: Sorin Books.

3. Bernstein, Judith R., PhD. 1980. *When the Bough Breaks: Forever after the Death of a Son or Daughter.* Kansas City: MO: Andrews McMeel Publishing.

4. Bowlby, John. 1982. Attachment and Loss: Retrospective Prospect. *American Journal of Orthopsychiatry* 52 (1980): 664-664-678.

5. Caine, Lynn. 1990. *A Compassionate, Practical Guide to Being a Widow. P. 79*, New York:NY: Penguin Putnam Inc.

6. Campbell, Scott, and Phyllis R. Silverman. 1996. *Widower: When Men Are Left Alone.* Amityville, NY: Baywood Publishing Co.

7. Carter, Jimmy. 1998. *The Virtues of Aging. P. 22* New York, NY: Ballantine Publishing Group.

8. Claypool, John. 1995. *Tracks of a Fellow Struggler: Living and Growing through Grief.* New Orleans, LA: Insight Press.

9. Coleman, Sally, and Maria Porter. 1994. *Seasons of the Spirit.* Center City, Minn: Hazeldon Foundation

10. Henderson, John M., Bert Hayslip Jr., and Jennifer K. King. 2004. The Relationship Between Adjustment and Bereavement-Related Distress: A Longitudinal Study. *The Journal of Mental Health Counseling* 26, no. 2 (February): 98-105.

11. Johnson, Barbara. 1994. *Mama, Get the Hammer! There's a Fly on Papa's Head: Using Humor to Flatten out Your Pain.* Dallas, p. 46, 50, 58, TX: Word Publishing.

12. Johnson, Spencer. 1981. *The Precious Present.* New York, NY: Doubleday Books.

13. Kubler-Ross, Elisabeth, MD. 1969. *On Death and Dying.* New York, NY: Macmillan.

14. McConnell, Stephen D. 1998. Christians in Grief. *Living with Grief.* Washington, DC: Hospice Foundation of America.

15. Menten, Ted. 1994. *After Goodbye: How to Begin Again after the Death of Someone You Love.* Philadelphia, PA: Running Press.

16. Meyer, Charles. 1997. *Surviving Death: A Practical Guide to Caring for the Dying and Bereaved.* Mystic, Conn: Twenty-Third Publications.

17. Muller, Elizabeth D., Charles L. Thompson. 2003. The Experience of Grief after Bereavement: A Phenomenological Study with Implications for Mental Health Counseling. *Journal of Mental Health Counseling* 25, no. 3: 183-184-187.
18. Neeld, Elizabeth Harper, PhD. 2003. *Seven Choices: Finding Daylight after Loss Shatters Your World.* New York, NY: Tiime Warner.
19. O'Connor, Nancy, PhD. 1984. *Letting Go with Love: The Grieving Process.* Tuscon, AZ: La Mariposa Press.
20. Omartian, Stormie. 1999. *Just Enough Light for the Step I'm On: Trusting God in Tough Times.* Eugene, Oregon: Harvest House.
21. Reilly, Marla, S. P. 1996. *Now That I Am Old: Meditations on the Meaning of Life. P. 31, 32,* Mystic, Connecticut: Twenty-Third Publications.
22. Segal, Julius. 1986. *Winning Life's Toughest Battles: Roots of Human Resilience.* New York, NY: Ivy Press.
23. Shuchter, Stephen R. 1986. *Dimensions of Grief: Adjusting to the Death of a Spouse.* San Francisco, CA: Jossey-Bass.
24. Stalling, Elizabeth. 1997. *Prayer Starters: To Help you Heal after Loss.* St. Meinrad, IN: Abbey Press.
25. Staudacher, Carol. 1991. *Men and Grief: A Guide for Men Surviving the Death of a Loved One.* Oakland, CA: New Harbinger Publications.
26. Tatelbaum, Judy. 1980. *The Courage to Grieve: Creative Living, Recovery, and Growth through Grief.* New York, New York: Harper Row.
27. Tolle, Eckhart. 1999. *The Power of Now. P. 207,* Novato, CA: Namaste Publishing.
28. Wolfelt, Alan D., PhD. 2001. *Healing Your Grieving Heart. P. 44,* Fort Collins, CO: Companion Press.
29. Wolfelt, Alan D., PhD. 1992. *Understanding Grief: Helping Yourself Heal.* Muncie: IN: Accelerated Development Inc.

Chapter 3

GRIEF: A HEALTH HAZARD

The definition of *grievous* is *causing physical suffering*. We, who grieve the loss of someone we loved, know firsthand the truth of that definition. The acute suffering cuts to the core of our being. The pain reaches our very soul wherein lies our spirit and our own will to live. The suffering is so intense it takes our breath away. We struggle to take in air. We struggle to get up each day. We struggle to accomplish any of our normal daily activities. We struggle to live with the physical suffering.

> Those who hope in the Lord will renew their strength. They will soar on wings like eagles; they will run and not grow weary; they will walk and not be faint.
>
> —Isaiah 40:31

This passage from the Bible assures us of divine help as we deal with the suffering of life. It is the last part of this scripture, "they will walk and not be faint," that is a promise on which to cling as we, the bereaved, deal with the impact grief has on us physically and emotionally. We are weary. At times, we do not know if we can walk on. Some of us become ill enough to literally faint from the stress of the terrible loss. To be able to walk and not be faint of heart is an important goal for the survivor. At a time when we need the most strength and the best health possible to deal effectively with the grief, we find the grief experience itself takes its toll on our physical and emotional stamina.

Knowledge about the physical and emotional symptoms that are possible to be experienced due to grief better prepares you to do your grief work. This information helps mourners to make a self-assessment of physical and mental health to determine whether or not treatment or intervention is needed. Whenever these various physical and mental health issues were discussed in the bereavement groups I led, participants often expressed relief learning many of the symptoms they experienced were normal symptoms of the grieving process. The information is also helpful in determining unhealthy grief patterns.

Somatic Symptoms

A mourner may experience varied physical symptoms when processing grief. Some symptoms are short-term and experienced in the early part of the bereavement. These gradually disappear as the mourner progresses through the grief.

1. Fatigue and Low Energy

The most common short-term symptom expressed by individuals is extreme fatigue. Coupled with low energy and a lethargic feeling, the mourner cannot get daily routines accomplished. Tackling the simplest of tasks takes a huge effort. Losing the ability to meet the responsibilities that were second nature before the loss is distressing to most people. The exhaustion and lack of energy causes many to become more sedentary, thus, adding to the lethargic feeling.

2. Sleeping Problems

Second to the number of mourners who report fatigue and low energy is the complaint of sleeping difficulties. Sleeping problems early in the bereavement are to be expected, but when they become chronic, they can lead to insomnia. Early sleep problems can range from sleeping too much, but still being tired, to sleeping very little. Some people report not being able to fall asleep at normal bedtime, although they feel exhausted. Others report falling asleep but only sleeping a few hours. Many mourners report waking up in the middle of the night and not being able to return to sleep.

Chapter 2 discussed the hour of the wolf, as described by author Lynn Caine, when this pattern of sleep disruption makes an appearance. Inability to sleep the amount of time needed to restore the body leads to many other problems for the mourner such as poor concentration, lack of motivation, and daytime exhaustion.

Bowlby found in his studies on attachment and loss that mourners exhibited behaviors he called "searching," which interfered with their ability to sleep. He said some mourners might not want to sleep for fear they will miss the person who died, if they return. This is *not* crazy. It is part of what he termed the "searching and yearning" phase of grief. It may be conscious or it may be unconscious, but this searching phase renders the mourner unable to sleep well.

Dr. Alan Wolfelt determined in studying sleep patterns of the bereaved that sleeping is connected to feeling a loss of control. When you sleep, you are not in control. When you are bereaved, the last thing you want to do is to lose more control of your life. Therefore, there is an unconscious need to stay awake because of the fear of additional losses that may occur when you are not at the wheel of control.

3. Eating and Digestion Problems

Problems with eating and digestion are other common physical complaints experienced by the bereaved. Some people eat too much and are not conscious of how much they are eating. Others feel low-grade nausea and cannot eat normally. Thus, these folks lose a lot of weight, while the former find they gain weight. Constipation and diarrhea are both physical problems seen in many bereaved individuals in the early stages of bereavement. There is a tendency to seek out comfort foods. These foods are the worst possible diet for people under stress because they are high in fat, oil, sugar, and caffeine. A diet of these comfort foods while under great stress can escalate to stomach- and colon-related problems. Stomach pains, heartburn, and indigestion are other common digestion complaints with mourners. Poor eating habits coupled with great stress increase gastrointestinal complaints.

4. Other Physical Symptoms Impacted by Cognitive Distress

Headaches, dizziness, palpitations, nervous tics, elevated blood pressure, and difficulty breathing and swallowing are other physical symptoms the mourner may exhibit after experiencing a loss. The cognitive distress experienced by the mourner during the bereavement period has a great impact on these symptoms.

When my husband died, problems such as swallowing difficulty, feeling a constant huge lump in my throat, and feeling the need to swallow more often than usual were physical symptoms from this category that I experienced. The stress of dealing with the loss also brought on stomach distress and elevated blood pressure. I found it helpful to talk to my doctor and a therapist about these physical problems and follow their advice as to management of these symptoms from both a physical health approach and a mental health approach.

There are other symptoms that may be overshadowed by the prominent ones of digestion problems, low energy, and sleep problems. In fact, sometimes the mourner does not connect these physical symptoms to the experience of loss and its effect on the body and the brain's cognition. Poor coordination, mishearing communications, not seeing things correctly, loss of hair, and a distorted sense of time and distance are all physical symptoms that can be experienced during mourning due to cognitive distress. When concentration and thinking patterns are skewed, it is easy to see why poor coordination and misunderstanding take place. People suffering intense stress are more prone to accidents, to making mistakes at work, and to having difficulty in time management than those who have a lower stress level.

Serious Medical Illnesses

There are many medical illnesses that can arise when a person is under the traumatic pressure of bereavement. In the previous section, prominent complaints of a physical nature were discussed. Those complaints are generally of a short duration. However, serious problems can occur when these somatic symptoms continue for a much longer period of time. There are some serious medical illnesses that can be exacerbated by a lengthy time of distress.

1. Systemic Problems

Long-term stress takes a toll on the cardiovascular system. Prolonged high blood pressure and elevated stress levels impact the function and health of the heart. The respiratory and gastrointestinal systems are also negatively impacted by long-term stress. Any previously diagnosed breathing disorders can be aggravated by the stress suffered by the patient. Lower immunity compromises the respiratory system by making the mourner more susceptible to respiratory infections. Emotional stress plays havoc in the digestive system with the many upsets in life, producing a variety of gastrointestinal ailments.

During the twelve-year period of my husband's illness, although I never smoked, I developed serious respiratory problems, requiring hospitalization numerous times for chronic bronchitis. I was finally diagnosed with an asthmatic condition that the pulmonary specialist believed to be aggravated by my stress.

Another condition for which I was diagnosed and treated was irritable bowel syndrome (IBS). This physical ailment is often listed on the medical history section of the intake form of many clients I see for anxiety, stress, and bereavement issues. Although not the only factor in contributing to IBS, stress is definitely one of the factors. It is reasonable to conclude that some of these physical symptoms may surface in mourners who are living through one of the most stressful times in their lives.

2. Dermatological Problems

Another physical reaction produced by the stress of loss that was found by researchers was dermatological problems such as rashes, acne, skin eruptions, recurring psoriasis, shingles, and herpes infections. Hair and scalp problems were also noticed. It is not uncommon for intense stress to cause hair loss.

3. Endocrine System Problems

Researchers Hofer, Wollf, and Mason, in studying mourners, observed abnormal production of steroids—particularly cortisol, the stress hormone—which has an effect on every system in the body. Thus, the impact stress has on the endocrine system negatively impacts other systems of the body.

Susceptibility to illness was mentioned in both the research of P. J. Clayton and the research of Hofer, Wolff, and Mason as another result of long-term somatic symptoms. Stress affects the immune system, thus, lowering the mourner's resistance to many illnesses. It was noted by these researchers that the participants in their study were more susceptible to diseases from the common cold to more serious illnesses due to prolonged stress.

4. Chronic Insomnia

Sleep problems, which begin early on in the bereavement, may become chronic insomnia if not addressed and dealt with at the early stage. The failure to get adequate rest has a detrimental impact on the mourner's physical and mental health. The ability to function well mentally is greatly decreased when the body is exhausted. Chronic insomnia deprives your body of the rest needed for your heart, lungs, and other vital organs to maintain good health. A great deal of body repair takes place during sleep. It is important for the mourner to learn positive ways to deal with the insomnia and not just rely on medication, which can be habit-forming.

5. Musculoskeletal Symptoms

Illnesses of the musculoskeletal system, which can be intensified by the stress of bereavement, are back problems, neck pain, and increased pain in joints and muscles. When you are suffering stress and anxiety, you feel tension throughout your body. When the aches and pains of muscles, neck, joints, and the back occur, this contributes to insomnia and prevents the mourner from getting the rest the body requires. Thus, the effect is one of a vicious cycle with stress and anxiety producing tension, tension producing pain, and pain producing more stress and anxiety.

6. Cognition Confusion

Feeling out of sync with your body produces feelings described by many mourners as coming apart at the seams. The feeling of functioning in a drugged state, described by some of my patients as pulling their feet though sticky mud or thinking through a wad of cotton, contributes to a sense of unreality. These feelings, along with the many different physical complaints, greatly complicate cognitive functioning for the mourner. Problem solving and decision making seem impossible when you feel ill. Because your physical health is so important in successfully completing grief work, it is a must for the mourner to have a complete physical examination with the family physician as soon as is feasible after the death.

Emotional Symptoms of Grief

Death brings a plethora of feelings to the survivor. It is easy to become overwhelmed by these intense emotions. At the point of death of the loved one, the survivor loses a piece of his own identity. So grief work begins with the mourner caught in a morass of emotions. Recognizing and understanding these emotional symptoms helps the mourner to grieve in a healthier manner. Failure to deal positively with emotions or, worse yet, suppressing emotions is detrimental to the healing process. Suppressing emotions produces physiological symptoms that in turn produce serious disorders.

1. Sadness

One of the most common emotional symptoms is deep sadness. This begins at the time of the loved one's death. Participants of a research study reported that along with the sadness came a feeling of numbness and unreality. These feelings often spiral downward into depression. However, some depression over the loss is a normal reaction. It would be abnormal to not be sad or depressed over losing someone of such importance.

Even when the mourner accepts the death as a release for the deceased from the pain and suffering of disease, sadness and depression still occur because of the loss of the physical contact with the person in the mourner's life. It is important to monitor the depression and discuss it with a medical professional. After the early part of the bereavement, if the depression deepens or interferes with the mourner's return to normal daily functioning, a mental health evaluation should be sought to screen for possible treatment.

2. Responsibility Overload

Participants in the study of mourners conducted by Mueller and Thompson expressed the emotional sense of having tremendous responsibility placed on their shoulders. Although many of the mourners did not recognize the feeling as responsibility overload, it was described by many of them through the listing of tasks they had to assume after the death. Making decisions—starting with the arrangements for the body and the funeral services to deciding the order of service, music, flowers, and how to contact out-of-town family members—put a heavy burden on the bereaved at a confusing and most vulnerable time for them.

The participants also reported the responsibility the mourner felt for others. Feeling as though others were looking to them to be strong weighed heavily on many people. Mourners with small children were especially prone to feeling this responsibility. Many participants in the study mentioned feeling they had to put on a good face, be strong, be stoic when that was far from the way they wanted to react.

Assuming the responsibilities of the deceased person created another pressure for the mourners. In some cases, the deceased was the family leader or the one who handled the finances, so assuming this task was difficult for the person who had to take over that responsibility. If the wife/mother passed away, some of the male mourners felt overwhelmed taking over the childcare and the many household tasks the deceased previously performed. If the husband/father passed away, assuming the role of sole breadwinner, maintenance and/or repairperson, outdoor maintenance, automobile maintenance, and assistant in parenting tasks (if there were children) were all additional responsibilities.

A final responsibility mentioned by participants was the task of being responsible for their own life. This was peculiar to the loss of a spouse. Spouses feel a bond with each other and operate as a team in many ways. While many marriages do have a great deal of autonomy in the union, there are times when each spouse feels dependent on the other for opinions, advice, suggestions, care, or simply as a sounding board when making decisions. The loss of a life partner leaves the survivor struggling to assimilate the deceased partner's roles into their own load of responsibility. Where there was the companionship and knowledge that a partner was there to assist, that comforting thought is no longer available due to the partner's death.

3. Anxiety

Anxiety produces a wide range of emotions. Fear, panic, irritability, edginess, impatience, and restlessness are companions of anxiety. Worry and fear about the unknown and uncertain future distresses a large number of mourners. This emotion produces many of the physical symptoms discussed earlier such as loss of appetite, inability to sleep, and feelings of exhaustion.

The mourner must learn to stay in the present time, as discussed in an earlier chapter. Anxiety builds as you borrow trouble before it happens. Fear about the future can paralyze the mourner from being able to make decisions and function on a daily basis. Knowing the difference between productive worry (worry about the things you can do something about) and nonproductive worry (worry about things over which you have no control) helps the mourner to identify tasks he can complete. It liberates the mourner from the needless worry about those things beyond the scope of his responsibility.

Disorganization at its utmost, which occurs in the family when there is a death, brings about intense anxiety. The goal for the mourner is to once again achieve a reorganized state, which means reconciling the loss into one's life. The transitional stage between disorganization to reorganization is when anxiety is most likely to be a problem for the mourner.

4.   Erratic Behavior

Grieving people often exhibit erratic behaviors. Mood swings, unpredictable reactions, poor memory, and poor concentration are a few of the behaviors that confuse both the mourner and their family members and friends. Some survivors begin to question their own sanity because they are behaving in ways unlike their normal behaviors. Organized people become unorganized. Calm people become nervous. Confident people become unsure and dependent on others. Pleasant people become grouchy. Punctual people lose all sense of time. Mild-mannered people exhibit irritability and anger. These are all erratic behaviors, which may occur in many mourners.

Failure to complete tasks when a person normally was consistent and reliable can be very alarming to the bereaved and their family members. Forgetting what they have said and repeating the same story over and over is another upsetting behavior for all concerned. Some people report forgetting what they did on certain occasions. Being distracted and preoccupied, giving others a feeling the mourner is not paying attention to them, is another erratic behavior noted through family member observations.

People in my bereavement groups report feeling like Dr. Jekyll and Mr. Hyde. They describe drastic mood changes from their usual demeanor. The unexpectedness of these behaviors makes many mourners question their sanity. Some are distressed because they think they are falling apart. Unusual behaviors reported many times by mourners are failing to pay bills on time and writing checks but not signing them. Other comments include failing to remember certain events that happened after the death. Group members report mixing up conversations, starting projects/tasks and failing to complete them, missing events due to forgetfulness, being irritated by people they usually like, and feeling sorry for themselves. For people who normally operated daily in a rational manner, these behaviors are frightening.

The behaviors concerning memory and concentration upset older mourners the most. Many fear they are developing dementia since this is so out of character for them. A common question from many of my clients is, Am I coming down with Alzheimer's? This is another reason it is important to have a complete checkup by the family doctor so these possibilities can be ruled out, and it can be reinforced to the mourner that these are normal reactions to grief.

Mourner Wellness

As the mourner experiences the wide array of physical and emotional distress, it is to be expected that some feel their whole world has tumbled down about them, and there are no better days on the horizon. Is it any wonder that your energy is depleted and your resolve weakened? You are at a vulnerable time in your life. Many feel as though they are lost in a very large sea, adrift in a very small boat. You feel tempest-tossed and are sure you will crash upon the rocks of life as you struggle to regain your direction in life. Will you ever reach the safety of the shore? How will you be able to reach it? What can you do? How can you take charge of your physical and mental health and move toward wellness?

Moving toward wellness begins like any other journey—with the first step.

> Suffering touches every human life. What we decide to do with our personal suffering has much to do with the quality of our lives.
>
> —Sister Marla Reilly

There comes a time in the life of each bereaved person when he has to make a choice. The choice is really very simple. It is to curl up and die or to get up and live. Reconciling loss and going on with life is a process that is easier with support and assistance from others, but like so many other responsibilities in your life, it is one that only you can complete. I have used Barbara Johnson's quote with many of my support groups: "Only you can do it, but you can't do it alone." This emphasizes the importance of asking for and accepting help but first making that important choice to move forward.

Jesus said it best in Luke 4:23 when he said, "Physician heal thyself." If we want to be well, if we want to be healthy, if we want to get better, *we* have to make that choice. In order for us to attain physical and emotional wellness, there are several areas we must improve by taking positive actions.

1. Physical Care

The family physician should be made aware of the loss in your life. He will evaluate medications you are taking and make adjustments if needed. Grief takes a toll on the mourner's health; and it was found in a study done by Charlton, Sheahan, Smith, and Campbell that surviving spouses experienced more visits to the physician and received more prescriptions for various illnesses during the year following the death of their spouse than they had in previous years. There was also an increase in treatment for psychological illnesses during the post loss year for these patients.

Receiving a thorough physical checkup after a loss is especially important if the mourner served as caregiver before the death. Caregivers quite often neglect taking care of their own health because they are so busy caring for the loved one. After the death, it is not unusual to find the caregiver let many of his own health appointments go due to the responsibilities of taking care of the ill person.

Several studies validate the effect of loss on the health of survivors. The results are not surprising since we know that stress takes a toll on physical well-being. A study by Nicholas Christakis compared the mortality rates of the surviving spouses in different caregiver survivor groups. One group had assistance from outside sources such as hospice during their loved one's illness. The other group did not have this support. The study showed those without the hospice's help showed significantly higher death rates in the eighteen months following their spouse's death.

The assistance with nursing care, as well as an outlet for talking to someone about the illness, helped to relieve some of the stress for the caregiver. While both men and women in the strained caregiver group experienced a higher death rate, the death rate for surviving husbands was not as high as for surviving wives.

Perhaps one explanation for this gender difference can be taken from another study by Schultz, which found that women, more so older women, scored higher on the scale of feeling helplessness in assuming the role and responsibilities of the spouse. Living alone, especially if they owned a home, impacted this group's feeling of responsibility. This feeling built more stress contributing to higher risk factors for health.

The second group comparisons in this study of the impact of bereavement on health compared caregiver group to noncaregiver group. Again, the finding showed a higher death rate in the caregiver group during the eighteen-month period following the death of the loved one than in the noncaregiver group. However, an interesting difference between the two groups was the caregiver group reported significantly lower depression indicators after six months than the noncaregiver group. The conclusion drawn was the relief expressed by the caregivers that the loved one's suffering was ended was a factor in reduction of depressive symptoms.

The impact from the stress of caring for a loved one cannot be overlooked. A study done by the Yale School of Medicine validated that the survivor who has fulfilled the caregiver role suffered more physical and mental complaints than noncaregiver survivors. In this particular study, 20% of the respondents reported a decline in their health for a period of one year preceding the death. Thirty percent met the criteria for major depressive disorder at the time of the death. Additional impairment was noted to be higher in their social functioning, mental health, and general health perceptions.

Since my husband experienced a long period of illness before his death, I can relate to the reasons why many caregivers neglect their own health and checkups. There is always too much to do and too little time. There are enough visits with doctors, hospitals, and laboratories for the one who is ill; so your own symptoms go untreated. Many times, you simply fail to follow through with good health behaviors.

I felt physically and emotionally drained after his death. In the last year of his life, I was hospitalized three times for respiratory and colon problems. I was so exhausted after his death I did not know if I had the energy left to begin the grieving process.

Tending to my own health had only been done in stopgap measures. I let many routine physicals, eye and dental appointments, fall behind schedule during the lengthy illness he suffered. I was like an old car past tune-up time! I spent a great deal of time in the first year of my bereavement doing all the things that needed to be done to get me back in the best possible health. It was a full year before I felt truly healthy. It was important for me to reach this soundness of body to effectively continue my grief work. It is important for all survivors to start this different life following the loss with a complete physical examination, followed by doing all the things needed for optimal good health.

The next thing to consider in your physical care is diet. Healthy eating truly does do a body good. When you grieve, you may not feel like eating. You may grab the first thing that comes to hand, or you may skip meals. You certainly do not think about well-balanced meals. When you fail to eat properly, you are not giving your body what it needs to carry you through each day. Poor diet coupled with poor eating can diminish your coping skills.

Planning your meals is a smart move when you are having food issues. This planning may include being sure your kitchen is stocked with the right kinds of foods to eat in a different meal style. If you do not feel like going to the market, this is a great activity to give to some of the people who want to help you in some way. Many times, the thought of food makes the mourner feel ill. Large meals may be unappetizing. Good eating does not mean one has to eat three big meals a day. Small amounts, eaten more frequently, can help with appetite loss. Fruits, vegetables, grains, and dairy products are important parts of a good diet.

Drinking adequate amounts of water to hydrate the body is important too. Caffeine dehydrates the body. This is why excessive consumption of coffee, tea, and colas is to be avoided. A well-hydrated system is important in maintaining good physical health.

Skipping meals throws the metabolism off and contributes to overeating later and to decreased energy. If the mourner is taking medications, it is especially important to keep a balanced diet in order for the medications to work to full advantage.

Sugar, caffeine, oily food, sweets, and foods high in fat should be avoided as you get your body fueled to do your grief work. According to physicians, foods high in saturated fats are the worst offenders in artery and cardiovascular disease. These foods tend to be high in cholesterol, which contributes to clogged arteries and heart disease. Narrowed blood vessels do not allow the brain to receive as much oxygen as it needs, and the resulting feeling is one of fatigue and low energy. The American Heart Association's standard recommendation is for no more than 30% of daily calories from fat.

The stress of loss may interfere with your sleep patterns. So many problems surfaced due to lack of adequate rest. Again, diet can help with the sleep solution. The body may need more melatonin in order for you to feel drowsy enough to sleep. Some foods rich in melatonin are bananas, tomatoes, and rice. Adding more of these foods to your diet may help you with a natural solution to sleep problems.

In considering the best diet for bereaved people, it is somewhat amusing that when a person dies, the things most people do to assist the family through the initial days of loss—up to and including the funeral—can be the very things that are dietetically the worst for people under great stress. Our society immediately thinks about the physical comforts that can be provided for the families, and it is natural that the comfort foods rank high on the list of things to contribute. When someone dies, coffee is made by the gallons. Cakes, pies, and casseroles begin to pour into the home. The home of the bereaved is soon filled with a smorgasbord of comfort foods. However, knowledge of how these foods impact the health, especially of people under stress, can assist not only the bereaved families in choosing better foods but can also assist friends and other community helpers in selecting healthy fare to bring to bereaved families.

The third important component of physical care is exercise. Exercise provides the mourner a way to lessen the effects of stress and depression. It is also a key component in the program to improve your physical condition. It is very hard to get up and walk around when you feel totally drained and lethargic. However, inactivity breeds inactivity! Exercise on a daily basis helps you with your self-healing process. You probably will not have the energy to do extensive exercising, but it is vital for you to remain mobile. This does not mean you have to go to the gym or do anything particularly strenuous. It simply means that you must move it or lose it!

Walking is the very best exercise. Most people, if they are mobile, can do some walking even if it is limited. Twenty minutes of walking daily has a major effect on not only your energy level but also on your state of mind. The endorphins produced in the brain by exercise help in fighting depression, lethargy, and stress. Just as diet can affect your sleep patterns, so can exercise. You will find with some daily exercise that you may not only experience a better appetite, but also, you may find you are able to get more rest.

It is easy to find a million reasons for not exercising. This is true for people who have not experienced a loss, but it is even truer for the mourner. Mourners may give excuses such as, "I'm just too exhausted to move." "The weather is too hot/cold/rainy to go outside." "I just feel too badly to do anything physical." Some patients express, "It doesn't matter whether I exercise or not. My world is ruined anyway because my loved one died." These reactions are not abnormal; everyone who experiences a loss can sympathize with them.

However, the fact remains that the mourner is still among the living; and it is of utmost importance to keep the blood circulating, the heart pumping, the muscles stretching, and the lungs working to capacity. This goes back to something mentioned earlier in this chapter, which is making a *choice*. You can choose to not sit and let things happen to you but to be proactive. Good health does not just happen. It is greatly assisted by you making wise choices to take care of your body. You have to choose to take back control of your life and do the things that must be done to be productive and purposeful again.

Whatever religious beliefs you may follow, the body is the home for the spirit. When our spirit takes a serious hit, such as loss of a loved one, it becomes easy to ignore the maintenance required on the home of the spirit—the body. The Bible, in I Corinthians 6:19, says,

> Do you not know that your body is a temple of the Holy Spirit,
> who is in you, whom you have received from God? You are
> not your own.

Christian believers are admonished in this passage to honor God by caring for the body. But even nonbelievers can understand that what makes us what we are, our spirit, is housed in this physical shell. In order for us to function properly, that physical housing must be cared for and maintained.

2. Self-care

What can you do to give yourself the care you need in order to go forward from this terrible loss? Ted Menten, in his excellent book *After Goodbye,* said it best when he said,

> Wisdom is not knowing what the answer is, but knowing where
> the answer is—it is in your own heart.

No one knows what helps you more than you do. Self-care is very important, but it is hard for us to do because we are taught from the time we are youngsters that doing for self is selfish. Women appear to have a particularly hard time with this concept of self-care. In my practice, not only bereaved women—but also other women suffering great stress, anxiety, and depression—are often found to be running pell-mell, constantly doing for others and doing absolutely nothing for their own mental and physical health.

So the first hurdle to get over with the self-care concept is to learn it is imperative to take care of oneself in order to be of any help to anyone else. I am reminded of this every time I fly, and the flight attendant gives the demonstration about the oxygen masks. They always make the point, if you have someone with you who will need assistance, to put your own mask on first so you will be able to help. This is true in our lives. When we fail to do adequate self-care, we are refusing to put the oxygen mask on first.

Ask yourself this question as you start to assess the quality of your self-care: If I were treating my best friend like I am treating myself, what would I think of that behavior? If the answer is that you would be ashamed or you would not have her for a friend very long, there needs to be some changes made in how you care for yourself. Tending to your own emotional wounds is imperative to being able to handle the tough times in life. You would help anyone else in need, would you not? Why not meet your own needs?

It is vital for you to be compassionate with yourself. We do not have trouble being compassionate with others when they are hurting, but for some reason, we find this very hard to do when we are dealing with our own hurts. In Dr. Alan Wolfelt's book *Healing Your Grieving Heart*, he paraphrased one of the beatitudes by saying, "Blessed are those who learn self compassion for they shall go on to discover continued meaning in life."

Where do you begin? You must first look at the total self. This includes your past—before and after your loved one came into your life. What were your talents, hopes, dreams, goals, sensitivities, and passions? How have those changed throughout the years? What are they now? Self-care will help you answer those questions because it encompasses (1) reclaiming yourself, (2) redefining yourself, (3) nurturing yourself, and (4) doing cognitive self-care.

During the time you shared with your loved one, you invested huge parts of yourself in the relationship. That person is gone now, and there is a surplus of time, talent, and energy no longer being used in that particular relationship. Questions you must ask in order to reclaim yourself are,

1. Who or what am I today?
2. What do I need or want to change?
3. What goals do I need to set?
4. What do I think others want from me?
5. What talents, abilities, and/or gifts do I have?

These questions require you to identify the needs and resources of your body, mind, and spirit. Until you do this inventory of yourself, you cannot make a plan to move forward with your life.

Reclaiming yourself is recovering your identity. For example, before my husband died, many of my own personal interests, talents, and gifts changed in order to fit the needs of the relationship. To build a good relationship in a marriage, a person works to find common interests and develops new interests the spouse enjoys also. As a couple, we developed social contacts and recreational activities that were not of primary interest to me alone.

After his death, I found I no longer fit into the same mold of my old life with him. I was free to explore more interests I enjoyed previously that he did not enjoy. I reconnected with people from my past who were lost to me through the years due to different life circumstances. I also found the lifestyle of a single person was quite different from that of a married couple. Daily routines, personal living habits, and social activities required adjustments. For a while, I felt like a square peg in a round hole! My comfort zone was gone, and I no longer operated in automatic pilot. I had to develop into a new person in order to function successfully in this new life. This required me to take the wheel and change directions.

From working in my practice with people suffering many different types of loss, I find this to be true of them too. For example, after losing a child, parents find their activities drastically changed. This is especially true if the child is older and involved in a lot of school activities. Some parents have described it as losing their whole social network. One mother said her activities were gone after her son's loss. The other parents she and her husband did so many child-related activities with no longer had a common thread to bind them together.

During the process of reclaiming yourself, you will discover your roles have changed. This leads you to the next step of self-care, which is redefining yourself. A huge part of each person's identity is formed by relationships. When I lost my husband, I discovered I was not a wife anymore. If that was true, what was I? It took a long time to not only stop acting married, but to stop feeling married. When my parents died, even though I was grown, I lost my role as a child. Adjusting to not being anyone's child was a very difficult process. In each of these different losses, my roles changed drastically and had to be redefined.

The bond you had with your loved one was special. You had roles and duties to perform, and these were very much connected to that person. When he dies, your need for performing these roles and duties is no longer there. Your roles and responsibilities are changed, and you are left with the task of redefining yourself to fit your changing lifestyle.

This period of redefining yourself takes a long time, and it is ever evolving. Part of it involves integrating the deceased loved one from the present into the past. In the process, you are also sorting parts of your identity. You are selecting some parts of your old self to keep and adding new or rediscovered parts. This is a time when you are vulnerable and may be unsure of your decisions. You are not only forming a new self, you are forming new relationships also.

A couple of things are important to do during this time of redefining self. First, it is helpful to list three people you can turn to if you feel you need some direction. Just knowing there is a contingency plan helps relieve some of the stress of this period. Second, it is a good time to use some of your quiet time to reassess your priorities now that you have a different self. A simple list on a piece of paper listing *what's important* and *what's not important* will help you to realign your roles. Nothing quiets the fear of the unknown more than making some preparations for facing the task before you.

As you go through the process of reclaiming and redefining yourself, you will discover parts of you were not used in the relationship. There is someone inside you who is a unique and different person. Self-development begins. As it proceeds, you find this person may want to deal with life and all it has to offer in vastly different ways from your previous patterns. It is important to know self-development after loss not only entails reclaiming and redefining self, but also embracing the different self you have become.

I am different now from before the death of my husband and my parents. It does not mean I am better or worse; just that I am different because I am living a different life. In order to embrace this different person, a great deal of soul-searching and exploration of my inner self was required. I had to find the qualities I needed to go forward in the different life thrust upon me. I let go of some obsolete roles, and I grew in developing interests I previously did not pursue.

Reclaiming and redefining yourself is an exhausting process. During this time is it important to nurture yourself. The self-nurturing component of self-care is important because this involves soothing your soul. Dealing effectively with the stress and emotions of loss means you must be good to yourself. Allow yourself time to think, rest, and renew your energy. This is a time to pamper yourself. The idea that you shouldn't take time for yourself is not biblical. In fact, failure to do so can have devastating effects!

You have the perfect excuse for exiting out of the rat race that takes up much of your daily schedule and contributes to your stress. Again, rely on your own instincts as to what will help you the most. Some suggestions for this nurturing process that have not been mentioned in the other sections of diet and exercise are,

a. Create a haven for yourself.

This involves looking at your physical environment and selecting a room or a place in your home you can make your "battery recharging spot." Make this a comfortable place to sit or lie. Even if the rest of your home is chaotic or messy, this will be your comfort spot. It is just for you. It is your sanctuary. When you want to be alone with your thoughts, or have a cup of tea, or listen to some music, or just be, go to this place and take some time out from the hustle and bustle of the world.

b. Make some small changes in your physical environment.

This does not have to be a major overhaul of your house or apartment. Perhaps, adding a spot of color to a bland room will do the trick. Maybe adding a plant or something else of beauty to change the appearance will help. Some people get a comfortable chair to put in the room where they stay a great deal of the time. Perhaps putting something away that has been in your environment for a long time may be helpful.

I moved my husband's chair out of the den because it was a painful reminder every time I sat there. I also put away a few pictures. I moved my belongings to the guest room and began to sleep in there as opposed to the master bedroom. These were simply small changes I made, which helped me. Again, this is personal choice. Do what makes *you* feel better.

c. Develop new interests.

As you work on who you are and what you want, you will discover you have some interests you either have not pursued or you let go for various reasons. Begin to do something of interest to you. It can be a project around the home or elsewhere, but the key is that it must be enjoyable for you. There may be a class you always wanted to take. Perhaps there is a hobby you once enjoyed but stopped doing. Maybe you've thought about volunteering, but your family duties took too much of your time. Think about what interests you, and consider whether or not this would bring joy to you.

d. Plan minivacations.

This does not mean to go on a trip. It simply means that you plan each day to take one hour to do something you thoroughly enjoy. It could be sitting with a cup of soup. It could be watching one special television program. It could be reading. It could be a bubble bath or long shower. It could be gardening. It does not matter what it is as long as you have a plan, and it is something you want to do.

Cognitive nurturing is another important part of the self-care program. The goal of this kind of nurturing is to build self-esteem and confidence. It is also to take away living in fear. Cognitive nurturing helps you to feel you are exerting some measure of control in your life. This is best accomplished by sending more positive messages to your brain.

For example, instead of thinking of all the things you cannot do, list the things you can do. List the things you accomplished that are positive steps forward. It may be as simple as "I did not cry for one hour today."

Or it could be you washed your hair and dressed. Perhaps you took a short walk, or maybe you ate something instead of skipped meals. Thinking about the positive things you did in your physical environment to make it more pleasant for you is another great psychological lift, because it focuses on positive behaviors instead of negative ones.

Have confidence in yourself and the fact that your body and mind will point you toward the best help for healing. You may not be able to enjoy great pleasure at this time, but you can find joy in small comforts. When you find comfort, emphasize its power to yourself. Refuse to feel bad about having moments of joy. This is one of the strongest kinds of cognitive nurturing.

One form of cognitive nurturing I used was taking what I called *grief breaks*. Just as workers do a better job if given short breaks periodically, I did a better job handling my grief if I was able to mentally take a break from it. This requires taking control of your mental processes. I simply set aside a small portion of time I vowed to think about something else besides the loss.

Some things I did during my grief breaks were reading the comic page, reading an advice column, working a crossword puzzle, listening to one song, calling a friend, and watering my African violets. During these short breaks, I refused to think about my loss. None of these activities took very long. Although they required very little time, the positive cognitive gain I experienced was tremendous. I was soon immersed in the midst of my grief but felt renewed to tackle it. As I mentioned previously, techniques have to be personal because each person's grief is so unique. You are the best judge of what activities you can do during a grief break.

3. Expression of Feelings

A mourner wellness program would not be complete without avenues for the mourner to express the huge variety of feelings that assail him on a daily basis. As numbness wears off and feelings begin to surface, the emotional pain is excruciating. As in all other aspects of the grieving process, how you express your feelings is a very personal choice. With that being said, take the following suggestions as suggestions only. Each one of these ways of expressing thoughts and feelings has helped many people, but there is no clear-cut, one-size-fits-all method. Remember, you are the captain of your own ship. So as you are buffeted on the sea of grief, choose wisely the tools that will best help you navigate the treacherous waters.

Writing or journaling helps some people. If you are a writer and love to put things on paper, this may be the right choice for you. If you hate to write, this obviously would not be helpful. Writing about how it was or how it is can be very good therapy for the hurting soul. A popular writing book by Natalie Goldberg called *Writing Down the Bones* helps people learn to express core feelings in writing. This is the purpose of journaling. You are digging to the bare bones of your feelings and expressing them in written words.

When you are able to express the hurt deep inside, it can provide a tremendous relief. Grammar and punctuation do not matter. You are not writing this for anyone but yourself. Journaling not only helps you to express what you feel, but it gives you a way of looking back and seeing the progress you made. This is vital because the progress for a mourner is in such small, infinitesimal steps often mourners feel there is no progress being made. A journal gives positive feedback that some forward progress has occurred.

The importance of journaling is twofold. First, you must think about the loss and begin to sort the emotions. Second, finding words to express the pain is a huge step forward in dealing with the heartache. This is a difficult process. The beginning of many journals is disjointed and displays the confusion and frustration of the writer. As the journaling continues, the writing not only shows improvement, but the writer can clearly see the advances made in the thinking processes.

Another avenue of help is a support group. There are many different types of support groups, and you may have to visit several before you find the right fit for you. If the support group has a leader who is experienced in keeping everyone involved and not letting it become a litany of sob stories, it can be a very beneficial experience. Not only are there general grief support groups, but also there are specialized groups. Specialized groups may be by type of loss, age of survivors, or gender specific. The availability of support groups depends on the mental health resources in your community.

The benefits of a support group are many for those who choose to participate. First, it provides a place where the mourner can access people who understand him and accept his feelings. This provides a means of catharsis. Second, learning about and seeing others who have gone through the same experiences and have come out intact provides encouragement to the mourner that it is possible to go forward. Third, it is an opportunity to share practical information about resources and other options that may be available. Fourth, some support groups provide social and recreational activities. Sometimes friendships are formed in the group and carried over to activities outside the group.

If the mourner has few or no family members in the area, a good support group can be a godsend. Avoiding isolation is very important in dealing with grief in a healthy way, and support groups help the mourner by providing contact with others.

Some mourners do not feel comfortable talking about their feelings in a group and prefer individual counseling. This is also a good choice. It may be encouraged if the mourner is having complicated grief. There may be issues, which need to be addressed that would be best discussed in private sessions rather than a group setting.

The value of therapy is help in adjusting to the world as it is for the mourner. A skilled therapist can help the mourner to untangle some of the emotional knots of bereavement and to sort out those emotions. Loss brings the mourner to an emotionally negative situation, and the job of the therapist is to help the mourner go from negative back to zero. From that point, again, it is up to the mourner to make the choice to move forward in dealing with the loss. The direction of a good therapist can assist the mourner to unblock his ability to live meaningfully again, but the therapist cannot take the mourner to that place of meaning and purpose. This is something only the mourner can do.

Psychotherapy is an educational process rather than a medical cure. A therapist helps the mourner to clarify experiences, correct misconceptions, and relieve anxieties. Promotion of emotional growth is the goal of the psychotherapy. The therapist assists the mourner by asking good questions and helping the mourner to work out his own solutions. This enables the mourner to achieve growth. Pointing out important connections the patient may have missed helps the mourner to focus on his own good answers.

There are many different professionals in communities who are available to do individual sessions. It may be a minister, priest, rabbi, therapist, or someone from the medical field. The availability of resources depends on your location. Calling local clergy, local hospice or palliative care centers, or local mental health agencies can help mourners locate therapists who work with bereaved individuals.

Family and friends are other important outlets for mourners in expressing emotions. There are several cautions for the mourner if using family and friends as the main outlets. First, your need to talk about the loss may exceed your family and friends' desire to listen. People get tired of hearing the story over and over. You, the mourner, need to talk about it for much longer than they want to hear it. Telling the story is an important part of the healing process, and this is another way support groups and/or individual counseling can help the mourner. The second caution is to select someone who will keep your talks confidential. Sharing with someone who shares your information with everyone else can be problematic.

One advantage of talking to family and friends is they can identify with your loss because they too are experiencing grief from loss of the person. However, this is a double-edged sword. Because they are grieving too, they may not be capable of being a help to you. The other danger in talking to people you are close to is you may end up getting a lot of well-meaning but useless advice. You are not seeking a solution when you want to express your feelings. You simply want a listening ear. There is no magic fix for dealing with the pain of loss. There is nothing that will take the pain away, but talking about it helps the mourner to deal with it.

Mary Ann Vail of the Ministry of Consolation used the following poem in a presentation at Creighton University, and I found it to be the consummate how-to directive for what a mourner needs when trying to express feelings. It is titled "It Helps to Have Friends Who Will Listen."

It Helps to Have Friends Who Will Listen

When I ask you to listen to me and you start giving me advice,
You have not done what I asked.
When I ask you to listen to me and you begin to tell me why I shouldn't feel that way,
You are trampling on my feelings.
When I ask you to listen to me, and you feel you have to do something to solve my problems,
You have failed me, strange as that may seem.

Listen! All I asked was that you listen, not talk or do—just hear me!
Advice is cheap; twenty cents will get you both "Dear Abby" and "Billy Graham" in the same newspaper.

I can do for myself. I'm not helpless.
Maybe discouraged and faltering, but not helpless!
When you do something for me that I can and need to do for myself,
You contribute to my fear and inadequacy.

But when you accept as a simple fact that I do feel what I feel,
No matter how irrational, then,
I can quit trying to convince you
And get about the business of understanding
what's behind this irrational feeling.

And when that's clear,
The answers are obvious and I don't need advice.
Irrational feelings make sense when we understand what's behind them.

Perhaps, that's why prayer works sometimes for people, because God is mute
And doesn't give advice or try to fix things.
He just listens and lets you work it out for yourself.
So, please listen and just hear me.
And if you want to talk, wait a minute for your turn and I'll listen to you.

—Author Unknown

The author of this poem apparently knows firsthand how important it is to talk about the loss and to have a good listener. The expression of the feelings and the telling of the story over and over bring a release to the mourner that is paramount in moving toward wellness. While expressing the emotion does not take the pain away, it does help to provide the strength to bear it. In the words of Frances Ridley Havergal: "Sorrow which is never spoken is the heaviest load to bear."

Education about the impact of grieving on physical and mental health is a positive, beneficial action for the mourner to pursue. Knowledge is one of the most important tools human beings can use to reduce anxiety, fear, and stress. Loss puts each of us in uncharted waters, and few of us are prepared for the life-altering effect of loss. If we learn to recognize problematic symptoms, we are better able to plan interventions. If we know what symptoms to expect, we are not taken off guard and are better able to plan coping strategies. Knowledge enables us to exert some measure of control over an uncontrollable situation. It is not necessarily the fear of the unknown that haunts us but the fear of not knowing what to do about it. The goal of this chapter is to give the mourner knowledge, thus, providing a valuable tool in the mourner's survival kit. The attainment of knowledge helps us to navigate the storm of bereavement. In the words of Louisa May Alcott: "I am not afraid of storms, for I am learning how to sail my ship."

Chapter 3 References

1. Blair, Pamela, PhD, and Brook Noel. 2000. *I Wasn't Ready to Say Goodbye: Surviving, Coping and Healing after the Sudden Death of a Loved One.* Milwaukee, WI: Champion Press LTD.
2. Bowlby, John. 1982. Attachment and Loss: Retrospective Prospect. *American Journal of Orthopsychiatry* 52 (1980): 664-664-678.
3. Bowlby, John. 1982. Attachment and Loss: Retrospective Prospect. *American Journal of Orthopsychiatry* 52 (1980): 664-664-678.
4. Bozarth, Alla Renee, PhD. 1990. *A Journey through Grief.* Center City, MO: Hazelton.
5. Caine, Lynn. 1990. *A Compassionate, Practical Guide to Being a Widow.* New York:NY: Penguin Putnam Inc.
6. Charlton, Rodger, Kelly Sheahan, Gary Smith, and Ian Campbell. 2001. Spousal Bereavement Implications for Health. *Family Practice* 18, no. 6 (June): 614-615-618.
7. Christakis, Nicholas A., Theodore J. Iwashyna. 2003. The Health Impact of Health Care on Familes: A Matched Cohort Study of Hospice Use by Decedents and Mortality Outcomes in Surviving, Widowed Spouses. *Social Science and Medicine* 57: 465-466-475.
8. Claypool, John. 1995. *Tracks of a Fellow Struggler: Living and Growing through Grief.* New Orleans, LA: Insight Press.
9. Clayton, P. J. 1974. "Mortality and Morbidity in the First Year of Widowhood." *Archives of General Psychiatry* 30: 747-748-750.
10. Hofer, M. A., C. T. Wolff, and J. W. and Mason. 1972. "A Psychoendocrine Study of Bereavement Part II: Observations on the Process of Mourning in Relation to Adrenocortical Function." *Psychosomatic Medicine* 34, no. 7 (July): 492-493-504.
11. Johnson, Barbara. 1994. *Mama, Get the Hammer! There's a Fly on Papa's Head: Using Humor to Flatten out Your Pain.* Dallas, TX: Word Publishing.
12. Kushner, Harold. 2002. *When All You've Ever Wanted Isn't Enough: The Search for a Life That Matters.* New York, New York: Simon and Schuster.
13. Lukas, Christopher, and Henry M. Seiden. 1987. *Silent Grief: Living in the Wake of Suicide.* New York, NY: Macmillan Publishing Company.
14. Menten, Ted. 1994. *After Goodbye: How to Begin Again after the Death of Someone You Love.* Philadelphia, PA: p. 126, Running Press.

15. Meyer, Charles. 1997. *Surviving Death: A Practical Guide to Caring for the Dying and Bereaved.* Mystic, Conn: Twenty-Third Publications.

16. Muller, Elizabeth D., Charles L. Thompson. 2003. The Experience of Grief after Bereavement: A Phenomenological Study with Implications for Mental Health Counseling. *Journal of Mental Health Counseling* 25, no. 3: 183-184-187.

17. Prigerson, PhD, Emily Cherlin M. S. W., Joyce Chen, Kasl, Stanislav V., PhD, M. P. H. Hurzeler, and Bradley, Elizabeth H., PhD. 2003. The Stressful Caregiving Adult Reactions to Experiences of Dying (SCARED) Scale: A Measure for Assessing Caregiver Exposure to Distress in Terminal Care. *American Journal of Geriatric Psychiatry* 11, no. 3 (June): 309-310-319.

18. Rando, Therese A. 1986. *Loss and Anticipatory Grief.* Lexington, Mass: Lexington Books.

19. Reilly, Marla, S. P. 1996. *Now That I Am Old: Meditations on the Meaning of Life. P. 67*, Mystic, Connecticut: Twenty-Third Publications

20. Schulz, Richard, PhD, Beach, Scott R., PhD, Bonnie Lind MS, Lynn Martire PhD, Bozena Zdanuik PhD, Calviin Hirsch MD, Sharon Jackson PhD, and Lynda Burton ScD. 2001. Involvement in Caregiving and Adjustment to Death of a Spouse. *The Journal of the American Medical Association* 285, no. 24 (June): 3123-3124-3129.

21. Shuchter, Stephen R. 1986. *Dimensions of Grief: Adjusting to the Death of a Spouse.* San Francisco, CA: Jossey-Bass.

22. Stalling, Elizabeth. 1997. *Prayer Starters: To Help You Heal after Loss. P. 20*, St. Meinrad, IN: Abbey Press.

23. Staudacher, Carol. 1991. *Men and Grief: A Guide for Men Surviving the Death of a Loved One.* Oakland, CA: New Harbinger Publications.

24. Staudacher, Carol. 1987. *Beyond Grief: A Guide for Recovering from the Death of a Loved One.* Oakland, CA: New Harbinger Publications.

25. Tatelbaum, Judy. 1980. *The Courage to Grieve: Creative Living, Recovery, and Growth through Grief.* New York, New York: Harper Row.

26. Wolfelt, Alan D., PhD. 2001. *Healing Your Grieving Heart.* Fort Collins, CO: Companion Press.

27. Wolfelt, Alan D., PhD. 1992. *Understanding Grief: Helping Yourself Heal.* Muncie: IN: Accelerated Development Inc.

Chapter 4

THE GRIEF ROLLER COASTER

Author Karen Linamen says there is good news and bad news about grieving. She says the good news is that grieving is not unlike an arcade game—the pinball machine. The bad news is we are the pinball! We may be able to see some grim humor in this analogy, but it is no laughing matter when we find ourselves plunged into grief and bouncing back and forth emotionally like that pinball.

Plunging from highs to lows emotionally happens when we go from one phase of grief to another, then back again. We talked in chapter 1 about the phases of grief and how we tend to ebb and flow in and out of those phases. We skip some phases and go back and forth into others numerous times. We find ourselves in denial some days, exhausted on many days, and then energized by a burst of angry energy at other times. We may think we have accepted the loss one minute, only to discover we are still wallowing in doubt, fear, and uncertainty the next. We berate ourselves for our inconsistent behaviors and question our own sanity.

When discussing the phases in chapter 1, it was pointed out that grief is very messy. It is not a neat, tidy process. Emotional pain is not organized. It spins us out of control and throws us off balance from our normal routine behaviors. Ms. Linamen described our reactions as being the ball in a pinball machine. I often call it riding the grief roller coaster.

The Grief Roller Coaster

The roller coaster ride of grief is a fearsome ride. It makes you not only fearful and unsure of yourself; it creates feelings of dread, panic, and anxiety, because you never know what is coming next. When will the next sudden drop occur? You never fully relax, because just when you think your emotions have stabilized, you find yourself plunging into the pits of despair.

Up and down, up and down go your emotions. Your behaviors follow suit and are just as unpredictable. When this happens, pay attention to your emotions. Do not be discouraged by the irregularity of your behavior patterns. Eventually, your emotions will level out, but not until you work through all of them. Allow yourself to fully experience the feelings. Healing comes to you through admitting and expressing the feelings.

These up-and-down emotions are a normal part of the grief experience. As time passes after the death, you may feel you are getting better. After a while, you begin to string together more good days than bad. You begin to feel the hand of grief loosening its grip on your heart. Then, without warning, the grief returns with a vengeance, knocking you down in your progress. Out of nowhere appears the pit of depression, and you plunge back into it. Brook Noel, in the book *I Wasn't Ready to Say Goodbye*, calls these events the ambush. This is a very good name for it because when it happens, you will feel that you've been ambushed in a very cruel way.

You just began to feel you had a handle on the pain; then the handle fell off! Why does this happen? There may be various reasons for the return of the despair. Sometimes there are no reasons for the resurgence of grief except to say it is the nature of the beast. Other times, you may be able to pinpoint a reason for the plunge.

Often the grief resurfaces because of some inconsequential occurrence. It may be a spoken word or phrase that reminds you of the deceased. Perhaps your loved one's favorite song came on the radio. Or while rummaging through a drawer, you came across an old greeting card from your loved one. A sad movie may strike a chord of sorrow in your heart. Maybe you bumped into someone who triggered a strong memory of the deceased. Sometimes, there is absolutely no identifiable cause for the sudden intense longing and pain. It just resurfaces of its own accord.

Grief intensifies when this happens, and the mourner suffers resurging loneliness, sadness, and despair. When you think you are doing better, this is quite disconcerting. Clients say to me, "I thought I was doing so well. Now it's worse than ever." or "I've made no progress." The valleys on the roller coaster ride are discouraging moments to the mourner.

Most people feel these downs show a lack of progress with their grief. However, that is a misconception. At the beginning of this roller coaster ride, your changing emotions are constant and full of ups and downs. A pictorial example of the ride at this time would look like this:

Figure 4.1

These ups and downs are the normal ebb and flow of emotions when you are newly bereaved. As you can see, the changes are close together, and there is a great deal of difference between the highs and lows. Is it any wonder you feel you are on the roller coaster? There are so many feelings assailing you they keep you off balance.

As the ride through this grief journey continues, your roller coaster track begins to look more like this:

Figure 4.2

It is important to note in this drawing that even though there are many down days, the ride at the peak begins to be longer. This means you begin to have a longer period of time between the drops in mood. Also, look at the valleys of the ride. As more time goes by, the valleys, while low, are not quite as low as they were in the first drawing.

With more time and grief work under your belt, your ride begins to look like this:

Figure 4.3

Again, you can see a marked improvement in the duration of the good days, a lessening of the severity of the bad days. This shows that progress is being made, even though those down days are discouraging to you when they come.

The final drawing of your roller coaster ride illustrates the pattern you will follow, I believe, for a lifetime. This ride, unlike the carnival ride, which has a beginning and an end, is a lifetime ride. It looks like this:

Figure 4.4

So do you ever get off the ride? No. You spend the rest of your life exhibiting this last pattern. Why do I think this is true? I think it because I have lived it. After the loss of my loved ones, my moods followed these patterns and still do today.

Alan Wolfelt, PhD, says, "Mourning never really ends. Only as time goes on does it erupt less frequently." The last diagram of the roller coaster pattern represents a reconciliation of the loss into the mourner's life. There are long periods of functioning normally. There are long periods when the loss is not uppermost in your mind. But because you loved that person and have so many memories of him, there will be times when the sadness, grief, or sense of loss returns. Grief revisits us throughout our lives.

There are many triggers for these downtimes. Some have been previously mentioned. The lifetime triggers are the special days and milestone events that occur in every family. Holidays, graduations, births, birthdays, important anniversaries, and the anniversary of the death are a few of the special days. You have so many memorable times connected to these dates. Loved ones come back to the forefront of your mind when these days arrive. Dealing with these days will be discussed in a later chapter, but special days must be mentioned here because they are one reason the last pattern of the roller coaster ride has the continued small dips over the life span of the mourner.

Why is it not disconcerting to think we stay on this ride forever after a loss? I believe it is comforting to think I operate on the last pictured pattern of the ride, because I loved those I lost. This tells me they are still very much a part of me. They are present in my heart, if not in my physical life. I loved them then, and I still do. That love does not keep me from living, enjoying, and going forward with my life. However, occasionally, I have moments when I am moved by memory to shed a tear and think about how it was. The fact death did not take away the relationship comes home to me when this happens. Death simply took the life. I carry the loved ones with me every day. It is just as writer Elizabeth Stalling said, "We come to discover we don't necessarily have to see what we love in order to know it is safe in our hearts."

Understanding the roller coaster ride of emotions is an important concept for the mourner. It allows us to own our grief. It allows us to grieve thoroughly and to fully experience the avalanche of emotions assailing our minds. It enables us to understand our sense of well-being will return. Each time we feel better, it lasts a little longer. Next time, it will last longer still. So it goes throughout our lives. Fully understanding and allowing yourself to grieve is the cornerstone for emotional health.

The Transition to Healing

The grief roller coaster is our transition to healing. In the book *The Courage to Grieve*, Judy Tatelbaum discusses the disorganization of grief and what disorganization does to our lives. As we move through grief, she says we move toward reorganization.

The concept of grief as a process of moving from disorganization to reorganization is used in many of my support groups. Since many people are visual learners, drawings and diagrams help them better understand their behavioral processes.

In my work, I use her disorganization-to-reorganization concept to construct a diagram for the mourner to use to visualize the process.

The transition-to-healing diagram also uses the works of Wolfelt and Rando. I have simply applied their ideas to a visual aid, which helps mourners to use a concrete tool to understand the process they are going through with their grief.

The Transition to Healing

(Transitional Period)

DISORGANIZATION--RE-ORGANIZATION
(The Loss)   (Healing/Reconciliation)

Embracing the loss

Grieving the loss

Attending to secondary losses

Adjusting to their absence

Reviewing your life with the loved one

Letting go of the past

Developing coping skills

Finding purpose

Reinvestment

Figure 4.3

The transitional time between disorganization and reorganization is the emotionally difficult period I refer to as riding the grief roller coaster. This is the time you go through major upheavals in your life. This is when you struggle to gain your equilibrium. This is when you strive to get life to make sense once again.

Accomplishing the tasks listed in the transitional time requires many activities and changes on the part of the mourner. Studying the diagram, you can identify and discuss the many behaviors challenging you and bringing stress into your life as you work to accomplish the tasks. As each mourner uses the diagram, he will put his own activities in the transition section.

Transitional Behaviors

As you ride the grief roller coaster, many behaviors are exhibited. Some behaviors are healthy and help you move toward the goal of healing. Others are unhealthy. It is imperative for the mourner to grieve in a healthy manner in order to successfully make the transition. It is also important to understand the difference between healthy grief and unhealthy grief in order to identify when assistance is needed with the healing process.

Healthy Grief

Healthy grief is a natural process moving us through our adjustment to the loss. It enables us to successfully reconstruct our lives. Healthy grief is productive because it allows us to eventually return to the mainstream of life. Healthy grief entails making changes and adjustments to enable you to be productive and happy once more.

Think of the grieving period as a convalescent time. You were grievously injured emotionally by the loss of your loved one. If you had surgery, you would require a time of convalescence to let your body recover physically. It is the same with grief. You are in emotional convalescence; therefore, you must practice all the things we discussed in chapter 3 concerning good self-care.

If the grieving is healthy, the mourner shares the grief outside his inner self. He does not hug it close and tamp it down, pretending it is not there. The mourner does not run from the pain but embraces it, talks about it, and shows it. Elisabeth Kubler-Ross said of dealing with the pain:

> You will not grow if you sit in a beautiful flower garden, but you will grow if you are sick, if you are in pain, if you experience losses, and if you do not put your head in the sand, but take the pain and learn to accept it, not as a curse or punishment, but as a gift to you with a very, very specific purpose.

Dr. Kubler-Ross means pain is our source of healing. We are in grief boot camp, and just as the marines say no pain, no gain, we must embrace and deal with the pain if we are to gain progress in our quest for healing. Hiding the pain or running away from the pain does not neutralize it or make it go away. It is always there in your shadow.

The healthy mourner is able to relinquish the physical relationship with the deceased and make the adjustment to the new environment without the him. Saying good-bye is never easy. Of saying good-bye,

Khalil Gibran in *The Prophet* said, "Ever has it been that love knows not its own depth until the hour of separation."

Often, it is not understood the intensity of our love until the separation takes place. So much was taken for granted. So much was not spoken. The task is not to continue wallowing over long in what is missing and to focus on the beauty and wonderment of the gift that was ours. Death will never separate us from that love.

Yes, acknowledging your loved one's death is most painful. However, the breadth and depth of your love for them guarantee some things go on forever. You have memories, stories, thoughts, and a love that transcends the bonds of death and life in your heart. Even though your loved one was taken from you, your relationship and love can never be taken.

Healthy grief enables the mourner to complete the process of redefining one's self and recreates an identity that can function successfully in the new world, which began at the moment of loss. In a research study by Gamino and Lewis analyzing the impact the death of a loved one had on a group of mourners, researchers found being able to redefine the identity was most important in successful grief. The circumstances of the deaths experienced by the participants were varied from illness, trauma, violence, and accidents. Some 45% of the mourners reported they successfully completed this transitional task, thus, enabling them to go on with life and recreate themselves. They also reported accomplishing this by finding some meaning in the loss and by remaining connected with the loved one in a nonphysical way. Those who were not successful were found to be struggling with the adjustment and change in their own identity.

This study validates the importance of the goal of healthy grief, which is to experience personal growth through positive reconciliation of the loss. Just as change of any kind brings loss, it also brings new life. Although you may not want a new life, or were not searching for one, you were given new life by the death of your loved one. Being able to readjust your roles and go forth in a new direction is something each mourner must do in order to have a successful reconciliation of the loss.

Mourners who are healthier in their relationships before the death are found to grieve in healthier ways—thus, making the transition more successful—than those mourners experiencing complications in their relationships. Problems in communication styles before the death also create complications for mourners after the death. Your attachment style makes a huge difference. The more positive your attachment style, the fewer problems the mourner will experience after the loss.

Wayment and Vierthaler studied the attachment styles of mourners and the impact of these styles on grief. They found when the mourner had a secured attachment style, it did not lessen the grief, but it did lessen the depression. Securely attached individuals were most likely to display what is considered a normal grief. This is described as intense grief at the time of loss with the gradual incorporation of the loss into the mourner's sense of self, along with being less susceptible to more pathological reactions such as depression.

During healthy grief, the mourner also grieves secondary losses. This means grieving not only the loss of your loved one, and all the things you did and had together, but also grieving the things that might have been. You grieve the "nevers" the loss creates. It is these secondary losses that account for those dips on the roller coaster ride throughout your life.

When someone you love dies, it creates a string of losses. The person is gone. So are all the things you shared with them. The hopes, the dreams, the future plans, the possibilities are all gone. It does not mean life is over for you because you are left behind. It does mean however that life is and will be different from the point of the loved one's death. Healthy grief recognizes this and deals with it head-on. Knowing renewed grief will come and keep on coming throughout the years better prepares you to cope successfully at those times.

My husband died when our son was thirteen. As life moves on, there are numerous nevers surfacing periodically, which touch my heart due to secondary loss. As a couple, we did not see our son graduate from high school or college. We did not attend his wedding together as the parents of the groom. We did not celebrate the birth of a grandson, his namesake, together. We were not together for the birth of our granddaughter. Our son's graduation from the police academy was another milestone missed as parents together. Missing the enjoyment of being with each other for many family celebrations and occasions throughout the years makes a long list of nevers. When these events occur, you experience the dips in the roller coaster ride. The missing loved one comes to mind on all these occasions. This is why the ride continues across the life span.

It is these secondary losses that are so hard to deal with when parents lose a child. Losing a child creates many nevers. Failing to address these losses in healthy ways creates roadblocks on the journey of grief for many parents. Failure to understand how these milestone events renew your grief leaves you unprepared to face the resurgence of grief. Thus, it is important to realize losing someone you love does not happen in one clean break. The hits keep coming. It is like kneeling in the sand on the beach at the water's edge and being hit by one wave after another.

Knowledge of healthy grief patterns prepares you for the task ahead. It is important to understand there are choices. Only you can make those choices. Benjamin Franklin once said, "While we may not be able to control all that happens to us, we can control what happens inside us." Knowing and believing you have a choice, and thus, some control, is encouraging. This is positive thinking. This creates positive self-talk. Understanding your choices is a valuable tool to use when processing grief. It is a key survival skill.

Viktor Frankl, psychologist, survived the Nazi concentration camps during World War II. He said he did it by knowing the Nazis could take his liberty but not his freedom. He controlled his own mind. He said this enabled him to survive a hellish existence.

Just as Frankl's ability to choose to control his own mind helped him through unimaginable horrors, your ability to make choices as to how you will grieve will help you through the hellish experience of grief. Choose wisely the grief behaviors you will use.

Unhealthy Grief

Death is not a popular subject. Most people find it depressing or stressful to talk about it. This is why we are woefully unprepared to deal with it. Comedian George Carlin once said,

> Americans do not do well with death. We call it a "terminal incident." We may refer to it as "organismically challenged." We use any word but the D word.

Because of this avoidance of the subject of death and all things having to do with it, we may fall into unhealthy grief due to our ignorance of the grieving process. Unhealthy grief is nonproductive behaviors impeding progress toward readjustment and reconstruction of life after the loss of a loved one. Unhealthy grief is counterproductive in helping the mourner adjust to life without the presence of the deceased. It is also referred to as complicated or problematic grief.

Risk Factors for Complicated/Unhealthy Grief

There are several risk factors determining the proclivity for complicated grief. Therese Rando, a leading expert in the area of complicated grief, has identified several. They are,

1. A sudden unexpected death
    Traumatic deaths, sudden deaths, and violent deaths fall into this category. The suddenness does not give time to prepare for the loss. The mind can only absorb so much at one time, and the lack of time for preparation leaves the survivor without a buffer. The body goes into shock as psychological protection.
2. The youth of a deceased person
    When the deceased is a teenager or a young adult, it is much harder to make sense of the death. It is hard to find meaning in the passing of one so young and full of life. The senselessness of the death and the loss of the promise for one so young can lead to complicated grief issues.
3. Death from an overly long illness
    The length of the illness takes its toll on the survivors. It was painful watching the loved one suffer. The survivor was under emotional stress. Perhaps death was a mercy. There may be a feeling of relief it is over, but also a feeling of guilt for feeling relieved. Another factor is the stress put on the caregiver through such a long illness, which may put the survivor at an emotionally and physically fragile stage by the time the death occurs. Thus, the mourner is not in the best health—physically or mentally—to begin the grieving process.
4. Loss of a child
    Losing a child is extremely difficult. As mentioned in previous pages, the loss of the future is a bitter pill to swallow. There are so many nevers to mourn. The loss of an innocent child seems to be an abomination. It is against the natural order of life. Parents do not expect to outlive their children.

5.   The perception of preventable death
     When the mourner has the perception the death was preventable
     in some way, it is hard to accept the loss. Death from risky
     behaviors, carelessness on the part of the deceased or others,
     suicide, homicide, and reckless driving are just a few of the causes
     of death that complicate acceptance of the loss by the mourner.
     This compromises the ability of the mourner to get past the anger,
     guilt, and blame.
6.   An angry or dependent predeath relationship with the deceased
     If the relationship was conflicted before the person died, there
     may be a sense of unfinished business complicating the grief for
     the mourner. Also, the mourner who depended very heavily on
     the deceased to make the big decisions of life and to take care of
     daily life is predisposed for unhealthy grief, because major role
     revisions are in store for the mourner. His world is in total disarray,
     and the dominant force in his world is gone. The dependent
     personality is at a loss as to what to do next.
7.   Prior or concurrent mourner liabilities
     Sometimes the mourner is not in healthy psychological shape at
     the time of the death due to other losses. Long-term or ongoing
     mental health problems may have been diagnosed in the mourner
     before the death. The loss exacerbates the problems, and unhealthy
     grief ensues.
8.   The mourner's perceived lack of social support
     Some mourners are alone, separated by long distances from
     family. Some have no family. Others withdraw into isolation and
     refuse to let anyone into their world of grief. Whatever the reason,
     a lack of social support or a perceived lack of support on the part
     of the mourner can be a risk factor for unhealthy grief.
     These risk factors do not mean a mourner will experience
     complicated grief, but they are indicators that the possibility
     does exist under these circumstances for unhealthy behaviors to
     emerge. Knowledge of these factors can be helpful to families,
     friends, and professionals who want to help.

Rando explains complicated grief in the following way: "When life's
emotions are unexpressed or unacknowledged, they become locked in
frozen blocks of time." She goes on to say that these frozen blocks are

used to build a wall between the mourner and successful healing. The goal then is to melt the wall by the expression of the grief and the sharing of the pain with others.

Forms of Complicated Grief

Rando, in her work, cites four categories of complicated grief. These are important to understand in order to identify behaviors characterizing unhealthy grief. *Symptoms* make up the first category. Second, there are the *syndromes*. Third are diagnosable *mental or physical disorders*. Fourth is *death*.

Symptoms

Symptoms are individual behaviors that do not fit together with other behaviors to form a set pattern. For example, a mourner may refuse to part with any of the deceased person's belongings. Two years later, nothing may be changed in the room of the deceased. One woman left her husband's boots by the backdoor for five years after his death. This is a symptom of complication in the grieving process, but there may not be many other negative symptoms with this tendency to enshrine the deceased. As in the case of this individual mourner, she behaved normally in going on with her life except for this one symptom. It was only when she began a new relationship that friends pointed out these boots may be a complication for the new person. This was a linking item she had refused to let go of for five years.

Some mourners may refuse to change their daily routines to accommodate the loss. They may steadfastly hold to doing things the way the deceased person did them. Mourners with this symptom may base every decision on what they think the deceased person would do. All other behaviors may be viewed as normal, but the rigidity in changing routine demonstrates a complication in the process.

One widow revealed to me her husband's closet was still intact three years after his death. She returned to work, had many friends, went to church, and socialized; but she never got around to clearing out his personal effects. She appeared normally adjusted to outside observation. However, this one symptom revealed she had serious adjustment issues.

Symptoms refer to psychological or social behaviors or physical symptoms that reveal a failure to complete these tasks of mourning:

1. Accepting the reality of the loss.
2. Reacting to the separation from the loved one.
3. Remembering the person who died.
4. Relinquishing old attachments.
5. Readjusting in order to move on to the new life.
6. Reinvesting time into other relationships and interests.

Behaviors exhibited by mourners experiencing difficulty with these tasks are varied. The following are symptoms of unhealthy or complicated grief:

1. Avoidant behavior
2. Lack of self-care
3. Prolonged denial
4. Self-destructive thoughts
5. Displaced anger
6. Self-medication

Avoidant behavior

The behavior exhibited in this symptom is one of shutting everyone out of the mourner's world. Friends and family are avoided for a prolonged period of time (over three weeks), and the mourner isolates from outside contact. This is cause for concern, and outside professional help is needed.

Lack of self-care

Lack of self-care is a symptom that calls for immediate intervention. When the bereaved person becomes more slovenly with his appearance to the point of not bathing, brushing his teeth, combing or washing his hair, shaving, and tending to general grooming habits, it denotes depression. A day or two of sloppiness is nothing to become alarmed about, but prolonged lack of care for personal hygiene and/or eating and sleeping properly are clearly warning signs that professional help is required.

Prolonged Denial

Long-term denial of the reality of the death is another cause for concern. While not necessarily dangerous to the mourner per se, it is not helpful for processing the grief if the mourner refuses to accept the death. This is when professional help and a support group can help the mourner move through this phase.

Self-destructive Thoughts

Self-destructive thoughts are always a cause for concern, but it should be noted that it is not unusual during grief for the mourner to have thoughts of suicide. Most bereaved people have a passing thought they would like to go away from the turmoil. Comments like "I don't want to wake up" or "I wish I were someplace else" and "Why go on?" may be said or thought by the mourner during the early part of grief. However, these thoughts should pass quickly. They do reflect the need to explore the depth of the sadness. It is natural to experience these passive and passing suicidal thoughts. It is not natural to make plans to take your own life when someone in your life dies.

Suicidal thoughts can be an expression of wanting to find relief from the pain. It is important to talk about the death and the pain in order to heal. If you think about taking your own life more than just in passing, you need help. If the thoughts are persistent or obsessive, a professional should be consulted. Always err on the side of caution by seeking help.

Displaced Anger

Another negative behavior, which goes with the symptoms of complicated or unhealthy grief, is displaced anger. It is important to find appropriate outlets for the expression of anger if the emotion exists. Anger in and of itself is not a bad thing. Anger is the alarm system for the body to alert you something is not going as expected. With that being said, however, it is urgently important to have a positive way to express the anger. If this does not happen, anger can be displaced onto other relationships or other environments. Displaced anger often rains down on other family members, friends, coworkers, and, sometimes, even strangers. It is problematic if it is hurting you in personal or professional areas. It is a signal that it is time for professional help.

Self-medication

Another symptomatic behavior indicating the need for help is self-medication. It is easy to turn to alcohol and/or drugs to help cope when devastated by grief. Self-medication also includes the abuse of prescription medications such as antianxiety medications, sleep medications, and antidepressants. Any method to lessen the pain is tempting. This is dangerous thinking. Abuse of any of these substances—be it alcohol, drugs, or medications—is an attempt to distance yourself from what you need to feel.

Some mourners need to be on medications from the doctor for temporary relief; however, the physician should always monitor this. The amount taken should not be increased simply to make the pain go away. The last thing you need is to numb your feelings. That is not healthy grief and does more harm than good. Bob Deits says in *Life after Loss*, "To take control of your grief, you must face your loss head on with all your senses working. You can't do that while you are blissfully tranquilized."

Be wary about prescriptions. Never take someone else's medicine. Mourners are often offered sleeping medications or antianxiety pills from friends or family members to help them get through the visitation, funeral, and early home visits. It is never a good idea to take someone else's medications. If you go to the doctor for a prescription, be sure you know what he is prescribing and the effect it will have on you. You need to be alert. You need to know what is going on and to feel what you need to feel.

Some people have no recollection of the arrangements, the visitation, or the service because they were in a medicated fog. This is a detriment to their grieving process. Later, they will often ask, "What happened? Was the service nice? Who came?" This indicates the mourner missed an important step in the grieving process—the chance to say good-bye and to join with family and friends in remembering the life lived.

Using alcohol to deaden the pain is very dangerous. The use of alcohol is a form of avoidant behavior. The use can escalate before you realize it. One drink turns to two, then three, then a bottle. Before you know it, you are on the addiction highway. It is a very rough road. Alcohol masks the painful feelings and is a crutch. You may get temporary relief, but it is a postponement of the pain that must be felt. It can also cause a new set of problems for you personally and professionally.

Syndromes

Syndromes are a second type of complicated mourning. Patterns of behaviors grouped together form a syndrome. While the symptoms discussed in the previous paragraphs were lone behaviors, syndromes consist of a cluster of behavior patterns. There are three general types of syndromes. In each type, there are different sets of behavioral patterns.

First, there are the *expression syndromes*. The syndromes of expression are absent grief, delayed grief, and inhibited grief. Second are *skewed thinking syndromes*. These syndromes are unanticipated grief, displaced grief, replacement grief, conflicted grief, minimized grief, distorted grief, and somatic grief. Third is the *closure syndrome*. The closure syndrome for this category is chronic mourning.

Expression Syndromes

The expression syndromes include the types of behaviors that exhibit a failure to find appropriate ways to express the loss. Being able to put the pain into words or behaviors is very difficult for some mourners. Social norms, personality traits, mourner temperament, and family patterns of handling loss predispose some mourners to have difficulty expressing or showing emotional behaviors.

1. Absent Grief

Absent grief is an extreme avoidant behavior. The mourner believes exposure to the pain would simply be too hard to bear. This person becomes so entrenched in the denial of the pain he often refuses treatment, believing exposure to the pain will be detrimental to him. He does not want to work through it. It is a phobia manifestation. Without help, he fails to address the loss, and feelings are tamped down. This sets him up for the pain to resurface in some other manner in life, usually with negative consequences.

An example of this was a man who lost his father in an automobile accident when he was sixteen years old. He had to shoulder many of the family responsibilities and be the man of the family. He went on with his life and never fully processed his grief. When he came for counseling, he was suffering the loss of a son in the military. As he worked to process this tremendous loss, he began to talk a great deal about how he felt as a young man losing his father. He became very emotional about it and surprised himself with how much emotion he still carried over a loss that occurred over forty years ago. Anger, feelings of abandonment, bitterness poured out of him; and he found it hard to decide if it was over his father's death or his son's death. His journey of grief over losing his son uncovered for him an old grief he never addressed.

2. Delayed Grief

Any grief set aside will resurface because grief must be faced. Grief helps the mourner to achieve a certain degree of closure. In delayed grief, denial is strong. The mourner hopes the pain will go away or hopes, with more time, he will be better able to deal with it. There is the idea given enough time to get some equilibrium, the pain will lessen on its own. It can be likened to procrastinating about a particularly unpleasant task. It is an "I'll do it later" approach to grieving. It is not uncommon to find mourners in delayed grief appearing stuck in their grief months later with no real progress being made.

The woman described earlier who still had her husband's closet intact after three years exhibited a symptom of complicated grief instead of the syndrome of delayed grief, because she did not appear to be stuck. She made significant progress in other areas of her life. She did some of the adjustment tasks. Without other behaviors exhibited besides the closet issue, she does not fit the profile for delayed grief.

While a study done by Bonanno and associates showed no major adjustment problems for participants at the five-year point, due to delayed grief, there were two interesting findings. First, the participants experiencing delayed grief were found to have negative facial expressions at the six-month interview. At five years past the death, it was noted these participants were associated with a greater number of somatic complaints. Second, those who showed more dissociation of negative emotions at six months were associated with reduced depression at five years.

So while the delayed grief hypothesis did not show major adjustment problems at the five-year mark, the progress or lack of progress at the six-month time did seem to have an impact physically and in the diagnosis of depression at the five-year benchmark.

3. Inhibited Grief

In inhibited grief, the person knows there is internal turmoil associated with the loss, but despite conscious efforts, he is unable to express the grief or unable to cry. Schuster calls this inability to cry "dry grief." He points out that it is not necessarily important for a person to cry. Crying does not denote the depth of the feeling of loss. He does point out feeling unable to cry, wanting to cry but not being able to do so, distresses the mourner.

There are several reasons for inhibited grief. Sometimes detachment began before the death, and this interferes with the process of showing emotion. Also, it is not the personality makeup of some individuals to show emotion. Some mourners possess more stoic personalities than others. Some people are culturally taught to be less emotional in stressful situations.

There are a wide variety of reasons for not being able to show emotion. Each person's way of expressing grief is unique. However, when the mourner *wants* to express the emotion and cannot, it is categorized as inhibited grief. This can be treated with several approaches such as a vocal approach, directed imagery, and using tangible representations of the deceased.

Caregivers are sometimes presented with this problem. The caregiver tended the loved one for a length of time and became physically and mentally exhausted. The caregiver saw the pain and suffering of the loved one on a daily basis. When death finally comes, the caregiver may find it difficult to cry. There is nothing wrong with this unless the caregiver feels the *need* to cry. Often, in treatment, bringing a belonging of the loved one to the session and talking about it will bring forth the emotion of tears.

Skewed Thinking Syndromes

Skewed thinking syndromes are patterns of behaviors exhibited by the bereaved that show distortion in the thinking process, thus, hindering the successful completion of the tasks of grief. These skewed thinking syndromes are unanticipated grief, displaced grief, replacement grief, conflicted grief, minimized grief, distorted grief, and somatic grief. While some lone behaviors may be seen throughout the grieving process, these syndromes cluster groups of skewed thinking behaviors together. Successful completion of grief means the mourner does not suffer long-term physical or mental ill health from the loss. The bereaved is eventually able to function normally in the new life without the deceased.

1. Unanticipated Grief

Unanticipated grief follows sudden, unexpected deaths. Deaths such as automobile accidents, plane crashes, homicides, and suicides cause this kind of complicated grief. While sudden deaths always bring unexpected grief, this is different from the unhealthy aspects of unanticipated grief. The unhealthiness of this particular grief is that after a lengthy period of time, the mind cannot come out of its denial and shock mode to continue with the grief process.

When this happens, the mourner may withdraw from other important relationships, fearing loss. This can turn into a lifelong fear of loss. Always fearing loss keeps the mourner from forming close relationships and commitments.

Fear of association with the cause of death may become a phobia for the bereaved. For example, fear of flying may occur after losing a loved one to a plane crash. Fear of driving or riding in an automobile after losing a loved one in a car accident may become a phobia. If a child was killed, the fear of letting other children in the family participate in normal activities may arise. The parents may also fear letting the other children out of their sight.

A family, whose young adult daughter was kidnapped, never to be seen again, had tremendous problems from this type of complicated grief. In the early days, the search was to find her. Hopefully, she would still be alive. As months went by, hope dimmed of finding her alive. Leads dried up, and the police were unable to determine not only where she was, but who took her.

Finally, a good lead came in as to the identity of the abductor. Unfortunately, he was killed when they tried to take him into custody. The girl was never found. The family refused to believe the girl was dead. They spent thousands of dollars on searching for her and placing advertisements over a wide area.

At last, most of the family gave up the search and accepted her death and the idea they were not likely to ever find her body. Everyone accepted this, except her father. He continues to place ads over several states, offering a reward for information. He believes she is still alive somewhere and will someday be returned home. That was seven years ago, and his search continues. This loss became his life. He lost many relationships. His entire focus is to find his daughter.

2. Displaced Grief

When the mourner suffers displaced grief, the initial cause of the grief is not fully processed. The mourner directs intense feelings toward other things in his life. Problems for the mourner may surface at work or in personal relationships. The mourner, by expressing anger in other areas, avoids addressing the anger connected to the loss. This vents some of the rage felt by the mourner but does not fully alleviate the anger. The pain is directed outward; thus, the cause of the pain becomes something out there." Feelings of depression, bitterness toward others over perceived slights, anger over the unfairness in the world, and disenchantment are all ways of projecting the unhappiness inside the mourner onto other sources. Self-hatred and feelings of failure and self-pity rise up in the mourner who is displacing grief.

An example of a mourner with this complicated grief syndrome was a man who was previously very active in his church before the death of his child. He became angry with the medical profession and doubted the care she was given. He then became angry with God and anything to do with His church. He became bitter with his friends because it seemed to him they never had bad things happen. Their families were intact. He dropped out of church, isolated himself from his friends, and ended up divorcing his wife. All the things he needed the most to help him heal, he rejected. Displaced anger kept him from healing.

3. Replacement Grief

The mourner falling into the unhealthy pattern of replacement grief is trying to circumvent the grieving process and get things back to normal quickly. Some mourners will try to quickly find a replacement for the roles filled by the deceased. One example of this is the widowed person who immediately becomes involved in a relationship or marriage to get some stability back into life as soon as possible.

While reinvestment is one of the tasks to be completed in the grieving process, it should not be done too quickly. In replacement grief, the mourner prematurely reinvests emotions in another relationship or activity. Early remarriage is simply one example. Another behavior is jumping head over heels into activity. The mourner may become a workaholic, working long hours and going above and beyond the call of duty. This occupies time and keeps the bereaved too busy to feel anything. Others jump into excessive volunteering or any number of activities that absorb large quantities of time and energy, thus, enabling the mourner to avoid doing the needed grief tasks.

Another behavior of replacement grief of which to be aware is impulsive living. The mourner begins to take risks. "You only live once" may be said. "Life is too short. I need to experience the thrills." These are just a few of the statements heard in replacement grief. The mourner may begin to spend money excessively. "You can't take it with you" seems to be the mentality in this behavior. These are warning signs that the mourner needs help in getting the grieving process back on track.

4. Conflicted Grief

Conflicted grief is seen most often in love/hate relationships. The relationship with the deceased one was ambivalent. Often, there was a good reason for the animosity toward the deceased. Perhaps the deceased was cruel, abusive, or difficult to get along with throughout the relationship. Sometimes a relationship is estranged for a length of time before the death. Upon the death of this person, the survivor is flooded with many emotions and does not know how to handle them. There may be great anger at the deceased. The survivor may suffer guilt for not having a closer relationship. The mourner has conflicting emotions of love and hate for the one who died. Initially, the survivor may not feel a great deal of pain, then later feels a great deal of sadness and guilt about the hate part of the relationship. Professional help is of great assistance to the bereaved in processing these feelings and eliminating the feelings of guilt, blame, and anger.

A man whose wife betrayed their marriage, then died suddenly before they were able to resolve the marital problems discussed the conflict he felt. He was saddened by his loss, but on the other hand, he was very angry with her and had no means of addressing his grievance. He felt so betrayed and distrustful but could not tell her how humiliated he felt. He felt as though their problems were hanging in the air and would be there—unresolved forever. Therapy to help him address the hurt and anger was needed to enable him to resolve his grief, frustration, and anger.

5. Minimized Grief

The mourner who minimizes grief downplays the pain felt from the loss and the duration of the pain. There is great effort put into putting the best face forward to the outside world. Great pretense is practiced to make others think the mourner is doing much better emotionally than expected. Many people experiencing this type of unhealthy grief convince themselves they have gotten over it rather quickly and are moving forward at a very fast pace. This is another form of denial of the deep hurt. As long as the impact of the loss is minimized, the mourner cannot truly accept the loss and make the adjustments necessary to successfully complete the grieving process. People of faith sometimes exhibit this type of complicated grief because their faith teaches them to be happy when someone leaves this world for the next. Therefore, they feel the need to show minimal grief and put on a happy face.

6. Distorted Grief

This unhealthy pattern of grief contains underlying feelings of great anger and/or guilt. The mourner may exhibit a great deal of overactivity without a sense of loss. It is different from absent grief in that the mourner experiences specific changes in behaviors. Hostility toward certain persons may develop for no obvious reason. Self-destructive behaviors may surface. The mourner may unexpectedly develop a symptom the deceased had prior to the death. Due to the anger, hostility, and possibly self-destructive patterns found in this unhealthy grief, professional help is of utmost importance.

A mourner experiencing this pattern came to treatment after losing a spouse. He previously was not very social when his wife was living. After her death, he began to work more hours and added a long list of social activities to his calendar. He filled every moment of his time with activity. He began to drink, go to the casino, and spend money on a much more lavish lifestyle than he and his wife lived.

He expressed anger at old friends and did not want to socialize with them. They were still couples. He came to therapy because he was miserable. He felt he made changes, but he was not progressing. He did not see the changes he made were negative choices based on his distorted grief.

7. Somatic Grief

Somaticizing grief brings a host of difficulties to the mourner's life. The grief is converted into physical symptoms because the emotional issues are not being handled in a healthy manner. These are not benign minor complaints but chronic patterns of major ailments that have no organic basis. Psychological as well as medical help is needed to resolve this grief.

Closure Syndrome

Some mourners recoil with the mention of the word *closure*. It does seem impossible to achieve. The one who died is gone forever, and the mourner never fully gets over it. Closure does not mean getting over the death. Closure means letting go of the physical relationship and learning to live with the loss. Closure means returning to the mainstream of life but not as the person you were. It means returning to life as the different person you became with the last breath your loved one took in this world. Mourners who are not able to do this after a prolonged period of adjustment time are said to have chronic mourning. The behaviors seen in chronic mourning constitute the closure syndrome.

Chronic Mourning

The goal of grief is to lead the mourner to a successful reconciliation and assimilation of the loss into daily life. Prolonged grief that does not lead to a successful conclusion, as described, is chronic mourning. When this syndrome is exhibited, the mourner knows the grief has exceeded the bounds of normalcy but cannot or will not progress forward. Sometimes this is called being stuck.

Examples of behaviors that fit into this pattern may be (1) refusing to move, give away, or clean out a loved one's belongings a year or two after the death; (2) failure to pay attention to the lives of others and becoming more self-centered after the initial mourning time; (3) refusing to accept help from anyone; (4) isolation from activities within the family and social structure; (5) establishing a shrine in the home of the loved one's belongings; and (6) idealizing the loved one to the point of perfection.

It is during the unhealthy grief behaviors of chronic mourning that self-pity occurs. At times, grieving is like climbing a glass mountain. It is a slippery slope. You inch your way slowly up the mountain, gaining footing with a great deal of exertion. Then, as described in the roller coaster ride, you slide back down that mountain. If you are not careful, you fall into the pity pit. The result of self-pity is more loneliness due to the alienation of family and friends. When you continue to be self-centered, constantly wearing your grief, excluding the feelings of others, visitors and friends begin to drop away from you.

You become tedious and boring. Few people will continue to interact with you. Self-centered people become tiresome and lose the companionship of others, which is so desperately needed at this lonely time.

A woman who lost her husband made it very hard for her friends to continue being the friends she needed. She was finally persuaded by her family to seek counseling because they could see her many friends deserting her and understood why.

She had many people giving her support from the time of her husband's death throughout the ensuing months. Friends included her in all social activities. Many people took her out to dinner, ran errands for her, entertained her in their homes, and visited her frequently. Transportation was provided for her so she would not have to drive after dark or go home alone. Yet each time she was with friends, the litany continued about how lonely she was, how some people had ignored her, and how miserable her life was with few people helping her. Little notice was given to the friends and family who were steadfast and loyal. Emphasis was on those who were not there.

As months and months went by, and the first year passed, patience on the part of many wore thin. She continued to lament that no one understood or cared about her feelings. She showed no interest in others or the problems in the life of others. It became more and more of a chore to spend time with her.

Unfortunately, many of her friends did drop her, which gave her justification in her eyes for her complaints. This behavior continued for two years. During this time, she never entertained her friends or reciprocated their hospitality in any way.

Through therapy, she was led to see how her behavior toward others was affecting her life. She slowly began to make changes. She eventually came through her grieving process, but the time she spent in the pity pit cost her many good relationships and pushed some of her best friends and even some of her relatives to the edge of endurance.

To avoid the pity pit, which is a trap in chronic mourning, you must think of others. When you can look outside your suffering to the problems and suffering of others, it brings healing. Galatians 6:2 admonishes us to "Carry each other's burdens and in this way you will fulfill the law of Christ." It is when we think of others that we are able to lighten our own load.

Chronic mourning can become a means of control for the mourner. Endless grieving or the refusal to make the choice to live again becomes a way of exercising control over others. Author Doug Manning says, "Nothing feels as good as suffering in silence, especially if everyone knows you are."

Self-pity keeps the mourner in power because the rest of the family continues to try to appease the mourner. All attention is focused on the bereaved person. Others do all the work trying to bring happiness to an unwilling soul. The dependent personality can become more and more helpless. By controlling others, the dependent person never has to assume responsibility. The power exercised by the mourner keeps the family focused on dancing to his tune. The mourner's needs and wishes are the center of attention. Others take a backseat to the chronic mourner. The danger of using grief as a means of control is it drives away the people who mean the most to you and who can help you the most with your grieving process. It hurts relationships and makes the mourner a burden for everyone else.

Turning inward for a while is normal. It is necessary to do this in order to progress toward assimilation of the loss. It is a survival technique. It is a valuable coping skill when used correctly. But beware of the danger of prolonged self-interest. Falling into the pity pit, continuing with chronic mourning, drives away what the mourner needs the most to recover—other people!

Beware of becoming a chronic mourner. People who suffer the martyr complex even before bereavement seem especially prone to this. They cannot feel good unless they feel bad. These mourners are miserable and make others miserable too. They wear out the sympathy and empathy of others. They give up on life and remain stuck in the tragedy of the loss. Thus, they waste something precious—their time on earth.

Diagnosable Mental or Physical Disorders

This form of complicated grief is due to diagnosed mental problems or physical disorders. This means the mourner has a mental disorder that fits a Diagnostic and Statistical Manual of Mental Disorders, Fourth Edition DSM-IVR diagnosis. Or the mourner has a serious physical diagnosis, which will impact the grieving process.

If the disorder is a diagnosed mental problem, the mourner should be under the care of a doctor and/or a therapist to deal with the diagnosed illness. As part of the treatment plan for that particular diagnosis, the bereavement issue should also be addressed due to the impact it has on the primary diagnosis.

If the disorder is physical in nature, the medical professional treating the physical illness needs to be informed of the bereavement issue so the best course of treatment can be planned. As discussed in the previous chapter, it is of great importance for a bereaved person to have a physical checkup after a loss. This is especially true if the mourner is taking medications for a physical condition that may be affected by the emotional stress accompanying grief.

Death

Death is the ultimate complicated grief. Failure to successfully cope with the pain and the adjustment to the world without the loved one can lead to death in some mourners. Suicide is one such example. If the mourner suffers a diagnosed mental illness as discussed above, the inability to accept the loss, the pain, the suffering may lead the mourner to take his own life. This is why it is important for others to be alert to the actions and reactions of the bereaved. If there is any doubt about the stability of the mourner, it is imperative to get professional help.

As far back as 1944, EricLindemann, MD, of Harvard Medical School, found mourners were at high risk for myocardial infarction, cancers of the gastrointestinal tract, hypertension, neurodermatitis, rheumatoid arthritis, diabetes, and thyroid malfunction. This shows a serious physical risk for life-threatening diagnoses in mourners.

There are many statistics to support that bereavement can lead to death of the mourner. One study showed an increase of almost 40% in the death rate of widowers over the age of fifty-four during the first six months of bereavement. Another study of bereaved relatives found over a six-year period that 4.8% died within the first year of loss as compared to only 0.7 of the nonmourner group of people—the same age and living in the same location.

Another study by the Institute of Medicine found the mortality rate among young widowed males under the age of forty-five was seven times higher than for the married control group. The death rate for heart attacks was ten times higher for young widowers than for married men of the same age. Another study showed a death rate of 34.5% over five years for bereaved individuals as compared to a rate of 6.9% among those who were not bereaved.

The use of drugs and alcohol was discussed previously. This can lead to death. The death may be accidental because of the inability of the mourner to determine the quantity consumed, or it may be from combining drugs and alcohol. Prescription medications and alcohol are a potentially lethal combination. Caution is vital if the mourner is known to be using both of these substances or either one in large amounts.

Death by suicide among mourners is another type of complicated grief. Studies cited by Neeld show the suicide rate among a group of 320 bereaved spouses was 2.5 times higher in the first six months after bereavement and 1.5 times higher in the first, second, and third years after the death. This indicates the danger exists longer than many may expect. It also indicates the need for sustained mental help for this group of individuals.

Accidental deaths may occur in this type of complicated grief. When under great stress, concentration is greatly affected. Inattention to surroundings, lack of focus, and poor concentration raises the chances of an accident for the mourner. It may be a fall, car accident, or an accident operating machinery. Grief affects our attention to our surroundings, and inattention can make one more accident-prone.

As you travel through grief boot camp, the goal is to survive something that seems impossible to survive. You experienced an amputation of a vital part of your life. The suffering is tremendous. Practicing healthy grief behaviors is not easy. It is much easier to fall into some of the unhealthy patterns described in this chapter.

How do you go on in a healthy way? A philosopher once said there are three important things we all need in our lives: (1) something to love, (2) something to do, and (3) something to hope for. These three things can get you through the worst of times. Death, war, disease, and all the tragedies of life can be overcome—if we keep love in our life, purpose in our steps, and hope in our hearts. Hope is coming through the fog and being able to see a horizon. Love! Action! Hope! These enable us to stay the course on the fearsome ride that is the grief roller coaster.

Chapter 4 References

1. Bartocci, Barbara. 2000. *Nobody's Child Anymore: Grieving, Caring, and Comforting When Parents Die.* Notre Dame, IN: Sorin Books.
2. Blair, Pamela, PhD, and Brook Noel. 2000. *I wasn't ready to say goodbye: Surviving, coping and healing after the sudden death of a loved one.* Milwaukee, WI: Champion Press LTD.
3. Bonanno, George A., Nigel P. Field. 2001. Examining the Delayed Grief Hypothesis Across 5 Years of Bereavement. *American Behavioral Scientist* 44, no. 5 (May): 798-799-816.
4. Gamino, Lewis, Nancy Hogan, and Kenneth Sewell. 2002. Feeling the Absence: A content analysis from the Scott and White Grief Study. *Death Studies* 26, no. 10 (November): 793-794-813.
5. Kubler-Ross, Elisabeth, MD. 1991. *On Life after Death.* Berkley, CA: Celestial Arts.
6. Linamen, Karen S. 2001. *Sometimes I wake up grumpy and sometime I let him sleep.* Grand Rapids, MI: Fleming H Revell, Baker Books.
7. Manning, Doug. 1979. *Don't Take My Grief Away: What to Do When You Lose a Loved One.* San Francisco: CA: HarperCollins Publishers.
8. Neeld, Elizabeth Harper, PhD. 2003. *Seven choices: Finding daylight after loss shatters your world.* New York, NY: Tiime Warner.
9. Rando, Therese A. 1996. Complications in Mourning Traumatic Death. In *Living with Grief after Sudden Loss: Suicide, Homicide, Accident, Heart Attack, Stroke.* Bristol, PA: Taylor and Francis.
10. Rando, Therese A. 1986. *Loss and Aanticipatory Grief.* Lexington, Mass: Lexington Books.
11. Schroeder, Joel and Ruth. 1997. *The Power of Positivity.* Mission, KS: Skillpath Publications.
12. Shuchter, Stephen R. 1986. *Dimensions of Grief: Adjusting to the Death of a Spouse.* San Francisco, CA: Jossey-Bass.
13. Stalling, Elizabeth. 1997. *Prayer Starters: To Help You Heal after Loss.* St. Meinrad, IN: Abbey Press.
14. Tatelbaum, Judy. 1980. *The Courage to Grieve: Creative Living, Recovery, and Growth through Grief.* New York, New York: Harper Row.
15. Wayment, Heidi A., Jennifer Vierthaler. 2002. Attachment Style and Bereavement Reactions. *Journal of Loss and Trauma* 7, no. 2 (April): 129-130-149.
16. Wolfelt, Alan D., PhD. 1992. *Understanding Grief: Helping Yourself Heal.* Muncie: IN: Accelerated Development Inc.

Chapter 5

SPIRITUALITY AND LOSS

Dr. Alan Wolfelt says, "Mourning is a spiritual journey." I found that to be so very true. Spirituality is the umbrella to health and healing. It is your greatest resource in managing pain and suffering as you go through grief. Therefore, it is of utmost importance to consider the composition of your spirituality at the time of loss. In order to accept loss and assimilate it into your present and future being, you must first understand your own spirituality. Once this is accomplished, you are able to heal your wounded soul.

Accessing these spiritually comforting agents of healing is important when doing your grief work. Jimmy Carter's book *The Virtues of Aging* discusses the components of a fulfilled life. According to Carter, this is a life of peace and contentment. He is not referring to a problem-free life. He is referring to a life that sustains peace and contentment through good *and* difficult times. No matter what circumstances arise in life, these components provide a healing and fulfilling effect on man. These important

qualities are patience, kindness, love, truthfulness, hope, endurance, and generosity.

None of the components discussed by Carter require fame, fortune, great education, or a competitive spirit. None of them require material gain, acquisition of wealth, or a certain level of superior intelligence for achievement. All of these qualities fit into a person's belief system whether or not that system encompasses a religion.

Does not a wounded spirit cry out for us to seek these components of a fulfilled life? In order to do this, you must access your spirituality. But taking it one step further, you must understand the difference between spirituality and faith.

1. Spirituality

Spirituality is the essence of who and what you are. It consists of your deepest values, hopes, goals, caring, and your sense of beauty and loving. Spirituality is the essence of what makes you *you*. It is the core of your being. It is your center of peace, harmony, and wellness for the mind and spirit. Your spirituality is unique in that it is a reflection of your thoughts, feelings, and beliefs. Your spirituality may be similar to others, but it does not consist of exactly the same components.

Spirituality enables you to continue living when difficult times come into your life. This inner core contains your *will to live*. It gives you the momentum to get up each morning, do what has to be done for the day, and then do the same the next day and the next throughout your life on earth. Not only does it give you the ability to do this, it puts joy and pleasure into an otherwise drab existence. When someone you love dies, it is this center of being that takes a massive hit. The will to live suffers a devastating blow. Pain and suffering become your constant companions.

One of the promises in Psalm 23 is "He leadeth me beside the still waters. He restoreth my soul." If ever there was a time for restoration of the soul, it is following a serious loss. Survivors struggle for restoration of the soul, the will to live—the will to go on with life.

There are many relationships, beliefs, activities, and people that contribute to our core of being. *Feeding your soul* means accessing and strengthening these qualities to enrich your spirituality. Just as grief has some common characteristics among mourners, many share common contributors to spirituality. However, just as each mourner's grief is unique, contributors to one's spirituality are unique to individuals also. For this reason, it is important for you to gain a clear understanding of your own personal spiritual paths to healing. It is also important to understand where faith fits into the spiritual pathways.

Thus, spirituality encompasses a wide range of emotions, values, beliefs, people, and activities. Religion, God, faith, scriptures, prayer, and any other connections to belief in higher powers are spiritual pathways. The impact of using these pathways to help heal your sorrow depends on your personal spiritual design.

2. Faith

Faith is an important component for many mourners' spiritual wellness. Mourners with strong faith use it as a tool for healing the wounds of loss. Faith and religion are not necessarily one and the same. Many people have strong faith but do not belong to any particular organized religion. For the purposes of this discussion, faith is defined as a belief in God as a higher power. Reference is made to the teachings of Jesus Christ and scriptures from the New Testament as well as scriptures from the Old Testament. People of different faiths may use the teachings of the holy books associated with their faith. The reference to faith in this chapter also refers to the belief in life after death. The faith discussed in this chapter is based on the premise that death is not the end of life itself, but merely the end of a physical existence.

Hebrews 11:1 says, "Faith is being sure of what we *hope* for and certain of what we do not *see*." Wolfelt, in his book *Understanding Grief*, says, "living with faith means embracing that which cannot be changed by your will and knowing life in all its fullness is still good." Both are good definitions of faith. Both quotes exemplify how a strong faith brings comfort when suffering the pain of loss.

Faith enables the mourner to believe things will improve and there will be better days ahead. Isaiah 40:31 promises believers strength to face what must be faced when it says, "they shall walk and not faint." This promise to the believer is to have the patience to endure when you think you cannot.

To have faith is to have hope. Joel Schroeder, in speaking of staying positive about life, said, "Many find their spiritual beliefs give new hope and a positive long term perspective." This is the essence of faith as a healing tool. When you have faith, the loved one is not gone, according to author Barbara Johnson, but "just gone on." This belief in an existence after death can bring great comfort to the mourner. Faith in the future brings the certainty there will be better days. The comfort in that belief strengthens the mourner through the troubled time.

Norman Vincent Peale says,

> Faith is another word for positive thinking. When real faith grips you, you develop a mind-set that looks for the best in everything, refuses to give up, finds a way around or through every obstacle, and presses on to victory. Such faith is the consequence of pouring down inside yourself the great truths of the Bible and thus being triumphant in human experience.

One cannot have faith without hope. A strong faith, as Peale points out, gives you the ultimate weapon in fighting frustration, mental anguish, fear, and pessimism. Hoping things will get better and *having faith* they will is a formidable tool for healing.

Faith knows there is a presence standing with you. Feeling isolated and alone during difficult days is frightening. The fear grief brings is paralyzing. There are new decisions to be made. There are uncertain times. The unknown future looms ahead.

"I am miserable. I am alone. I am frightened. I am suffering." These are some of your thoughts and feelings during the trying days following loss. Faith gives the peace of mind of having a power greater than you to depend on for guidance and companionship throughout the troubling time.

In the book *Just Enough Light for the Step I'm On*, Christian writer Stormie Omartian says much of our misery comes from feeling so alone with our troubles. She discusses the importance of faith in helping us through the dark times. We are always given enough light to find our way. She says we must have faith that light will be sufficient for the present place in our lives. Faith is the belief a higher power will be there with us as we travel toward healing.

The scriptures promise the body of believers again and again of the steadfastness of God. There are many references to the presence of God throughout the peaks and valleys of our lives. The biggest comfort of a strong faith is the *certainty* of that presence. Isaiah 30:15 assures us with these words:

Rest in the security of your Father's arms until you see His power transform your circumstances.

Questioning God and asking Him where He was when these tragedies took place are common questions from suffering people. In Philip Yancey's book, he discusses at length the question: Where is God when it hurts? Mr. Yancey emphasizes God's presence is the friend who sits with you, the clergy who prays with you, the tears shed for you, the arms enfolding you, and the hands reaching out to you. Others sharing your suffering by sympathizing and empathizing with your pain is God's way of saying,

"Lo, I am with you always."
—Matthew 28:20

Strong faith teaches us God works in many ways. Many of His tools are other people. Many of His ways are mysterious to us. This is where faith enters. We cannot explain everything in life. We cannot put reasonable answers to every question. Faith goes beyond reason.

Job recognized the power of suffering in life as a means of transformation. Unaided human intelligence is incapable of comprehending the mystery of death, misery, and suffering. Only faith can transcend reason. Faith can fill the vacuum created by death. Faith is assurance life will continue, and someday joy will return.

Faith is to believe in something for which there is no proof. Faith is belief in a spiritual presence. Faith believes there is a force greater than man. Faith does not only believe this presence exists, but it believes this presence is good. This presence has the ability to sustain us when we need the strength to deal with adversity.

Spirituality is a large umbrella of sources contributing to your sense of well-being and your "all is right with the world" viewpoint. Faith may be found under this umbrella. For most of us, faith is one of the most important sources of our well-being. Religion denotes adherence to an organized structure of faith. People perceive God in many ways. These many organizations and structures of beliefs make up a large array of religions. For this discussion, all people have a spiritual side. In this realm of spirituality, faith and/or religion may be discovered. It is the discovery of the individual's unique spirituality components, which give the mourner tools for healing.

Using Spirituality to Heal

Using spirituality to heal is vital to the bereaved. When a person hurts, who better knows what helps to ease the pain than the person himself? When I am anxious and hurting, I know what is comforting to me and what is not. I know what soothes me and what irritates me. Therefore, I am my own best source of healing. If given the proper understanding of spirituality, I find people in my support groups come up with very useful lists of spiritual ways to gain comfort and healing.

Proper understanding of spirituality means knowing the difference between spirituality and faith. Understanding spirituality enables the mourner to tap into the many contributors to peace of mind, thus, discovering the most soothing actions to take for healing. Spiritual understanding leads to individualizing helpful healing techniques for each mourner's spirit. This understanding also helps mourners to better understand where their beliefs, values, views of God, and their faith fall in their scope of spirituality.

1. Accessing Spiritual Resources

Dr. Nancy O'Conner, in her book *Letting Go with Love*, says the closer the loss is to self, the more devastating is the loss. She uses a diagram of concentric circles to represent the different losses experienced throughout life and the closeness of these losses to your sense of self. Her premise is the closer the loss to your sense of self, the more devastating it will be for you.

This visual of the concentric circles diagram clarifies the impact negatives in life have on well-being. However, I take this premise one step further with support groups struggling to find healing resources. My premise is to use the concentric circle diagram to identify the *positives* in the mourners' lives. I ask, "What are the important people, events, activities, and beliefs, which contribute the most to your core of well-being? I call this core the soul, the will to live, the center of peace and harmony.

If mourners put these listings in a linear model, from least important to most important, the resources are not as readily identifiable as they are on the circle of spirituality diagram. This visual model allows the mourner to reach a better understanding of positive influences on his spirituality. It also allows the mourner to see where the person who died fit into the mourner's spiritual framework and what other resources are left to use to fill the void caused by the loved one's death. (See Diagram 5.1)

It is important for each mourner to understand that the answers on his own diagram may look quite different from the sample diagram. For example, on diagram 5.1, job is not in the inner circle next to the core of being. If your job is greater in the impact it has on your inner self than is indicated on the diagram, you may put job in your inner circle.

SPIRITUALITY RESOURCES

Diagram 5.1

If you look closely at the items you put in the innermost circle, the person who died was in that circle. This is why the pain is so intense. Since you place him in the innermost circle, this means the loved one contributed greatly to your sense of contentment, happiness, and general well-being. Your soul is suffering because of the loss of such an important contributor.

In order to use this diagram to select the best sources of healing specifically for you, look at the other items you listed in your inner circle. You have other things or people to turn to in order to help yourself heal. These are the other spiritual contributors you picked as being most vital to your sense of well-being.

For example, if your spouse dies, you are devastated because that person was in your inner circle. Others, trying to be helpful, may suggest you go on a cruise or vacation to have a change of scenery. Chances are this is not going to be helpful to you. Why? The answer is apparent when you look at your circles. Unless you listed travel/vacations in your inner circle, it is not close enough to your core feelings to help you at this time. The person suggesting a cruise or vacation is suggesting you can replace the pain of a deep loss with an activity that is in one of your outer spirituality circles. Travel may at some times in your life give you a sense of peace and well-being, but it is not likely to be important in this situation.

When you lose someone from the inner circle, look at the other items in that same circle. This is where the key to helpful spiritual resources lies. If you are a person of strong faith, faith was probably listed in the inner circle. Turning to your religion, to God, the scriptures, your house of worship, your clergy, and prayer may be very beneficial—if they were listed in your inner circle. These are resources from which to draw strength.

My personal example fit this pattern when my husband died. I found my faith was a strong anchor for my feelings during such a traumatic time. My belief that God was with me was a great source of comfort. My belief that my husband's life had only ended physically, not spiritually, was another great comfort. Belief in afterlife continues to be a helping, healing resource for me because it is in my inner circle.

Other things in my inner circle—which provided great healing for me—were my family members, close friends, my child, feeling of being needed, and feeling of being loved. These inner core contributors were wonderful resources to help me through a most difficult transition. Turning to the other resources in your circle will provide help for you too.

Notice in the circles that hobbies, hunting, fishing, golf, and other activities are in the outer circles. This may not be true for some mourners. After the loss of his wife, a widower confided one of his most comforting activities was fishing. He said when he went to his perfect fishing spot, where it was quiet and peaceful, he felt soothed just sitting with his line in the water, listening to the frogs and looking at his reflection in the water. He said it didn't make him miss his wife any less, but when he left the spot, he felt renewed. He said he always felt that he could hang in there for another day after spending some time fishing. He felt strengthened to continue his grief work. This man put fishing in his inner circle because of the effect it had on his sense of well-being.

During group discussions, other mourners revealed activities such as gardening were very helpful to them. One lady said when she ran her hands through freshly turned soil in her flower bed and planted bulbs and seeds, she felt more relaxed and less frightened than at any other time. Her garden became a place of retreat and relaxation for her. She found great solace in the turning of the soil and the planting of future plants. Her hobby was a soul renewer. Needless to say, gardening was in her inner circle.

Using the spirituality diagram helps each mourner to discover individualized sources of comfort. Not only does this exercise help the mourner deal with loss, it is a source of identifying helpful resources whenever you suffer anxiety, depression, stress, or many of the other maladies—which affect us in this busy, hectic world.

2. Self-examination

In Wolfelt's discussion about the place of spirituality when dealing with death, he says, "Death calls you to confront your own spirituality." Identifying the components of your spirituality and using them to maintain a healthy soul forces the mourner to do a great deal of self-examination. It is by confronting your spirituality that you learn who you are, what you believe, and what you value.

Searching for meaning becomes a thought-provoking quest. Losing someone you love makes you look at your life and ask some hard questions. Why am I here? What is the purpose of my life? What am I doing with my life? What should I be doing with my life?

In the beginning days of loss, I felt ambivalent about life. I wondered, "Why go on living? My loved one is not here. What is the point? Why should I try so hard to do the right thing when fate is so unfair? Why was my loved one taken and other less-deserving people left in the world? Is it really worth the effort?"

I can relate to many of the feelings expressed by mourners. Some told me they felt deserted and alone with too much time on their hands. Time is a hard concept to come to terms with in searching for meaning. There was not enough time with the loved one; now there is too much time left without him. The disconcerting feeling of being adrift on the sea of doubts and questions plagues the mourner. Is it any wonder the meaning in life is lost? This feeling of disorganization produces apathy and a lack of interest in many of the people and activities, which once filled our lives with meaning.

Another part of self-examination is seeking purpose in life. The death of the loved one clouds your sense of purpose. The danger of losing a sense of meaning and a guiding purpose in life is profound. During traumatic times, humans hunger for meaning. If meaning can be discovered, it helps to make sense of what happened. If sense can be made of what happened, purpose can again be discovered.

Finding Meaning

Judith Bernstein, who wrote extensively about the loss of a child, says meaningfulness should have been included in the writings of Thomas Jefferson when he said we are all entitled to "life, liberty, and the pursuit of happiness." She believes it is the "pursuit of meaningfulness" that brings about any future happiness. Without meaning, nothing makes sense. Friedrich Nietzsche said, "It is not so much the suffering as the senselessness of it." Making sense of the chaotic events leads to acceptance of the different life, which must be led after the death of a loved one.

Pain and suffering do not bring all negatives into our lives. A German theologian, Helmut Thielicke, said, "American Christians have an inadequate view of suffering." This can apply to all Americans, Christian or not. None of us fully understand the possibilities in suffering until we are faced with it. Suffering people do battle on five different frontiers: (1) the frontier of fear, (2) the frontier of helplessness, (3) the frontier of meaning, (4) the frontier of purpose, and (5) the frontier hope. The result of the suffering and the response to it by mourners depends on the outcomes of the battles they fight on these frontiers. This chapter discusses at length the frontier of meaning and the frontier of purpose, because it is in fighting on these frontiers that the mourner meets the enemies of fear and helplessness and wins the battle of hope.

Viktor Frankl, who survived the Nazi death camp of Dachau, said he concluded the search for meaning is the primary force in life. He found people without goals were unlikely to survive the camp. His goal was to tell the world about the experience. Many who failed to give meaning to the situation gave up and perished. This meaningless existence did not aid their chances for survival.

Meaninglessness is not a psychological disease. It is not a diagnosable ailment. However, it has a major impact on the emotional and spiritual health of a person. Psychologist Carl Jung wrote,

> About a third of my cases are not suffering from any clinically definable neurosis, but from the senselessness and aimlessness of their lives. Meaning makes many things endurable—perhaps, everything.

Doing something meaningful fills the empty void created by the loss of your loved one. The cosmic force of meaning in life is important, but during bereavement, the immediate focus is on what we do *today*.

Making sense of the loss does not come all at once. It comes by making sense little by little. This is the reason what we do today is the immediate goal. I could not make sense of my husband's death and immediately know my goal in life. However, an immediate goal for me was to be present emotionally for our young son. He was a contributor to my inner core in the spirituality diagram. Turning my focus to him gave me an immediate goal and gave meaning to my life. I came to believe the words of Viktor Frankl: "Despair is suffering without meaning." Without meaning in my life at that critical time, it truly would become a life of despair.

The importance of making meaning of the loss to reconciliation by the mourner is emphasized in the theoretical perspectives of research into meaning reconstruction. This research emphasizes responses to bereavement from the perspective of the mourner striving to make sense of the problematic events. Neimeyer, Prigerson, and Davis studied the importance of meaning making to healing through the organization of the mourner's experiences into narrative form.

When the mourners used their own words to organize their experiences in narrative form, the mourners were more likely to conclude some meaning to the loss. Telling the story in this organized manner helped mourners gain clarity in making sense of the loss. With this clarity, they were better able to find meaning in it. When the mourners were able to establish meaning, improvement in healing took place.

This research connects to the beliefs expressed by Tatelbaum in *The Courage to Grieve*, in which she says the task before the mourner is to move from the chaos of disorganization to reorganization in the mourner's life. Organization of the mourner's experiences into narrative form, as emphasized by Neimeyer's research, would take place in the transition period between disorganization and reorganization. The establishment of meaning in the loss is a huge step toward the reorganization of the mourner's life.

Davis and Hoeksema found putting meaning to the loss was easier if the death was predictable in some way. It was also easier done if the death was consistent with the family's perspective on life and their spiritual beliefs. The age of the deceased made a difference in assigning meaning to the loss. As mentioned previously, the younger the person who died, the harder it is for survivors to make sense of the loss. These researchers also found the religious survivors made sense of the loss 2.65 times more over the nonreligious group.

Julius Segal cites studies of people under severe stress, which showed the ones who were able to identify a rationale for the suffering experienced a significant increase in their capacity to endure and recover than the ones who failed to make sense of the situation. Another important finding was the positive impact on the mourners in knowing the loved one's life had meaning. Rabbi Kushner echoes this finding when he says, "It is not so much the fear of dying that haunts men as it is the fear that their life will not have mattered."

More research on meaning making in the aftermath of violent death was done by Marilyn Armour. She too found making meaning of the loss was very important to the survivors. Her study covered a time span of 7.5 years past the death. She found the pursuit of what matters was intense in the survivors and was a form of coping.

The participants engaged in a number of meaning-making ventures during this time frame in order to reconstruct self-identity. The participants found meaning by participating in various actions. Some formed groups to inform, help, and comfort others with similar loss. Others sought to fight for what's right. This meant the formation of groups to correct wrongs in the legal system, get new laws passed, and toughen up enforcement of existing laws. Other corrective activities related to the availability of mental health resources in the communities. These actions exemplify the variety of ways the survivors gave meaning to the loss of their loved ones. It also gave the survivors a meaning and purpose in life because of the time and energy they invested in the pursuit of these actions.

In the search for meaning, the mourner is actually seeking two things: (1) What was the meaning of the life of the one who died? and (2) What is the meaning in life for the mourner now that the loved one has died? In searching for the answers to these two questions, the mourner achieves additional wisdom. This happens when limitations are accepted and also with the discovery of how to be comfortable with the way life operates.

How does the search for meaning contribute to the gain in wisdom? The search causes the mourner to examine values, beliefs, and relationships. For many, this is the first time to put attention on forming, reestablishing, and maintaining a set of cherished values. During this self-examination, you clarify many things about your belief system such as (1) what you believe, (2) what matters to you, (3) your relationship to God, (4) your relationships with others, and (5) what you are willing to give of yourself in commitment and time.

The wisdom gained from this introspection of your thoughts on meaning helps to put a different perspective on the loss and the effect of the loss on you. The visitation, cards, flowers, funeral, and eulogy reenforce to the mourner the importance of the loved one's life. Knowing our loved one's life truly mattered and left an impact on others is a soul-soothing piece of knowledge. Someone once said the only legacy worth anything is our footprints for others to follow. Knowing the life, which is now over, left lasting impressions on those left behind and made a difference in the world because they were in it for a time is the most valuable inheritance left to the mourner.

The search for the meaning of the life lost and your life yet to be lived leads to consideration of your purpose. This is a good thing. In our society, we are often so caught up in all the things to do in order to make a living, we fail to really live.

It is a sad commentary on our culture when it takes a tragedy to make us stop and assess our lives to determine what our life goals should be.

We are creatures of habit and prone to fall into familiar routines and schedules. We become caught up in the mundane routines of living and do not often take the time to stop and look at the big picture. Where are we in the scheme of things? Am I being a good steward of my time, talent, and energy? Am I making a difference in the world?

Death is the great equalizer. It plays no favorites. It comes to rich and poor alike. It comes to the educated and the uneducated. It comes to the famous, infamous, and the not famous. We all face it. It is not avoidable. We live as though our time is endless. We fritter away time like money on a spending spree. Eventually, death, the bill collector, is at our door. It comes for a loved one or for us. If it comes for a loved one, we are given more time to examine and evaluate our life habits. We are given time to search for meaning and establish a purpose.

Seeking Purpose

As the mourner struggles with the loss of meaning, it soon becomes apparent purpose has changed. A great deal of meaning and purpose is tied to the person who died. After the death, life takes on shades of gray. The sun does not seem as bright; colors appear dulled; music is not as sweet; and joy is gone. Time spent with the loved one now hangs there empty and unused. Questions such as, what matters? and why am I here? begin to surface.

Your daily investment in your loved one is no longer needed. Now it is time for reinvestment. Reinvest in what? How do you do it? What must your goal be now that the focus of your life seems unclear? What will put the color back into life? How do you find the zest for living? These questions are part of the makeup of your spiritual journey. Just as you search for meaning in the loss and meaning in your life, you also search for purpose. You have more time ahead of you. What will you do with it? Did your purpose end with the death of your loved one?

"There is a test for whether or not your purpose is done. If you are alive, it is not finished." These are the words of Doug Manning in *Don't Take My Grief Away.*

This gives us the answer to that last question in the above paragraph. As long as you are on this earth, there is a purpose for you. It is not always easy to know that purpose. The longer you live, the more you will become convinced your purpose changes with life circumstances.

Manning also says in his book there are two great days in each person's life. One is the day you were born. The other is the day you discover why you were born.

Knowing why you were born determines who you are as a person. It not only determines what you do with your life and how you live it, it determines what you leave behind when you make your exit from this world. Knowing and fulfilling your purpose is the greatest achievement you can attain.

In a newspaper article from *Chicken Soup for the Soul*, a man wrote about how he came to understand what heritage meant. He said most of his life he thought knowing about your heritage meant boring family reunions, old family pictures, and hearing about people you really did not know and perhaps did not care to know.

As he matured and reached adulthood, he married, had a family, and assumed all the family responsibilities expected of him. At some point, he and his wife decided to build their own home to save on the cost. Both of them worked full time, and they also had two small children. His father was a retired contractor and helped all he could, but the brunt of the work fell to the man and his wife. They struggled using all their extra money and time working on the house. Progress was going slowly, and they became extremely weary.

Then his wife had to have surgery, he and the kids got the flu, and all work on the house had to stop. They decided it was time to call in professional help to finish the walls in all the rooms. They worried about how much this would cost but could see no way to get this huge job finished before winter with their present circumstances.

The finisher did the work in one week. Of course the couple was pleased, because the amount of work done would have taken the two of them six or seven weeks of laborious work. However, they dreaded getting the bill and knew it was going to put a huge dent in their house budget.

When the finisher brought the bill, they could not believe their eyes. It was extremely reasonable. So much so, the man questioned the finisher about the bill being correct. The finisher told him the bill was for materials only. He did not charge for the labor of installing the Sheetrock. He told the man when he was young and starting out in the business, the man's father hired him when no one else would. The dad took the young finisher under his wing, trained him, gave him advice, and helped him get established in his line of work. His closing remark was, "I was never able to do something to repay your father, but I can do something to help you."

After he left, the man thought about what the finisher said to him. He thought about his definition of heritage. This experience with the wall finisher made him realize he was reaping the benefits of his heritage. His father made a difference in the life of someone else. This came back to him, not his father. He was not deserving of the benefit, but it clarified for him the importance of purpose in life. He decided then and there he would redefine his purpose and think about how fulfilling his purpose would impact his children and loved ones when he left this earth. Purpose and heritage intertwine to leave a worthy legacy.

In finding what matters to you, you will find your way to your life purpose. Candy Lightner, in speaking about death, said, "Death changes us, the living. In the presence of death, we become more aware of life . . . . It can inspire us to decide what really matters in life—then to seek it." Loss impairs creativity and dulls imagination, removing motivation from the mourner. The inability to see possibilities for future growth, along with the lack of impetus to make these adjustments, impacts the mourner's ability to see a purpose to life.

Achieving the ability to live in the *now*, as discussed by Eckhart Tolle in his book *The Power of Now*, enables the mourner to reach a level of personal integrity, which promotes the acceptance of the *now* and the *what is* of present life. The next task is to restore creativity in order to look at the present situation and determine where to go from this point. In other words: What has to be done differently? What must change? What new things are coming your way? Dr. Renee Bozarth says, "Every loss creates a space and in that space, something new and wonderful may happen."

Restoring creativity in order to make changes does not take away from the enjoyment of what you had before the loss. It does not replace grieving. Grieving is vital. However, it does mean both grieving and the resulting reappraisal of your life leads you to growth and renewal of purpose. You grieve because you want more of what you had—time with your loved one. You heal by being cognizant of what you have left in your life—blessings of relationships and more time to fulfill your purpose. Finding your purpose allows you to see what your life can be, if you come through your tragedy with the determination to meet the challenge.

As I look back on my struggle through the early days of bereavement, and the subsequent years that have followed, I completely agree that loss creates a space. In that space, something different and wonderful may happen. I do not think this takes away from the love I held for those I lost. I loved them dearly then, and I love them yet today. However, because their physical presence is gone from the space in my life they previously occupied, I had to be creative and imaginative in reforming my life and in determining the changes I had to make.

From the point of losing two special grandparents and a husband in the space of one year, to losing both parents close together in very recent times, I see that my purpose in life has taken many twists and turns. Because I was able to reassess my life at these important times, I have evolved into a very different person from the young widow I was twenty-six years ago. I cannot be that person now because what made me who I was and what helped determine my purpose is left in the past. I have to be different because I am living a different life.

I began a renewed life after each devastating loss. I had to do so because my life had a piece the size of my loved one missing from it. Each of my loved ones is gone physically from this place, but they remain in my heart forever. That does not preclude me from adding other relationships, other people, and other activities as I strive to fulfill my purpose.

I see purpose in life as living fully. It does not matter the length of life, but it does matter if one lives fully. I believe God made us with our own unique gifts and talents, and we are to use those to better the lives of those around us. We are given precious time. Each person's time allotment may be different, but the amount of time does not really matter. It is the time itself that is important.

The lives of my loved ones were important. They were not rich, famous, noteworthy, or achievers of great worldly acclaim. But each of them lived fully and left their mark on the world. They made an impact on the hearts of many who knew and loved them. They each had various amounts of time given to them, and I believe they fulfilled their purpose in life because they lived and touched the lives of others.

This belief was validated as I stood at the funeral home during each of these losses, receiving the callers who came to pay respects. I heard from many people I did not know of various kindness and good deeds done by my loved ones, which I had not previously known about until that time. My heritage, the legacy they left to me, was each one's fulfillment of his personal purpose. The lives they touched rippled across the waters of time. These ripples washed over me and led me to strongly believe that the fulfillment of one's purpose in life is the richest legacy to leave behind when death comes.

Even the stillborn child or the child who does not live many years is an important life and fulfills the purpose for which it was created. That child touched the lives of many, and because it existed, it left an impact on the lives touched by him. Although these young lives did not exist long on this earth, because of their existence, others grieved and made changes in their lives as a result of that young life. Every life, no matter the length, leaves a lasting impact. That is purpose fulfilled.

Faith Crisis

Some people of faith suffer a crisis with their beliefs in the aftermath of loss. Very few people are comforted by comments such as, "It is God's will" or "They're in a better place" even if the mourner is a devout believer. Those who believe in heaven are caught in a double bind. Heaven is a reward for believers. It is a good place to go. There is no pain, no suffering, and no loss in heaven. So why am I so upset that my loved one has gone there? The believer may ask.

The believer bases his whole life on the promise of eternal reward, but when the time arrives for the reward to be claimed, it is disconcerting to discover it is not the happy time anticipated. It is like the old saying, "We all want to go to heaven. We just don't want to die to get there."

Disruption in the believer's life is just as painful and gut-wrenching as in the life of the nonbeliever. At the time of the loss, believers and nonbelievers are suffering the absence of the one who died. It is a pain of separation. The sorrow has little to do with where the deceased went and a great deal to do with the fact the loved one is physically gone. They are with us; then they are not. Because of the suddenness of that transition, the mourner is stricken. There is no way to fully prepare for it.

Faith does not take the pain away from loss. Faith is a way of coping with the loss. Believing that faith will remove the pain and prepare the believer for the loss is a misconception on the part of the believer. Believing your loved one's departure from this life to heaven will be an occasion to celebrate with great joy is another misconception. While assurance of the destination of the loved one is a comforting part of faith, being happy about the leave-taking is a misconception. This misconception leads to a crisis in faith in some believers.

People of strong faith sometimes suffer two different forms of complicated grief. One is distorted grief. As discussed previously, distorted grief contains repressed anger. Faith causes the believer to feel safe under God's care. Then a loss occurs, and God does not appear to be very helpful to the mourner. The believer feels he must continue to acknowledge the goodness of God, but he is in a dilemma because his true feelings do not match up to his actions. He can become bitter, irritable with other people, and suffer noticeable changes in his personality. In reality, the mourner has anger over the loss and may harbor anger toward God. The believer does not see his perception of faith, and the position of God in his life may be incorrect. Therefore, blame is assigned to God.

The other form of complicated grief, which may be experienced by the believer, is minimized grief. The mourner with deep faith becomes confused by the chaotic emotions following the loss. The believer thinks if his faith is strong enough, he should not be so shaken. To the world, the mourner pretends he is doing much better with the loss than he is in reality. He may give lip service to faith being a great help, when deep down, he does not feel faith is helping at all. He continues to minimize the depth of his grief in order to keep up the mask of the faithful believer. By not allowing himself to fully express his grief, he is avoiding the grief.

Often, the believer mistakenly thinks since going to heaven is a good thing, he should not feel so bad about his loved one going there. In actuality, he feels terrible about the loss. It hurts deeply. The believer may fall into the "feeling bad because you feel bad" syndrome. This is mistakenly thinking the loss should not hurt this much. It is thinking it is wrong to feel so badly, if one is a true believer.

It is important for the mourner suffering a faith crisis to understand faith does not take away the wound. Loss hurts. It hurts intensely. Faith is not the shield from hurt, but it can be a tool to help heal the hurt. The crisis is created because the believer has the wrong perception of what role faith plays in helping one through the rough times of life.

My support groups discussed at various times the role faith plays in processing grief. Many mourners expressed disappointment in God or feeling let down by God. Hopefully, the believer comes to understand God is not insurance against harm. Faith in God is not like buying "a piece of the rock," as an insurance advertisement promised. Faith in God does give you a rock to anchor yourself during the stormy time of resolution of the grief. When mourners are able to change their expectations of faith, faith becomes an asset. Failure to do this creates a continuing faith crisis.

The mourner who has strong faith but experiences a crisis of faith exhibits this in many ways. He may have a deep anger toward God. Questioning God and His ways may lead the believer to doubt his faith. He may doubt God is good or merciful. He may doubt God's plan for his life or even that there is a plan. The faithful believer in crisis may experience difficulty in praying and problems in returning to worship.

A crisis of faith, which is not addressed, can take a serious toll on the mourning believer. This is questioning something that previously was at the core of the believer's being. First, the believer lost a loved one; now he is in danger of losing another valuable component of his well-being, which is his faith.

1. Anger

Anger and resentment can boil inside the person of faith who feels God let him down. "What kind of God are you?" This is the question, which goes through the minds of many mourners. In the book of Job, Job was numbed and shocked over what happened to him. Since he was a good and faithful servant to God, was this God's reward for him? His life was turned upside down. Everything seemed hopeless. Job struggled to come to terms with reality.

One of the things Job did, which mourners often do, was retreat to the past. He remembered how good things used to be. He lived on memories. This relegated God to the past. God was good at one time but not now. Anger and resentment arise when the believer does this.

Many believers are victimized by false promises of religious zealots or their own conjecture. Some religions preach the mantra if you are good enough, bad things will not happen to you. A faith, which teaches believers sins cause God to bring tragedy as a punishment, does not present a loving god to turn to when suffering and despair occur.

A believer who expects God to deliver him and his from all that is tragic in life—simply because he is a good person—has expectations that will not be met. This unrealistic expectation of God can shake the faith of the strongest believer and leave him with feelings of anger and resentment toward God.

How God works in each person's life and how God helps when difficult times come is not subject to our demands. What faith means to you, what you expect from God in the valleys of your life, and what vision of God you take with you into the shadows has a lot to do with whether or not you will be angry and resentful of God.

2. Questioning

The questions all mourners have can be especially difficult for the person of deep faith. Many believers are taught not to question God's ways. God is omnipotent. Rev. John Claypool says some believe in unquestioning resignation. However, he says the Bible does not forbid questioning. The Word of God does not demand unquestioning acquiescence. Claypool's god and the god of many believers is a god of love—a father who pitieth his children rather than an unfeeling force who knocks us about for the fun of it.

Throughout the Bible, examples of the questioning of God are given. Job cried out to God to question why he had so much agony. Jesus cried out from the cross questions of why. Asking the question is not wrong. What the believer expects as far as answers does affect the faith of the believer.

In my practice throughout the years, the universal question asked by hundreds of bereaved patients is, why? Why was my loved one taken? Why did they suffer? Why did this happen? Rev. John Claypool gives an excellent answer to the questioning in his book *Tracks of a Fellow Struggler.*

Claypool lost a young daughter to leukemia, and following her death, he had many questions of God. He says it is futile and unproductive to try to explain tragedy in a comprehensive way. There is never a rational explanation for grief and loss. However, he does believe someday God will give an accounting. "It will not be until all the facts are in," says Claypool, "but it is valid to ask." He goes on to say he believes when the account is given, it will all fit together, but not at this point in time.

As for me, I concluded with the questioning I did after my losses, the why of loss did not matter. If God told me why my loved ones died, it would not make me feel one bit better. I would not feel less pain. My pain was the pain of separation from the ones I loved. There is no reason that could ever be given, even a seemingly very good reason, which would lessen my suffering about no longer being with them.

My second conclusion is my human mind is only capable of understanding things of this world. I see the here and now. God sees the here and forever. The answer to "why?" may not be understandable to me now, even if it were given. Someday, all will be made clear. I have a feeling when I arrive at that point, it will not really matter.

3. Doubt

Believers suffering anger at God and questioning His ways may begin to doubt their faith. To the person whose faith has been a vital part of his life, doubts can be most unsettling. One of the challenges is to go on living and believing although there are no explanations. It is at this point the believer is questioning a belief in something that cannot be seen and cannot be proved because of the occurrence of a concrete event in life, which requires an explanation in the believer's mind.

This time of doubt is when the believer is most likely to jump to conclusions, misinterpret events, and make false assumptions. Doubt slowly puts a wedge between the believer and his faith. It can be likened to the old adage, "Feed a fever; starve a cold." In this case, it is "Feed doubt; starve faith."

Doubt is negative thinking. Doubt is building fear and anxiety into life by worrying over what Claypool calls the "great not yet." We doubt because we want explanations *now*; then we can *live*. The challenge to the doubter is to *live*, then *interpret*. Doubting the outcome, being negative about what lies in store, feeling abandoned by God leads the believer further and further away from the faith needed to meet the challenges with hope.

Doubt keeps the mourner from using his faith to move in a forward-looking direction. Forward-looking means focusing on the *results* of the positives in your journey. It means knowing there is hope. Doubt dwells on the *causes*. Dwelling on the causes puts a huge roadblock in the journey toward healing. The more the believer allows doubt to take hold, the larger the roadblock becomes.

Your belief system has a great impact on the journey of grief. Doubts undermine this system. When tragedy happens, it is normal to feel life has stopped. In actuality, life as you knew it came to a standstill. Your new life began moving forward from that instant. This is when the questions and doubts begin to surface. Doubt as to God's care, concern, love, and help creates difficulty in the new journey and impairs the ability to fully utilize one's faith. The doubting believer must work to feed faith.

Remembering the past goodness of God reminds the believer more is to come. Isaiah 53:4 tells us: "Surely He has borne our grief and carried our sorrows." Further assurance is found in Psalm 23:6: "Surely goodness and mercy shall follow me all the days of my life." These two verses are reminders to the doubters of the good gifts in the past from God and the promise of more good things in the future. By doubting, the believer is saying the blessings are over, and there will be no good things to come. Faith emphasizes good things came from God in the past, and good things will come from God in the future.

4.   Prayer Crisis

Communicating with God is something people with faith do on a regular basis. Everyone has his own way of praying. It is a deep personal and private ritual. There are many names for God. The body of believers uses a wide variety of these names to call upon God. When suffering stress, anxiety, fear, uncertainty, and any number of other experiences in life, the believer calls on God for blessing, guidance, requests, and for renewal of the spirit. Sometimes when bogged down by grief, the person of faith finds he is unable to talk to God. Anger toward God, questioning, and doubt can impact the ability to pray.

It is not always the lack of desire to talk to God but is often the inability to put the words together. The believer may not be angry with God, but he is often so befuddled with grief the words will not form. Just when prayers are needed most, he simply cannot put together a coherent thought. Thus, the inability on the part of the mourner to think clearly and concisely may affect his ability to talk to God.

It is normal to find it hardest to pray when you are suffering deep hurt. God sees into the heart and knows the thoughts and feelings you have. You may want to scream and yell. These thoughts are not sweet prayers, but they can serve as prayers also. Remember God knows your heart and your emotions better than you do yourself. He understands. He is always there. He listens.

A woman whose daughter went through a debilitating illness for two years thanked her fellow church members for praying when she did not have the strength to pray. Her comment made me realize the importance of helping the mourner with a prayer crisis. Other people picking up the baton and offering prayers of intercession are ways for the believer to feel the power of prayer when he is not able to deliver the prayer. Her admission of experiencing times she was too exhausted to pray, but still needed the prayers, indicated another reason some people cannot pray during crisis.

The faith is strong, but the crisis is in being too exhausted to pray. This is when fellow believers can come forward with what Yancey called "shared suffering." This means your pain is important to others, and they share it with you and help you carry the load. Prayers of intercession are wonderful examples of shared suffering.

When a mourner wants to pray, but simply cannot find the words, it helps to have a short prayer in mind to use to call on God. One example is Psalm 6:2: "Have mercy on me, Lord, for I am faint." This prayer says it all. The mourner in prayer crisis needs only to repeat this verse, and communication with God has begun. God knows your heart and your sorrow and knows the full scope of your supplications.

5. Worship Difficulty

Returning to worship presents a problem for some believers. Many people return to their house of worship immediately, drawing great strength from the familiar readings, scriptures, prayers, and rituals. Others are terrified of the thought of returning to worship, fearing their emotions are too out of control to be in public.

Those who find comfort are reminded of the transcendence of God. They find solace and understanding. They feel closeness in the fellowship of the body of believers. It draws them closer to God and brings a sense of peace.

For the believers who are experiencing a crisis in faith, the effect is quite the opposite. Some mourners report anger at the scripture readings. They report feeling indignation over references in the readings or service to the justice and mercy of God. Anger at God is the mourner's reaction.

Others report being reminded even more of their own loss when they observe other intact families worshiping together. Hurt and envy are unpleasant emotions brought on by these observations. These two ugly emotions cause the mourner to feel guilt that such hateful thoughts come to mind while in the house of worship.

If the funeral service was held in the house of worship, many report difficulty with returning to worship due to being reminded of the service. If the loved one was a regular attendee of the services, there are many memories of past services in which the deceased participated to remind the mourner of the now missing person. The absence of the loved one at service reemphasizes the loss.

Other problematic behaviors mentioned by bereaved believers who have difficulty returning to worship are stares from others, questions, and callous comments made by people who mean well but say all the wrong things. Fear of being embarrassed by showing emotions during the service is also a reason many mourners give for hesitating to return to worship services.

There are many solutions for resolving the issue of when to return to worship and how to return to worship. Thinking about the things you fear happening and developing a plan for dealing with these fears is one important step. The following are suggestions made by Charles Meyer, which the mourner may consider.

Decide why you are going.

Once you know why you are going to worship, you will not be quite as frustrated with what other people say or do. If you see it as a positive step toward healing, this gives you a sense of purpose about returning to the house of worship. You may be going because it is a safe place to make your public debut after the loss. What could be safer than God's house? He knows what you feel. He does not care if you cry. He understands. The service itself may be what you need to feed your sagging spirit.

Prepare responses to others.

Planning ahead for questions such as, How are you doing? helps you to feel more confident. Your first inclination may be to give a biting retort such as:

> How do you think I'm doing? I've cried my eyes out, snapped at my kids, kicked the dog, and run off my best friend! I've just lost someone I loved dearly and feel as though I've been kicked by a mule!

While you may silently want to say this, a planned answer helps you to remain calm and to reply with decorum. Some examples are, (1) I feel as well as could be expected. (2) I have good days and bad days. (3) I'm doing so-so. (4) I'm fine. I stress to clients when using this last one to remember *fine* can stand for fearful, insecure, needy, and emotional. Only you know what fine really means.

Return to worship gradually.

Perhaps a few test visits to the house of worship will help you to actually return. You may inquire about going to the house of worship when there is no activity. You may wish to sit in a pew for a while alone. This gives you a chance to acclimate yourself to the environment. It also allows you the privacy to be emotional, if you wish.

Another option is to attend a different service than the main service or the one you usually attended. For example, a midweek service, an evening service, or an early service may have a smaller crowd and be more comfortable for you. If you and your loved one always attended the early service, going to the later service would be a different ritual for you.

Go with a friend.

Having someone to attend the service with helps reduce the anxiety of going alone. The friend can be a buffer between you and curious members. A friend can be prepared to hand you tissues, hold your hand, steer you through the crowd, or to give you moral support for a difficult outing. Be sure the friend understands your misgivings about going to worship and will move you on, if someone detains you longer than you prefer. The last thing you need is a friend who makes the situation worse.

Leave the service when you want.

It is important to understand, unlike many places, worship service attendance is optional. You are free to come and go whenever you choose. I do not know of any houses of worship that have chains attached to the pews. Whenever you do decide to go to the service, stay only as long as you are comfortable. If you decide the opening songs and scriptures are all you can take, leave. If at any time during the service you feel the urge to leave, get up and make a quiet exit. Choosing a seat nearest the exit is important when you first enter the sanctuary. If you decide to leave, do not feel embarrassed about it. God is all that matters. He understands and knows your heart.

Stay through the service.

This may sound contradictory to the previous suggestion, but it is not. Staying through the service means you have a right to be there, and you have a right to express your emotions if you need to do so. Stay as long as you are receiving something beneficial to you. Of course, if your crying becomes loud and is disruptive to others, leaving is probably the best option. However, softly crying and wiping your eyes bothers no one and is no reason to leave, if you do not wish to leave.

After the death of my mother and father, my sister and I wanted to do something for the church in memory of our parents. The church desperately needed new choir robes, and since my parents enjoyed the music, we donated new robes as a memorial tribute to our parents.

Although the robes were ordered in December, they did not arrive until spring. Easter Sunday was the debut of the new choir robes. I always sit on the second row of the sanctuary, so I was in plain view of the whole congregation when the choir made this first appearance in the new robes. The minute I set eyes on those lovely robes, the tears started falling. Fortunately, I had a good supply of tissues. I sat through the entire service, softly crying and mopping my eyes.

Compounding the difficulty of being so emotional was the fact everyone knew I worked as a bereavement therapist. I provided therapy for many who lost loved ones and taught numerous workshops for the church on dealing with loss. There I sat with running mascara and a red nose. Did it hurt anything for me to be so emotional? No! In reality, not many people noticed my emotional behavior. As I thought about it later, I realized I provided an example of the many things I stress to other mourners: (1) Feel what you feel. (2) Cry when and where you need to cry. (3) God knows your pain, and it is okay with Him for you to express it. (4) No matter who you are or what you do, when loss comes to you, you will have pain and suffering like everyone else. There is no way to circumvent grief. Loss and grief are vital parts of living just as birth and joy.

Go someplace new.

It may be hard to return to your regular place of worship. You may consider going to a different one. Going to a different one for a while does not mean you have to permanently change places of worship. Do what feels spiritually right for you.

I counseled with a couple while she was in the last stages of cancer. They had a forty-eight-year marriage. She was to the point of acceptance of her impending death. He was not. The early part of therapy consisted of bringing him some of the peace she felt and being sure she was able to express all she wanted to express. When one partner accepts and the other does not, it can affect the communication process between them. It is important for all the things that need to be said to come forth so nothing is held back. Holding back communications produces later regrets. So the early therapy consisted on getting him to the place where he could enjoy the time left and not waste it worrying about the future.

The couple was very active in their church, and the church body was supportive of them throughout their last days together. After her death, he had a serious issue with returning to church. Each time he tried, there were so many memories of her there and the activities they did together; he could not bear the pain.

One day, he announced to me he made a big decision. He was not going to that particular church again. He selected several other churches to visit. The process of selecting churches to attend served the purpose of reinvesting some of his time. He attended quite a few and met many new people. He finally moved his membership to one he particularly liked. He became very active in the new church and made many friends in the membership. This solution worked well for him. He was able to continue to practice his faith but in new surroundings. This also enabled him to make new friends and begin to move forward with his life.

Does this mean moving to another place of worship would work for everyone? No. Many people of faith gain comfort in the familiarity of the house of worship they attended regularly. But for this mourner, he needed to do what was spiritually right for him.

The Benefits of Faith

When faith is an important part of your spirituality, there are many benefits to derive from it. Faith sustains and gives hope to the mourner. Without faith, the negatives of worry, regret, guilt, and depression take over. Why? Without faith, the world is viewed without hope. Faith believes there will be better times. Faith believes the bad times will not last forever. Faith believes the dark clouds will pass, and the sun will shine again. Faith believes you only *walk through* the valley of the shadow of death. Faith does *not* believe you pitch your tent in that valley and stay there. Faith believes you do not walk alone.

Lacking faith puts you in a negative frame of mind. Negativity leads to negative feelings of anxiety, fear, guilt, and depression. When you lose faith, you lose faith in yourself and faith in God. Your energy is spent on negative attitudes. Negativity pulls the force of your energy into a slow downward spiral of depression. Your spirit plummets into the lowest of valleys.

Faith brings hope to the hopeless. Faith lifts the spirit and infuses it with a sense of promise. Faith lessens pain, strengthens the courage to meet the challenge, and assures the believer of the arrival of better days.

Another benefit of faith is leading you to the acceptance of the changes in life. This enables you to pursue a new direction and purpose in life. Jimmy Carter said,

> Faith . . . in God . . . will permit us to take a chance on a new
> path, perhaps different from the one we now follow. It may be
> surprising where it leads.

While he was referring to the benefits of faith in making life changes in general, it does illustrate a deep faith and trust in God leads you to changing directions in life because you believe God is in control and has a plan for your life. This gives your life meaning and purpose. This is the quest for mourners.

Research supports the benefits of a strong faith for mourners dealing with the aftermath of loss. A 1991 research study of parents who lost children—and cited in the work of Bernstein—found up to eighteen months after the death of a child, parents who attended worship more regularly and professed a strong faith had lower levels of grief reactions. The reactions measured were guilt, anger, loss of control, and despair. The parents who attended worship less regularly or professed ambivalence about faith had higher levels of those grief reactions.

Another study of bereaved parents whose infants died two months earlier found the parents were not necessarily consoled by their religions, since their pain at the two-month time span was still intense. However, the more religious parents were found to be less anxious and depressed than the ones with a weaker faith or no faith.

An additional observation—made in studying the impact of faith on the bereaved parents—was the parents who were also strong believers in God were more apt to turn their parental responsibilities over to God, so to speak. In discussions with these parents, they indicated their trust in God was such they saw Him as a loving, caring parent. They expressed some degree of comfort in believing the child was in good hands with God. They also professed the belief there would be a chance for them to be together with the child again someday.

One of the needs for the suffering mourner is for the pain to be honored. The body of believers associated with the mourner's faith meets this need by providing a support network for the mourner during this period of suffering.

Henri Nouwen talks about the "wounded healer" who is another believer who suffers with you because he shares the suffering. Wounded healers have suffered pain and sorrow too. They can be truly empathetic with your pain. The wounded healer helps the mourner to return from his journey of suffering. Nouwen says, "Suffering has a meaning to us. No man can stay alive when nobody is waiting for him. Everyone who returns from a long difficult trip is looking for someone waiting for him." The wounded healer is someone who is waiting for you to return from your journey and understands the pain.

The woman mentioned previously who thanked her fellow believers for shouldering her suffering throughout two long years of personal tragedy emphasized the importance of being wounded healers. Wounded healers are people who have also known suffering and hurt and are there to help when there is a crisis.

It may be a faith crisis, prayer crisis, doubt, anger, or questioning. Whatever the crisis, just as this woman indicated, knowing there is a body of wounded healers taking your suffering upon their shoulders—interceding and providing for you as you struggle—enables you to return from a long difficult journey. Faith provides the mourner with a network of believers who will share the suffering and use their own experiences with difficulties to bring spiritual support in the time of need. Sharing sufferers and wounded healers are found in the groups of strongest faith.

One of the greatest benefits of faith is the promise it gives the mourner for the future. From personal experiences, I know at the time of the loss, it is hard to see past the pain. The future does not exist at that moment. The great not yet John Claypool speaks about yawns before the mourner like a black abyss. The suffering, which comes with the loss, clouds the view of any brighter days.

The scriptures are filled with God's promises. They echo throughout ages recorded in the Bible. Some comforting ones for mourners are,

> Genesis 28:15
> I am with you and will watch over you wherever you go.
>
> Isaiah 41:10
> I will strengthen you and help you; I will uphold you with my right hand.
>
> Isaiah 46:4
> I will sustain you and rescue you.
>
> Joshua 1:5
> I will never leave or forsake you.

Each one of these scriptures promises companionship on the journey and strength to complete the task of mourning. None of them promise protection from hard times; but they do promise sustaining love, strength, and guidance. My faith in these promises sustained me in some of my darkest hours. As long as I had God, I felt safe in His care. His love was a comforting presence in my journey. Faith served as an encourager for me to press forward. Being able to reach for God's hand in times of loss and knowing His promises were not empty promises gave me hope for better times in the future.

More importantly, faith enabled me to calm my fears and stay in the present moment. Fear of the future is enormous when you lose a spouse. There are so many uncertainties to face. Faith, with its promise for the strength and help to handle whatever came, enabled me to put aside those fears and do the tasks that needed to be completed at that moment in time. There is an old saying, which best illustrates the power faith has over fear:

> Fear knocked at the door.
> Faith answered.
> No one was there.
>   —Old Saying

Tomorrow is always a time of uncertainty no matter the circumstances. Ordinarily, you are able to ignore the uncertainty of life as long as problems do not arise. When death comes, anxiety rises as you realize how unpredictable life truly is. Henry Ward Beecher said,

> Every tomorrow has two handles. We can take hold of it with
> the handle of anxiety or the handle of faith.

Faith enables the mourner to handle tomorrow confidently in the belief this too will pass. There will be good times once more.

Just as faith assists you to quell fear and misgivings about the future, it also has a huge impact on your adjustment to the loss. There are so many changes to make. The changes begin at the moment of the death of the loved one. These changes invade your life in big ways, little ways, obvious ways, and subtle ways. You find yourself constantly making adjustments. From setting the table for one less person to changing legal documents, the adjustments flood your life with new challenges, new processes, and new patterns. Faith is a valuable resource in making these adjustments. Why? The courage to face and to meet the challenges of the adjustments comes from faith.

A research study by Walsh on the effect of one's spirituality on adjustment to loss validates the importance of a strong faith. Two groups of participants were tracked over a fourteen-month period following the death of a loved one. One group reported no spiritual beliefs. The other group reported strong spiritual beliefs. Both groups were given a grief assessment at the beginning of the study to measure their level of adjustment.

The finding at the end of the fourteen-month period was the group with no spiritual beliefs failed to make significant progress in adjustment to the loss as indicated on the grief assessment. The group with strong spiritual beliefs showed significant progress in adjustment to the death when rated with the same assessment.

The conclusion of this study was people who profess stronger spiritual beliefs seem to resolve their grief more *rapidly* and *completely* after the death of a close person than do people with no spiritual beliefs.

Another positive impact faith has on the mourner's adjustment to loss is the element of hope faith brings to the believer. Mourners are often referred to as survivors. The word *survivor* denotes one who withstands or bears difficulty and makes it through the situation. Survivors are hope-based people. They are people who know there will be better days ahead if they have some reason to hang on in the present situation.

Much as Frankl said about the death camp survivors, the ones with purpose and hope fared much better than those who gave up or had no goal for the future. Faith gives purpose and hope in troubled times.

Faith faces impossibility with a sense of possibility. Faith works miracles. Faith is the antidote to despair. With so many adjustments flooding the mourner's life, he has to cling to a strong hope and belief that all is not lost. There is a new dawn on the horizon.

Changing Perspectives

William James, sometimes called the father of American psychology, said,

> The greatest discovery of my generation is that human beings
> can alter their lives by altering their attitudes of the mind.

This quote applies to many areas of our personal lives; but in discussing how spirituality, faith, and loss intertwine, it bears great consideration by the mourner.

Death, naturally, focuses the mind on a huge negative—the loss. Believers and nonbelievers alike do this. However, the stunning thought in the quote by James is the realization that the power to successfully handle the loss lies in the mental perspective of the mourner. This is where faith makes a difference because of the positive feeling of hope faith nurtures in believers.

It is normal to review the past life with the deceased and to feel the good times are behind us. However, using faith to change the mind-set of negativity helps the mourner to calm anxiety and fear. The change in perspective, which most helps the mourner, is the change from focusing on *the death and what it took away from life* to focusing on *what the life of the loved one gave* to the mourner and others affected by that life.

Faith enables the mourner to feel God's presence no matter what is happening in life. Regardless of the situation, faith helps the mourner to focus on the *blessings*, not only in the past but also in the present. Wherever you are, there is God. There is always an abundance of God's blessings. The positive perspective of faith allows the mourner to see and feel God working in daily life.

Faith of this degree knows nothing in the future matters at this point, but everything in the here and now does. Grace is being given daily in the many blessings showering over the believer. Do we always see the blessings? Are we grateful for them? Often, the answer is no. The mind-set of negativity can divert the focus from *what we have* to *what we have not*. Faith is positive thinking at its best.

All problems cannot be solved in an instant. We have many steps to take in the journey, and the grace needed is given *as we need it*. Believers who are able to function from this positive mind-set have hope during the difficult times. The quality of hope comes from the sense of God's presence in the life of the believer. As the saying goes, "If God is with us, who can be against us?"

Brook Noel, who lost a child, described her struggle with such a devastating loss and how changing her perspective brought peace to her. Adopting the perspective of walking in the here and now—and not demanding complete grace and all knowledge and understanding at one time—enabled her to find the peace she sought. It also strengthened her faith.

She finally turned to God in the present and said,

> I do not understand. I am ready to quit trying to understand. You know more than I. I am ready to accept that. I will understand as I am ready. The right time. The right place. I ask for *peace.*

She said when she did this, blessings poured over her. Instead of viewing life as a certainty with clear answers and plans, she changed her perspective to accept the uncertainty of life and to simply accept "I don't understand." Her focus turned from the turmoil of questioning and doubt toward *finding peace.*

Noel found when the change in perspective was accomplished, renewed faith was gained. Her comment was,

> With peace comes renewed faith—a faith that Someone is standing over me and will lead me to what I must know, as I must know it. It is a faith where I surrender the unknown without expectation. I trust the process that all will unfold in its own time.

The two major changes in the perspective of the mourner as he goes from a negative mind-set to a positive one are (1) understanding life is a gift and (2) developing gratitude for the gift.

Life is a Gift

Nothing brings forth the realization of the preciousness of life like facing death. Like many things in life, you do not always fully appreciate something until you lose it.

I lived a number of years in a rural area where the electrical service was interrupted periodically by the weather. It is amazing the many ordinary daily activities, which require electrical service. Cooking, cleaning, ironing, heating, cooling, and all tasks involving water use were impossible to do when the electrical service failed. Our water came from a well, equipped with an electric pump. Not only could we not run any electrical appliances, but our water supply was stopped too. Several times a year, I was rudely reminded of the precious gift of electricity by having it taken away for a period of time.

This example of the blessings of electricity can be likened to life. Life is a blessing. Each day is precious, but often, we fail to appreciate it. Life is a gift from God, but unfortunately, we fail to understand that perspective until life is taken away. Do you think about life as a gift? Are you grateful for each day?

Since my husband had many years of serious health problems before his death, I learned to appreciate the gift sooner in life than many others. During his years of ill health, we knew our time together was precious. Each day was a blessing and gave us something priceless—more time.

Our son was a baby when his father was injured. The gift of life given by God enabled his father to live long enough for our son to know him. The gift of extra years allowed us to make memories, say important things to each other, and to fully enjoy family time together, because we understood the blessing of time. We learned to be conscious of the finiteness of time before it was too late.

It's been said until you face death, you do not truly know how to live. Once you see death face-to-face, you know the gift of life is indeed precious. Death emphasizes the importance of many things you overlooked before it entered your life. Facing death enables you to use time wisely. Understanding time is finite keeps you from squandering precious time on unimportant things.

Rev. John Claypool, grieving the loss of his young daughter, preached a sermon after her death about the gift of life. He used a wonderful personal story, which helped him come to terms with her loss. It bears repeating because of the point it drives home. That point is the importance of developing the perspective of seeing life as a gift.

John said when he was a young boy, times were hard. World War II started, and gasoline was rationed. The Claypool family did not have a washing machine, so getting to and from a laundry posed a problem.

A family friend was drafted, and the Claypools offered to store his furniture in their basement while he and his wife were away. Along with the household furniture, the couple owned a washing machine. In return for the favor of storing the furniture, the couple suggested the Claypools use the washing machine while they were away.

One of John's chores was helping with the laundry. The use of this machine was like manna from heaven. What a wonderful windfall for the Claypool family!

A few years went by, the war ended, and the couple returned to retrieve their stored belongings. This included the washing machine.

John was more than upset. He had forgotten the washing machine did not really belong to the Claypool family. When it was taken away, John was upset and said so quite loudly.

This is when his mother gave him food for thought. She told John to remember the machine was never truly theirs. She went on to say they were indeed fortunate to ever get to use it in the first place. The use of the machine was a gift. She admonished John to be grateful for the gift of having it and understand it now was with its rightful owner.

As he mourned the loss of his young daughter, he said the memory of this event in his youth helped him to realize his child's life was truly a gift from God. It was not a gift he earned or deserved, but God had bestowed the privilege of having her in his life for a while. How ungrateful to be angry over such a wonderful gift! He started out being angry and bitter toward God because the gift was taken. Then he realized he needed to change his perspective and to take the road of gratitude for the gift. It had returned to its rightful owner.

John Claypool's story strikes a chord in my life and in the lives of others who suffer loss. The gift of our loved one's life was precious.

Something so valuable is hard to give up. However, with the perspective of life as a gift comes the understanding of how much we were blessed to have this gift of life for the time we had it. If given the choice of never having the gift at all in order to avoid the pain of loss, how many of us would make that choice? Not many! No matter how long or short the loved one's life was, it was a valued gift and brought joy by being ours for a while.

The perspective of life as a gift put a new slant on my losses. Of course, I wanted my loved ones with me longer. You did too. My conclusion is anger and bitterness over the loss negates the joy of the gift. I loved these precious people in my life. If I had a choice, I would not give up the opportunity to love them for any lessening of the suffering following their loss.

Gratitude for Life

The other change in perspective is closely tied to viewing life as a gift. It is accepting the gift with gratitude, no matter the length of the gift. John Claypool testified to this in his story of loss. Every life is precious. Some are longer than others. As was discussed earlier in this chapter, all life has meaning and purpose. The lives of others leave footprints in our lives. It is these footprints, which impact our lives in so many important ways.

Claypool's struggle was to be *grateful* for the joy in receiving the life of his daughter into their family while dealing with her loss. This struggle led him to understand the scope of God's blessings in our lives. It also led him to strengthen his faith and rethink his *expectations* of God.

My own father was diagnosed with pancreatic cancer after only a few weeks of illness. When the specialist gave us the news, it shocked the whole family. My dad experienced no noticeable illness until about two weeks before the diagnosis. By the time the cancer was discovered and diagnosed, he was given only a few months to live.

We came home from the medical center and began to prepare for what was to come. One morning, my dad and I were talking about arrangements he wanted to make. Hospice, a nurse, reviewing medical powers of attorney, and being sure my mother had support and help for what lay ahead were all topics he wanted to cover. After talking about these tasks, he began to talk about how he felt about the frightening news. I will never forget his words. He said,

I was shocked about what the doctor said. Of course, I'd like to live longer. I know at my age (75) these things happen. But, I have no regrets about my life. I've loved your mother ever since the day I saw her over fifty years ago. We've had a good life together. I've done a lot of things I wanted to do. You and your sister brought us a lot of happiness. I've seen you, both, through school. I've seen you, both, married. I've seen my grandsons born and grown. I've even seen my first great grandson. God has been good to me. To be mad at Him because I have cancer would be terrible. I'd like to live, but it's not my decision. I've had many blessings.

My dad's diagnosis was near the end of May. He died in early August. The talk we had was one of the last times he was able to sit in his recliner before he became bedridden. When he died, I knew he left this world feeling a sense of peace because his life had meaning, and he fulfilled his purpose. I also knew he left with the perspective clear in his mind of the precious gift of life. He was grateful for it.

There is not a passing day I fail to think of my parents. They knew love and great joy in life. They understood the gift of life and from whence it came. They both led meaningful lives, touching many people and fulfilling their purpose. Most of all, they were grateful.

This perspective helps me deal with the tremendous losses in my life. Continuing to make self-examinations, to make adjustments, to find meaning, and to realign my purpose with each loss enables me to continue to see the promise in the future because of the enormous joys in my past.

Staying healthy spiritually is a must for the mourner. My faith gives me great comfort when times are sad, but it sustains my spirit on a daily basis. The twenty-third Psalm is my favorite scripture because there are so many reassuring verses in it. "He restoreth my soul" gives me what I need when I hurt. This is a task all mourners struggle with—to have their souls restored. "Thou art with me" is another important promise to me as I travel through the valleys of death. "Surely goodness and mercy shall follow me all the days of my life" assures me there are more joys ahead of me. There are more blessings to come. These are the assurances of faith. Faith enables you to reach for the Hand of God and feel the warmth of His Hand clasping yours.

Chapter 5 References

1. Amour, Marilyn. 2003. Meaning Making in the Aftermath of Suicide. *Death Studies* 27, no. 7 (July): 519-518-540.

2. Bartocci, Barbara. 2000. *Nobody's Child Anymore: Grieving, Caring, and Comforting When Parents Die.* Notre Dame, IN: Sorin Books.

3. Bernstein, Judith R., PhD. 1980. *When the Bough Breaks: Forever after the Death of a Son or Daughter.* Kansas City: MO: Andrews McMeel Publishing.

4. Blair, Pamela, PhD, and Brook Nocl. 2000. *I Wasn't Ready to Say Goodbye: Surviving, Coping and Healing after the Sudden Death of a Loved One.* Milwaukee, WI: Champion Press LTD.

5. Bozarth, Alla Renee, PhD. 1990. *A Journey through Grief.* Center City, MO: Hazelton.

6. Carter, Jimmy. 1998. *The Virtues of Aging.* New York, NY: Ballantine Publishing Group.

7. Claypool, John. 1995. *Tracks of a Fellow Struggler: Living and Growing through Grief.* New Orleans, LA: Insight Press.

8. Coleman, Sally, and Maria Porter. 1994. *Seasons of the Spirit.* Center City, Minn: Hazeldon Foundation.

9. avis, Chris, Susan Nolen-Hoeksema. 2001. Loss and Meaning: How Do People Make Sense of Loss? *American Behavioral Scientist* 44, no. 5 (May): 726-725-741.

10. Finkbeiner, Ann K. 1996. *After the Death of a Child: Living with Loss through the Years.* Baltimore, MD: The John Hopkins University Press.

11. Johnson, Barbara. 2004. *Laughter from Heaven.* Nashville, TN: W Publishing Group.

12. Kushner, Harold. 2002. *When All You've Ever Wanted Isn't Enough: The Search for a Life That Matters.* New York, New York: Simon and Schuster.

13. Manning, Doug. 1979. *Don't Take My Grief Away: What to Do When You Lose a Loved One.* San Francisco: CA: HarperCollins Publishers.

14. McConnell, Stephen D. 1998. Christians in Grief. In *Living with Grief.* Washington, DC: Hospice Foundation of America.

15. Meyer, Charles. 1997. *Surviving Death: A Practical Guide to Caring for the Dying and Bereaved.* Mystic, Conn: Twenty-Third Publications.

16. Neeld, Elizabeth Harper, PhD. 2003. *Seven Choices: Finding Daylight after Loss Shatters Your World.* New York, NY: Tiime Warner.

17. Neimeyer, Richard (. 2001. *Meaning Reconstruction and the Experience of Loss.* American Psychological Association.
18. Nouwen, Henri J. M. 1994. *Our Greatest Gift: A Meditation on Dying and Caring.* San Francisco, CA: Harper Collins.
19. O'Connor, Nancy, PhD. 1984. *Letting Go with Love: The Grieving Process.* Tuscon, AZ: La Mariposa Press.
20. Omartian, Stormie. 1999. *Just Enough Light for the Step I'm On: Trusting God in Tough Times.* Eugene, Oregon: Harvest House.
21. Peale, Norman V. 1990. *Words I Have Lived By.* Norwalk, Conn: C. R. Gibson Co.
22. Rando, Therese A. 1996. Complications in Mourning Traumatic Death. In *Living with Grief after Sudden Loss: Suicide, Homicide, Accident, Heart attack, Stroke.* Bristol, PA: Taylor and Francis.
23. Reilly, Marla, S. P. 1996. *Now That I Am Old: Meditations on the Meaning of Life.* Mystic, Connecticut: Twenty-Third Publications
24. Schroeder, Joel and Ruth. 1997. *The Power of Positivity.* Mission, KS: Skillpath Publications.
25. Segal, Julius. 1986. *Winning Life's Toughest Battles: Roots of Human Resilience.* New York, NY: Ivy Press.
26. Stalling, Elizabeth. 1997. *Prayer Starters: To Help You Heal after Loss.* St. Meinrad, IN: Abbey Press.
27. Tatelbaum, Judy. 1980. *The Courage to Grieve: Creative Living, Recovery, and Growth through Grief.* New York, New York: Harper Row.
28. Tolle, Eckhart. 1999. *The Power of Now.* Novato, CA: Namaste Publishing.
29. Walsh, Kiri, Michael King, Louise Jones, Adrian Tookman, and Robert Blizard. 2002. Spiritual Beliefs May Affect Outcome of Bereavement Prospective Study. *British Medical Journal* 324: 1-2-5.
30. Wolfelt, Alan D., PhD. 1992. *Understanding Grief: Helping Yourself Heal.* Muncie: IN: Accelerated Development Inc.
31. Yancey, Philip. 1990. *Where Is God When It Hurts?* Grand Rapids, MI: Zondervan Publications.

Chapter 6

DIFFERENT DEATHS—DIFFERENT GRIEF

Grief has many faces. It is the widow adjusting to living alone. It is the parent whose heart aches driving by the little league field. It is the daughter reaching for the phone to call her mother, only to remember her mother is no longer there. It is eliminating one place at the table. It is holding the folded flag from your loved one's coffin. Grief is missing the lunches with your old friend. Grief is realizing there is no one waiting for you at home. Grief is taking comfort in the smell of the loved one's clothing. Grief is the lump in your throat, the pain in your heart, and the tears in your eyes when you hear your loved one's favorite song.

Grief is more than sadness. St. Augustine pointed out, "Grief is a strange mixture of joy and sorrow—joy to be yet alive and sorrow to have life diminished by the loss of the one we love." Grief diminishes the mourner because life, as it has always been, is changed forever. The loved one who died no longer suffers. It is those left behind who are deprived of the release from suffering. The mourner is alive, yet life is empty and meaningless without the loved one. Being alive yet not fully alive deprives us of the joy of living.

Previous chapters discussed the characteristic behavioral patterns associated with loss. Mood swings, anxiety, depression, forgetfulness, and poor concentration are some of the more common emotions experienced after suffering the loss of a loved one. The phases of shock, numbing, denial, guilt, bargaining, anger, yearning, and questioning are other grief components. Actions and reactions to these phases are unique to each specific mourner.

You never fully recover from the trauma of death. The word *recovery*, as used by many people, in reality means reaching healing by integrating the trauma into your life, thus, enabling you to continue to live. Bernstein, in *When the Bough Breaks*, says,

> The process of integration involves changes in the person's view
> of the world, in the way they relate to others, in their values,
> in spiritual feelings and so forth. It's the difference between
> *stepping over* an obstacle and *being rerouted* by it.

In other words, the trauma causes you to readjust your life, not just picking up where you left off when the loved one died and going back to normal. It means readjusting your life by rerouting in a different direction. You are changed; your life is changed; and there is no return to the way things used to be.

Losing someone of great importance to you is disruptive to your entire life. Grieving this loss is normal behavior. O'Connor describes this period of great discomfort in life as a "state of dis-ease." The difference between this state of dis-ease and disease is you will eventually recover from a disease. As discussed in the description of the grief roller coaster, you never fully recover from the state of dis-ease caused by grief.

If you get pneumonia, it is a disease, which is treatable with medication. You can expect to recover and return to your normal self. However, the state of dis-ease caused by loss is a state you must assimilate into your life, thus, changing you from the point of the loss forward. You will never return to the old you. There will always be times in your life when the sorrow surfaces due to holidays, special events, or various circumstances.

Doing grief work to reach acceptance of the death requires the mourner to complete many different tasks. Talking about the loss, expressing feelings, realigning roles, reassignment of the relationship from the physical to the spiritual, redefining self-identity, sorting and storing memories, and reinvestment of time are some of the tasks discussed in chapter 2, which the mourner must complete during the period of mourning.

Discussion up to this point speaks of grief in generalities. The information thus far contains the basics of grief. The mourner must understand the reasons for grief, common characteristics of grief, behaviors exhibited while in mourning, and the goals to be accomplished during the grieving process. You must also understand your grief is yours alone. While all mourners experience similar emotions, actions, and reactions, you will have your own specialized technique of grief. This is the reason no one can truly say to you, "I know how you feel." No one does.

Second to understanding the basics of grief is the understanding of variations in the grief patterns produced by different types of loss. While the loss of a spouse, parent, child, sibling, and friend produce some similar feelings, each kind also brings emotions and adjustments peculiar to that type of loss. Suicide, murder, and other types of sudden, traumatic deaths have unique characteristics of mourning for the survivors, which are quite different from the impact suffered of death after a long debilitating illness.

While death brings chaos to the lives of all mourners, the method of death, the circumstances of the death, and the relationship of the deceased to the survivor greatly impact how the loss is integrated into the survivor's life. A mourner whose loved one died peacefully surrounded by family cannot possibly understand the emotions of the mourner whose loved one was murdered or died in a violent way.

Each of these losses encompasses a wide array of subject matter. However, for the purpose of this book, each loss will be addressed briefly. The goal is to make the mourner aware of the varied feelings and adjustments, which come with different types and circumstances of loss. This awareness enables you to gain insight into the different coping techniques needed to process different kinds of losses in life. Hopefully, it will also help the mourner and others to empathize with mourners suffering from these different losses.

Loss of a Spouse

The word *widow* is defined as "empty; without a mate." While commonly used as a term to describe a woman whose husband died, it refers to a male or female who lost a mate. In this discussion, the word *widow* will be used for both genders.

Someone once said losing a life partner is like being dismembered. When you are in a close, intimate relationship, it does feel this way. Sometimes married people joke about their spouse being the better half.

When death takes your spouse away, it does feel as though your better half is missing.

Marriage is a partnership like no other. A successful marriage involves a great deal of give-and-take, consideration of the other person's needs, compromising when disagreements arise, and tolerating each other's idiosyncrasies. Sometimes this partnership requires you to put your mate's wishes before your own desires.

There are times you need to be selfless and do activities your mate enjoys, but which are not your favorite pastime entertainments. There may be people your spouse loves and likes to be with, so you add them to your circle because of the spouse's feelings. In a good marriage, the spouse reciprocates this action. Marriage calls for a great deal of negotiation, tact, and diplomacy on the part of both partners—if it is going to be a successful marriage.

Losing a life partner is like losing your right arm. This was the person who comforted you when you suffered hurts and disappointments. He listened to your conversations, laughed at your jokes, and liked you for who you are. Your partner was your confidant, your cheerleader, your nurturer, your friend, and your lover. He filled so many different roles in your life; is it any wonder you are devastated at his death?

Losing a spouse brings forth feelings, which cross all barriers of race, color, creed, wealth, health, or intelligence. While culture does impact customs and rituals of grief, the pain is universal. It does not matter if you are rich or poor, the color of your skin, your nationality, or religious persuasion. Pain is pain. Losing someone dear to you and with whom you share such intimate moments hurts deeply.

The relationship between mates is so intensely personal and private the loss disrupts all aspects of your life. Marriage forges a bond, which not only establishes the home, but also is the foundation upon which your entire life is built. The joining of extended families, customs, beliefs, and values form a new nuclear home from which you and your spouse create your life together.

Marriage is a blending of two personalities. A good marriage allows each partner to maintain the individual personality traits, which served as the attraction in the beginning of the relationship. Often, the partner traits are very different but complementary, thus, forming a happy union. A successful marriage also continues to blend these two distinct personalities to produce a symbiotic relationship. Career decisions, social interactions, and parenting styles are life issues impacted by the bond forged between these different personalities.

While various feelings of grief and grief work tasks discussed previously are part of the grief of losing your spouse, there are some specific psychological phases peculiar to this type of loss.

Psychological Phases

Psychologically, after the death of a mate, you grieve not only for him but also for yourself. You realize how alone you really are. When the visitation and service is over, the visitors leave, the extended families go home, and everyone else returns to their normal routines—you are alone. The silence is deafening.

Your once familiar home seems to be an alien land. The bedroom seems so empty. The bed is huge, cold, and unwelcoming. You lie there at night hearing only your own breath in the stillness. There are noises you never heard before when your mate was present. Floorboard creaks, windowpane rattles, branches brushing the roof, the sighing of the wind, and the settling of the house for the night all come together to shout your aloneness to you.

Creeping into the aloneness is the feeling of fear. There is so much uncertainty. Can I make it alone? Will I have enough money? What if I get sick? What should I do about the house? Can I deal with the children on my own? Question after question comes to mind, and with the questions come fear and anxiety of what lies ahead as you face the world alone.

This self-grief includes the uneasy feeling of insecurity. Marriage gives security to both mates. The world may be a scary place, but with your partner by your side, it did not seem quite so frightening. You felt safe in the relationship with your spouse and did not have to pretend to be something you are not. Your mate met your need for belonging and the need to be loved. Your mate knew you warts and all and liked you anyway. The sense of belonging and being loved is a part of marriage, which brings a deep sense of security. Death takes the security away.

Also, included in the self-grief are the intense feelings of loneliness and longing after the partner's death. There is being alone; then there is being lonely. There is a huge difference between the two. You can be alone and become comfortable with your own company. However, being lonely is to desire companionship, yearning for close human contact and being deprived of it.

When my husband was hospitalized numerous times during his lengthy illness, I learned to enjoy my own company. He traveled to medical centers in Florida and Texas for some of his treatments. I could not always go with him due to financial concerns, family responsibilities, and my job. Sometimes he would be gone for a short while and at other times several weeks. I missed our time together and found it very lonely, especially in the evenings, when the daily tasks were finished. Learning to enjoy my own company simply meant I found things to do, which occupied my time and gave me pleasure. I developed many hobbies and interests.

However, the loneliness of those times was nothing to compare to the loneliness after his death. When I knew he was never coming home, I realized previously in his absences, I only learned to be alone. I had not learned what it was to suffer real loneliness.

Loneliness, especially for mourners who are left with no family, is a powerful emotional struggle. Couples, who are either childless or have children who are grown and live away from the parents, suffer this emotion intensely when one of them passes away. It is most difficult for those who were together for a lifetime. Marriages of great length have united the couple in so many ways and intertwined their lives so completely; the surviving spouse struggles with how to handle the intense yearning for the companionship of the deceased.

My parents were married fifty-eight years when my father passed away. My mother was sixteen years old when they married, and she commented they grew up together. She said it was hard to remember a time when they were not part of each other's life. His concern, up to the actual point of his death, was for her welfare when he could no longer be with her. She did amazingly well with her grief in the time after his death, but admitted to me some days it took her breath away when the pain of loss washed over her. She did not complain, but she did confide the loneliness was excruciating.

She lived a little over a year after his death. While I know the medical reasons she died, I believe the impact of his death had a great deal to do with the progression of her illness. I, her daughter, could only companion her so far. Because I was her child, and she was my parent, I could not totally fill the void my father's death created. The loneliness was one of losing mate companionship.

Dealing with the loneliness is complicated because it means you must come out of your comfort zone. When the spouse is no longer here for companionship, you must develop additional relationships outside of the home and the immediate family. Developing new friends and new relationships is scary. It requires you to risk rejection, and this is very frightening to the widowed person. Marriage provided security. Now the security is gone, and you are starting out on your own to make new relationships.

These new relationships are not necessarily romantic in nature. These are new relationships to provide social contact and company for you now that you are alone. Just as you lost the marriage to death, you will find you lose some of the friendships, which were attached to the marriage. Those friendships have to be replaced. Enlarging your circle of friends, both male and female, builds a foundation from which you can create your own social opportunities.

In learning to cope with the loneliness, you discover the importance of caring for others. When you reach out to fellow sufferers, your pain lessens. Pain shared is pain divided. This was a valuable lesson for me. Sharing my experiences, my actions, and reactions with others not only gave me relief—it helped others find their way on the journey. Listening to their pain and struggles gave me insights into life and the human condition, which I could use in my journey. It is not until you suffer loneliness that you are best able to identify it in other people and are better equipped to give assistance in their struggles. The reward for this ability is a lessening of your own load.

Another psychological phase after the loss of a spouse is anger and/or bitterness. While this is a common experience across all types of loss, there are some differences with the loss of a spouse, which bear mentioning.

Some mates are angry with the spouse who died. Since it feels like you lost your best friend, you might become angry because the spouse abandoned you even though you know this is a foolish thought. This does not sound rational, but remember, you are not always thinking in a rational way when you grieve.

Some widowed people are angry with themselves. In this type of anger, guilt creeps into the picture. Fearing you did not express your love enough when the spouse was alive may be one fear feeding the anger. You may go over in your mind things the spouse wanted you to do, which you failed to do. Now you regret not doing them. You direct the anger toward yourself for failure to do those acts of service. Some mourners carry anger for allowing themselves to be so vulnerable. Their thinking goes something like, "If I hadn't let myself care so much, this wouldn't hurt so badly." Of course, you see the fallacy in this thinking. Not caring would deny the mourner of many wonderful times and happy memories.

Bitterness creeps into the grief over the loss of a spouse when you see other couples happily going about the business of living. You feel terrible, and they seem to be completely unaware of how precious their time is together. They are oblivious to how quickly it can be taken away. Suddenly, finding yourself single makes the entire population appear to be paired into twosomes. One gentleman commented he became so angry at church he had to leave because he saw couples sitting together in their regular pews, unaware of how wonderful it was they could worship together.

Some bitterness is normal and is allowed just as having moments of self-pity is allowed. The mourner is to be cautioned, however, not to remain in the bitter state very long. Bitterness is like an acid. It eats you from the inside. Bitterness is not forward thinking. Bitterness is saying all the good things in life are in the past, and there is nothing good in store for you in the future. Bitterness is negativity at its worst. Do not fall into the bitter trap. Adversity can make you bitter, or it can make you better. The choice is yours to make.

A third psychological phase the bereaved mate experiences is a sexual blunting. Your intimate partner is gone. You hurt deeply. Because you are grieved, your sexual feelings may be frozen for a while. You have so many emotions to process and handle on a daily basis; you are exhausted mentally and physically. Your sexual energy goes away taking your desire with it because grief work is depleting.

At some point after the death of your mate, someone may approach you in a sexual manner. Often, it is someone you know. Usually, it is someone you least expect to approach you in this way. It might be one of your mate's friends, or it might be a person from your circle of couple friends. Understand this is not unusual. It does not have anything to do with a signal from you. If this happens, you may be shocked and begin to question your own actions. Thinking you did or said something to precipitate the advance is most upsetting. It did not occur because you sent a signal welcoming such an advance. Some people erroneously believe sexual contact might be helpful to you. Others simply take advantage of your distraught state. Being aware of the possibility of this occurrence better prepares you to rebuff the advance in a manner that is appropriate.

The sexual blunting suffered after the death of a spouse normally does not last forever, and sexual feelings eventually return as you process the grief. Humans are by nature sexual beings. Your sexuality is an important part of who you are and how you relate to others. This will be discussed more in depth later.

Gender Differences

Research and study of bereavement issues has focused on women more than on men. Carol Staudacher has studied gender differences extensively, and her writings give valuable information on this aspect of the loss of one's mate. She says one reason for the disparity between study of widowed women as opposed to widowed men is of the 13.7 million widowed people in the United States, 11 million of them are female. Statistically, females outlive males.

In studying the effects of grief on both genders, differences are noted. Although there are general gender-specific behaviors, there is indication the modality of grief expression relates to the personality of the individual as well as to gender. In Henderson, Hayslip, and King's study on the relationship between adjustment—and bereavement-related distress, they found some males and females reacted in similar ways depending on their adjustment before the death. Thus, well-adjusted males and females processed grief more successfully than males and females who were not well-adjusted at the time of the death.

Bowlby describes two adjustment modalities: (1) cognitive and (2) affective. Studies show males subscribe more to the cognitive modality because our society expects males to react in a cognitive manner, and males are more cognitive-oriented in expression. Females generally subscribe to the affective modality, which is more feeling-oriented. Societal conditioning strengthens this in females.

This is speaking in general of males and females. Not all fit into these modalities according to gender. There are females who process their grief in the cognitive manner, which is much less emotional. These females follow the cognitive pattern of goal-oriented activity, seeing the challenge in the change and remaining in control. A few males exhibit the affective modality, which is a feeling/emotional approach. Not as many males fit the affective modality as females who fit the cognitive modality. One explanation for this is the conditioning our culture gives males and females. Also, it is important to note adaptive strategies are influenced by temperament. Thus, some females may use the predominately male approach and vice versa.

Most men fit the cognitive modality of experience. They use goal-oriented activities to process their loss. Men, more so than women, shelve feelings in order to fulfill immediate responsibilities. This is not failure to face the feelings. Shelving the feelings puts the emotions on hold for a while until there is a more appropriate time to deal with them. When the mourner feels the time is appropriate, these emotions are released in small amount. This is called dosing the feelings. It allows the mourner to handle issues in small increments to avoid overwhelming the emotions, which interfere with functioning.

Modulation of feelings allows the male to maintain self-control and to feel he has mastery of his thoughts and feelings. These are familiar male behaviors; therefore, he is working within his comfort zone. Modulating feelings and having goal-oriented activities come from rational thinking and behavior. With this approach, it is difficult for the male to share his feelings with others. Because he does not share his feelings easily, other people may think pain is absent.

Predominantly, the male worldview is one of maintaining a sense of control. Changes are seen as challenges rather than threats. With a strong sense of control, the feeling of being able to master crisis is strong. This confidence overrides feelings of helplessness and insecurity. The masculine worldview comes about in part due to the cultural expectations society places on males.

Men are culturally expected to be thinkers rather than feelers. They are to be confident, assertive, courageous, and to remain in control of difficult situations. Goal-oriented and competitive behaviors are the norm. Males are conditioned to bear pain in silence, endure stress quietly, and keep a lid on their emotions. Often, the only expression allowed men is anger. These expectations make success possible, but they make coping with loss difficult.

Putting these expectations on the males of our society causes many problems when they suffer loss. Men are humans. They experience pain. Men often find being raised to be manly when suffering is difficult to do.

The fear of appearing unmanly makes it almost impossible for a man to show his emotions to others or to share his feelings for fear of how he will appear to others.

Grieving men most often express their grief through physical action. They problem-solve and develop an activity to carry out the solution. They are more likely to pursue a legal action following a loss. One example is a father who lost his child on a defective piece of playground equipment. He organized a class action lawsuit against the manufacturer to prevent further defective equipment. Saving other children from future harm gave him purpose and provided an action to relieve his stress.

Another expression of grief by men is solitary activity. In *Men and Grief*, Carol Staudacher cites more men than women visit the gravesite of the deceased alone. The visitation pattern for the men was going alone on regular intervals at a specific time. Men reported this private ritual as being helpful to them. Almost all of them reported talking to their loved one when they visited the grave. They indicated this ritualistic activity gave them an emotional release.

Comedian George Burns visited the grave of his late wife, Gracie, on a regular basis and gave her an update on what was happening in his life. He continued to do this until he became unable to perform this ritual due to his own health problems.

Although males may not show their grief and sometimes seem to take a shorter time to process it, this does not mean their grief is less intense and hurtful. When grief does not show, there are generally five coping styles the males use:

1. Remaining silent
2. Solitary mourning (silent grief)
3. Taking physical or legal action
4. Becoming immersed in activity
5. Exhibiting addictive behavior

Men are hesitant to show emotion because they do not want to be labeled unstable. They go to great lengths to mask fear because showing emotion or fear would be unmanly. Staudacher cites a sensory deprivation experiment in which both male and female subjects were used to illustrate a man's need to keep the lid on.

Each subject was put into a soundproof room, having little or no light and a monotonous background hum or no noise at all. Each subject was monitored while in the room. When the subjects were interviewed afterward, the women were more likely to verbalize their distress than the men. The men persisted in denying they had difficulty coping with the torment of sensory deprivation, even though they were observed during the experiment moaning and writhing.

The men were hesitant to express how tormenting the experiment was to them even when their discomfort was visible. This is a good example of a male's reaction to grief. The pain is there, but they are not likely to admit it verbally to others. They go to great lengths to keep the lid on their emotions when around other people. This is the reason support groups are predominately made up of females. Males do admit being in the company of other men is helpful although they do not specifically talk about the loss when they are with other males. The companionship factor of being with other males helps lessen the emotional pain by diverting the attention from it for a brief period.

The men studied by Staudacher reported the recognition of the enormity of their loss made them see they were never fully aware of the scope and depth of their spouse's roles in their everyday life. They listed four areas of major role loss: domestic partner, sexual partner, companion, and defender.

Losing the domestic partner left many males feeling at sea as to how to run the house on a daily basis. Although this varied according to age and previous division of household chores, the female apparently still does the major part of the household chores, even in the modern lifestyle of men helping with family tasks. Marketing, cooking, laundry, childcare, and keeping the social schedule were mentioned as areas of difficulty for the men. Some domestic chores were common problems for all ages. Younger widowed men usually had the compounded problems of child rearing, children's appointments, homework, and extracurricular school activities to juggle.

Several years ago, my parents lost the wife of their best friend to cancer. A few weeks later, the man returned to the routine of having Saturday morning coffee with my parents. One day, after they drank coffee and talked for a while, the gentleman looked at my mom and said, "Do you know where Sue bought my underwear?" This surprised my mother, but she told him it depended on the brand he wore. He told her the brand and said it was the only one he liked. He said underwear was never a problem when Sue was alive. He just went to his underwear drawer, and there was the clean underwear. When it wore out, there was new underwear in its place. Now he realized he did not have a magic underwear drawer. He understood how much he took for granted the importance of the small act of service she did for him in providing him with clean laundry and new clothes when the old ones became worn. Not only that, she put the clothes in the closet and the underwear in the bureau drawers for him. Mom told him where to buy the underwear, and he left, seeming relieved he had solved one problem.

This was a funny story and certainly does not speak of all men. However, in his generation, men did not worry about household chores. When his wife died, he was definitely missing his domestic partner. His life was in chaos! He learned too late to appreciate all his domestic partner did for him throughout the years of their marriage.

The second role the wife filled was of sexual partner. There is a great deal of comfort and security of a sexual nature in marriage. You know you are loved. Your spouse has seen you at your worst and not run screaming, so you are comfortable with your body and your looks. You have aged together. Both of you have seen your bodies go through the aging process and are comfortable about your body image.

Through the years, you discovered what sexually pleases each other. Knowing each other so well, there was no rejection in being turned down for sex at times. Also, it was not the end of the world if you could not perform. The sexual partnership in marriage is a convenient arrangement. At times, you took it for granted. Now it is gone. You miss the good night kisses. You miss cuddling under the blanket. You miss feeling needed and loved. You miss touching someone and being touched in return. You miss the close emotional bond forged by a satisfying physical relationship.

The third role linked very closely with the sexual partner is the companion role. Knowing you have someone with you, whether you are talking or sitting in companionable silence, is comforting. It is the little acts of companionship you miss the most. Someone bringing the paper to you; someone to share a cup of hot chocolate or coffee; someone to complain to; someone to share your thoughts, hopes, and dreams; and someone to hug when you need a hug are all parts of companionship. Being able to finish each other's sentences, having private jokes, and knowing each other's pet peeves are parts of the companion role. This is sorely missed when the mate dies.

The fourth partner role missed by men is the role of defender. It is comforting to know there is someone who will stand up for you when you need support. It is comforting to know there is someone you can count on when the chips are down. The defender is loyal and takes on anyone who maligns the mate. This is why it is dangerous to get between two married people who are having conflict. They may say terrible things about each other, but you will find yourself in a hot spot if you say something negative about one of them. The defender role is a security blanket for the spouse.

Females miss many of the same things mentioned by the men. The domestic partner role has quite different descriptions from female mourners because the household tasks the men supply usually are in the line of yard work and automobile and house maintenance. Females get help from the males with some childcare and other activities, but the help is usually asked for by the females rather than being voluntary done by the male. Many females indicate the males were receptive to helping but waited for directions from the female as to the type of help wanted.

In adapting to the loss of a mate, women more frequently use the affective modality of adjustment. Women do not feel it hurts their image by expressing their feelings to others. Most women will cry and share private thoughts with other women or counselors easier than their male counterparts. This is because most females are feeling-oriented. Also, it is a feminine custom to share many personal issues with other females. Female friends are accustomed to discussing life, marriage, sex, husbands, children, social life, worries, troubles, and men in general. The comfort of talking about personal issues with others is already established before a loss occurs.

Females usually have support networks with close relationships outside the immediate family. With these groups in place before the loss, females have immediate support networks to access. Females report more emotional distress, suffer more depression and anxiety, and experience more feelings of helplessness than men in the early part of loss. Many women are worriers by nature and become overwhelmed with the uncertainty of the future. Being able to express these emotions to others is helpful for the females.

For most women, there is no stigma attached to counseling, so they are more open to talking about their emotions. Therefore, more women seek professional help and participate in support groups. Hearing how others deal with common problems seems to be helpful to widows. Seeing others are surviving something so terrible is helpful too. It is assuring to know others know some of what you feel and to know survival is possible.

Women eventually get to the point of setting goals and problem solving, but this appears to come later in the process of grieving for females than males. Females start with the messy emotional stuff first. I felt if I could tear at my hair, cry and be a mess for a while, I would then be able to assess the situation and know what I needed to do. Problem solving and goal setting were accomplished later, but decisions I did not have to make immediately were put on hold. It was important for me to deal with the emotional distress first. Being able to express my feelings openly, to cry, and to talk to others about my loss enabled me to effectively take on the responsibilities facing me.

Another important factor for me was the ability to make a living, run the house, take care of our child, and juggle many activities by myself. I think many women are independent people who are also married. Women have so many hats to wear on a daily basis; the loss of a partner does not turn their entire world topsy-turvy. There is no denying a major part of the woman's world has been affected by the loss. But at least, most women have a good handle on daily life skills.

On the other hand, the male may be used to helping here and there with household chores, but few males run the whole show. Most males are adept at making a living, providing protection and maintenance, and assisting their spouses when needed. However, there are still a number of males who cannot independently run the household or take care of job duties and all the other responsibilities of daily family life alone. The life skills needed to accomplish these tasks single-handedly are unfortunately not being taught enough to the males of our society, even in these more enlightened times.

Adjustment Issues

Death of a spouse requires a huge psychological adjustment on the part of the surviving spouse. The quality of the marriage affects the extent of the adjustment necessary to process the loss. Deborah Carr and associates studied 1,532 married individuals ages sixty-five and older. They used a measurement instrument called the Changing Lives of Older Couples (CLOC) to gather baseline data on marital quality and mental health issues of grief, anxiety, and depression collected at six-, eighteen-, and forty-eight-month intervals following spousal loss. Their objective was to determine if psychological adjustment to widowhood is affected by marital quality. The three determiners of marital quality used were warmth, conflict, and instrumental dependence prior to the loss.

The results were hardly surprising. Widowhood was associated with elevated anxiety among those who were highly dependent on their spouses and lower levels of anxiety among those who were not dependent on their spouses. Thus, the males or females who were able to operate independently before the loss were much less anxious after the loss. Those widowed spouses who did not possess the independent life skills before the loss had higher levels of anxiety and a more difficult adjustment.

If the quality of marriage was poor, the levels of yearning were lower at the baseline. This finding is also validated in the material by Staudacher, which discusses the relief felt by the surviving spouse if the relationship was abusive or fraught with conflict.

In Carr's study, the levels of yearning were much higher in widowed people who reported few conflicts and great closeness in the quality of their marriage. The dependence of the surviving spouse on the deceased spouse also caused higher levels of yearning. An interesting additional finding was *women* who relied on their *husbands* for instrumental support had significantly higher levels of yearning than *men* who depended on their *wives*. However, the level of anxiety was higher in those men who were in the dependent role than men who were not dependent.

The loss of a spouse brings many adjustments to daily life. Finances must be assessed. The financial situation of the survivor determines many of the options available to you. Therefore, your financial situation might impact decisions concerning changes in your life.

A second daily life adjustment is the relationship adjustment in your life. There may be changes with in-law relationships. Other changes may be in your own family and extended family. You will also find changes to be made in friendships you and your spouse mutually enjoyed.

A third issue is the adjustment of your sexuality. You lost not only your best friend but also your lover. In the early days of your loss, sexuality is probably the furthest thing from your mind. However, with time, your libido will begin to return and may present issues for you to resolve.

Eventually, the issues of resocialization, dating, and possible remarriage will arise. While these last two may be issues in the far future, it is wise to be aware of these possibilities. Knowledge about these issues helps you make informed decisions.

Finances

Finances impact many decisions you make and the haste with which you make them. Few widowed people are financially independent enough to not have some financial concerns. Varying circumstances of loss affect the extent of the financial concerns.

The age of the deceased is one factor affecting the financial impact. If the spouse was young, and there are young children, there may not be enough financial security for the family following the death. The widowed spouse might have to downsize the home. This could entail moving to another location. Making a move at this time is complicated for the surviving spouse because you are not at your best mentally to be making business decisions. If minor children are involved, it is another disruption in their lives. This creates complications for them, especially if they have to change schools. Support resources from family and friends are greatly needed in this situation.

When minor children are involved, and there are little or no financial resources following the death, help in securing federal or state assistance is needed by the widowed person. Most states have some assistance programs in place for meeting medical needs of the children. In most situations, the children would be eligible for social security benefits, and sometimes the surviving parent is eligible for parent benefits until the children reach sixteen.

If the widowed spouse did not work before the death, work may have to be secured to meet financial needs. This greatly changes an already drastically altered daily routine. Again, securing employment and being able to perform satisfactorily on the job is extremely difficult, so soon after suffering a major loss. If the widowed spouse has been out of the workplace for a while, work skills may be weak or nonexistent.

If the deceased spouse was older and already retired, the surviving spouse may lose part of the retirement income. This must be explored to determine your options. The older widowed person too may have to move due to lower finances and/or being unable to maintain the property. The secondary changes, due to the huge change brought by the loss, add even more to stress and distress.

The bereaved group of widowed people who may suffer the most financially is the middle-aged group. Unless the surviving spouse is already working and has income and benefits, they may be in serious difficulty. Loss of income coupled with loss of insurance and benefits can bring about an immediate financial crisis. There are no social security benefits for anyone under the age of sixty-two unless you are disabled, have a child, or are a minor child. Unless financial security comes from a private source, the middle-aged widowed person can find it rough going financially.

The benefits the surviving spouse is entitled to receive become vitally important to the quality of life from this point forward. Knowing what you have and how to access it is valuable information. Both partners should be aware of the financial status of their life before death comes. Insurance policies, investments, stocks and bonds, and pension plans are tremendous security for the widowed person. Dying young does not give a person the time to accumulate much financially in these areas. Therefore, it is unlikely the young widowed person will have financial security in these forms.

An immediate expense faced by all bereaved families is the funeral expense. This can easily run into thousands of dollars, even for a very simple funeral. Generally, cremation is less costly but is often not a preference for the family. Most funeral homes require payment in full at the time of service. Not all funeral homes will take insurance policies, so this is a financial issue you have to resolve in the earliest part of your grief.

Additional expenses may come if your spouse was ill for an extended period of time or if hospitalization was required before the death. Medical bills can become huge in a very short period of time. Depending on whether or not you have medical insurance, and the type of coverage you have, you may be facing extra costs accumulated before the loved one passed away. This can be a crippling financial drain on the widowed survivor.

Unfortunately, for many mourners, their financial condition determines the pace of their adjustments. If you are forced to move quickly, you have little time to sort memories or belongings. If you must return to work immediately, you are in an emotional bind. You are expected to perform well when you cannot think straight. If you have children, the additional weight of their care and well-being rests heavily on your shoulders, thus, decreasing the attention you are able to give to your own grief.

While finances have to be considered, remember to focus your energy on the important things in life. You have faced death. Hopefully, you learned what to value. There is a way to resolve the finances. Love the children, love your friends, honor your spouse, help others, turn to your faith. Your character is being built by the way you live your life. If death teaches nothing else, it teaches us the truly important things in life.

Relationship Adjustments

After being widowed, you will find some of your relationships no longer fit into your new life. This may not be obvious at first, but as you emerge from the early fog of grief, you begin to notice subtle changes. Often, you may feel a need to make the changes in relationships because they no longer work for you.

One relationship, which may require adjustment, is the in-law relationship. This relationship can be one of your biggest supports, or it can be one of your biggest problems. If your in-law relationship was close, respectful, and healthy before the death, there is a good chance it will remain very beneficial to you. If the relationship was conflicted before the death, it may become even more conflicted after the death.

Your in-law family is your adopted family. When you wed your spouse, a large group of people came with that contract. Hopefully, it was a group of people you grew to love and respect. After death, they can be a source of support and strength in your journey of grief.

I was blessed with this kind of in-law relationship. My husband's parents, siblings, as well as their spouses gave a huge amount of love, care, and concern to us before my husband's death. This did not end with his death.

Being a young widow with a child, the assistance they gave me was invaluable. They helped with childcare, household maintenance problems, and many other crises, which followed my husband's death. They continued to maintain the close family relationship in all ways just as before the death. They continued to love me even though their son/brother was gone. They let me know I was still a daughter/sister to them, and they loved me for me, not just because of the marriage relationship.

Even after my remarriage several years later, they continued to include my new husband and me in all family celebrations. They attended our wedding, and we continued to celebrate holidays and family milestones together. My second husband and I were at the bedsides of both my mother-in-law and father-in-law when they died. To this day, we continue to be an active part of that loving family.

The benefits of a loving in-law relationship are tremendous. My son was reared with boundless love from all sides of the family, and our lives are enriched today because of the continued bond. He remains close to his aunts, uncles, and cousins on his father's side of the family; and now his children are added to the circle. Knowing your heritage and staying close to your roots are gifts to be treasured. When your partner dies, and there are children, it is important to give your children that gift. I was fortunate to have the opportunity to maintain the in-law relationship. My son is fortunate to remain connected to a vital part of his heritage.

When in-law relationships are not helpful, problems arise for the widowed person. One of the problems is difference of opinion on child rearing. If there are young children, the widowed person may desperately need help with childcare, but the in-laws may differ on parenting techniques. Sometimes the in-laws may be critical of how the widowed parent is parenting. If the relationship is good enough to allow discussion, this is the time to face the difference head-on and discuss why certain rules must be followed when the children are with the in-laws. If the topic cannot be discussed, then other arrangements must be made for the children's care.

If the widowed parent is being criticized, the ability to turn a deaf ear is invaluable. Depending on the type of criticism and validity of the complaint, the widow must decide the best actions to take to alleviate the problem without adding stress on the children. Of course, if no resolution can be found, it is natural for visitation to decrease, straining the relationship even more. Everyone loses in this type of situation, especially the children.

A word of caution must be made on the topic of taking care of the children. If the surviving parent appears to be in a poor mental state, and the children are being neglected whether it is the in-law family or the parent family, intervention must be made for the good of the children. Hopefully, both families can discuss this type of situation together and jointly seek a solution for the good of the widowed person and the children.

Another problem occasionally stemming from the in-law relationship is encouraging the widowed person to remain in the past. The in-laws may try so hard to keep their child's memory alive they refuse to accept any changes in the widow's life. They feel "staying faithful to the memory" validates how much their child was loved. The widow is encouraged to become a social recluse. Another benefit for the in-law family who encourages this behavior is keeping their grandchildren from having new adult relationships in their lives. It prevents a stepparent from entering the family circle, which the in-laws may see as taking the place of their child.

If this happens, the widow must recognize this behavior and refuse to play along with these tactics. Some of these behaviors are brought on by insecurity on the part of the in-laws. If they see you plan to keep them as part of your children's lives and your life, some of this type of pressure may cease.

Your in-laws may become less important in your life as you handle the many adjustments in your new life. This is especially true if they live far away from you. However, it is good for the sake of the children to keep them in touch as much as possible. It is important for children to be an important part of the families of both parents. Children can never have too many people to love and care about them.

Just as there are changes in the in-law family, there may be changes in your own family relationships. You may depend on your family more heavily for a while. However, it is important for you to develop independence as soon as you feel able to be on your own. It is easy to use others as a crutch during this difficult time. Some families take advantage of this as a time to control your life and keep you as the child. If you allow this to continue, you lose your independence; and if there are children, you abdicate your authority over them.

Staying dependent on your own family for a long period of time is not good for the other family relationships. If there are siblings, they may be resentful of the time and energy taken in resolving your problems. They may feel slighted due to the time and attention devoted to you. An overly dependent person in the family eventually wears others out with the pressure to sustain you. You do not want this to happen to your family relationship.

Healthy in-law and family relationships before the death are more likely to remain healthy afterward. Conflict in these two primary relationships before the death will probably give rise to more problems during the stressful time following the death. It is important for the widow to be clear to everyone about what is helpful and what is not helpful. Graciously turn down suggestions you do not want to do or are not ready to do. Be fair and firm. Realize everyone is hurting, and emotions are highly charged. Refrain from conflict as much as possible because additional stress is the last thing you need in your life. Having the backbone to say yes to what you want and no to what you do not want helps tremendously. Keep in mind this is a complete sentence. "No."

Relationships with married friends are other relationships that become less intimate. There are some couples you may be able to keep as friends and others you will not keep. Some couples will change their life patterns with you, but this is the exception rather than the rule. You present them with a challenge. They no longer know what to do with you. You remind them of the painful fact that death comes to all, and what happened to you could happen to them. Widowed men are included in social outings more often than widowed women. Many women do not want an extra female around when their mate is present.

Sometimes the problem does not lie entirely with your couple friends but with you. You may develop the fifth wheel syndrome. This is when you feel uncomfortable in the company of couples because it points out your single state. When others are in pairs, being the odd person is an uncomfortable position. As you feel more uncomfortable, you begin to stop accepting invitations to couple events.

Eventually, you will find you have more fun when you do things not involving couples. Fear of rejection is strong when you find yourself single again, so group activities are usually more comfortable for the widowed person. Pursuing new interests and hobbies is a big help when going through the changes in your social relationships. Finding new ways to express yourself by doing new projects can rejuvenate your spirit. There are many things you may have passed up because your mate did not enjoy those activities. Now is a time to try those things and add new friends to your changing life circle.

Sexuality

Sexual feelings and the desire for intimacy do not die with your partner's death although they are temporarily frozen. If an active and satisfying sex life was an important part of your life with your partner, it will continue to be a priority for you regardless of age. As time passes, sexual feelings begin to emerge. For the widowed person, this can be an upsetting, frustrating experience. The resurfacing of these feelings is something you may not know how to handle. You may have sexual dreams during this time. Not only do you feel frustration, you may feel guilty for thinking such thoughts when you are grieving a tragic loss.

"What is wrong with me?" you might ask. The answer is nothing is wrong with you. You are a human being, and human sexuality is a major component of who and what you are. You had a satisfying, intimate relationship. You lost your partner but not your need for intimacy.

Literature on bereavement often fails to deal with the delicate and personal problem of intimacy for the widowed. Survivors are left with many questions, but these questions go unanswered because people hesitate to talk about it. Widowed people are reluctant to bring up the subject because they mistakenly think they are the only one with the problem. Our society focuses on life and youth; so many other issues of loss, growth, and intimacy get swept under the rug.

In the United States, sex sells everything from toothpaste to cars, yet we are very puritanical in discussing sexual intimacy. As you grow older, it seems the expectation is neither do you have sex nor do you think about it. After your twenties, sex is a dead issue. Most adults think their parents only had sex to conceive them. The parents had sex more than once, if there are brothers and sisters, but the adult children do not recognize sexual intimacy as a life force across the life span. With this attitude, is it any wonder widowed people of all ages hesitate to ask about issues of a sexual nature after their loss?

What about sex after the death of your spouse? As was stated earlier, in the beginning of your bereavement, sex is the last thing on your mind. As Meyer says in his book *Surviving Death*, the "marriage bed is as empty as the rest of your life without the one you loved." Because you enjoyed intimacy with your loved one, an important need was met for you. We have a need to love and be loved. That need does not die with the death of your spouse. If you are healthy and physically able to have a sexual relationship, you may eventually seek one. This, like your grief, is a very personal journey. Only you can determine if and when you want to have an intimate relationship again.

There is a great deal of important information the widowed person should have pertaining to sexuality and loss. It behooves you to look at some initial reactions to the loss of a partner as it pertains to sexuality.

The first reaction is a loss of libido. Interest in sex is zero. Grief is so physically and mentally draining most people barely have the energy to get up each day, much less sustain a satisfying sex life. Intimacy appears to be a thing of the past to the newly bereaved. In the beginning, the widowed person does not think about it or care.

The numbness, which comes in the early phases of grief, drains your sensitivity and desire. It replaces those feelings with disinterest. You operate at this time as though your spouse is still around, so it would produce guilt for even thinking about sexual intimacy. The feeling of powerlessness leads to insecurity and more depressed mood. With so many tasks to attend to, the feeling of inadequacy for the task, and the numbing of your feelings, sexual desire disappears.

A different initial sexual reaction after a loss is sex as a form of searching. In searching, the widowed person seeks an intimate relationship like the previous one. However, the widow runs into several problems with searching sex. The loss of the partner can regress the widowed person to the time before sex began with the partner. All your sexual maturity is wiped away, and you feel uncertain. Some have said it is as though they are back to square one. Not being sure of your sexual knowledge and experience creates more insecurity problems.

Several things can happen during searching sex that derail the satisfaction of the sexual experience for the widow. One, there may be flashbacks of earlier times with the deceased mate. Needless to say, this ruins the attempt to be sexually active again and brings more despair. Second, mechanical difficulties may occur in this phase such as impotence, lack of lubrication, vaginismus, and premature or no ejaculation. These difficulties remind the widowed person even more of what was lost with the partner's death.

Some mourners dealing with the return of their interest in sex use sex as a distraction. Some widowed people indicate sexual activity helps assuage the intense time-consuming grieving process. Grief work is exhausting to the survivor. Some say the sexual activity provides a release, even if they were only going through the motions with a new partner. Obviously, this type of sexual encounter does not really meet the needs of the widowed person; but for some, it is a temporary release.

Occasionally, a widowed person will use sex as a means of expressing great anger. Indiscriminate sex with multiple partners may be a way of striking back for the loss. It is an attempt to prove you are really okay. It is a denial of your suffering. Some people reported it as a way to punish the deceased partner for leaving them. Some indicated it as a way of punishing themselves by having unenjoyable sex. Anger over the unfairness of the whole situation is another reason cited by people who participated in this type of sexual experience. This does not sound rational, but remember, grieving people often do irrational things.

A fifth initial reaction seen in some sexual encounters after loss is to use sex as a substitute for closeness. The widowed person really wants warmth, sharing, and closeness but sees sex as the only way to get these needs met. Sex is sometimes endured in order to get the closeness of sleeping in someone's arms.

The sixth type of sexual reaction seen after the loss of a spouse is sex as an expression of fear. People fear the present, the future, commitment, rejection, and being hurt again. When sex is based on fear, the person is likely to fear losing another partner and being hurt again. So he refuses to commit and strives to keep the sexual relationship superficial. Fear keeps him from bonding with any of his partners and eliminates the possibility of true intimacy.

The last sexual reaction to be discussed is sex as nurturing. This relates to the sex for closeness but is a much healthier approach to the intimate relationship. The desire to nurture and to be nurtured is so strong the widowed person may turn to a sexual experience to obtain the nurturing feeling. This is a give-and-take relationship. It involves caring for another person. Widowed people using sex for nurturing often speak of making love.

Of all the initial reactions, the reaction of sex as nurturing is the healthiest. It indicates the survivor may be ready for a long-term relationship. The giving and receiving in this kind of sexual experience indicates the mourner has made great strides toward building a new relationship. It signifies the mourner is ready to commit to an intimate relationship. It indicates less fear of being hurt again.

A word of warning is necessary to all widowed people who feel ready to have a sexual relationship. Keep in mind the necessity of safe sex. If it has been many years since you were single, the dating scene has probably changed quite a bit. If you were in a monogamous relationship, you did not have to worry about sexually transmitted diseases. However, finding a new partner means you are in new territory. If you do not know how to handle precautions, talk to your physician or a therapist before you begin a physical relationship to learn how to stay healthy. The sharp increase in sexually transmitted diseases in the older population indicates there is a lack of knowledge about the need for practicing safe sex.

Dating

There are some cautions in regard to the pursuit of a relationship after the death of a spouse. You are at a vulnerable time in your life and must be aware there are some unscrupulous people who will try to take advantage of you. Your sense of judgment may be affected by your emotional turmoil. Your need for love, care, and concern can lead you to make some poor choices. It is important to consider many things before you reenter society. What are these considerations?

Never date for the wrong reasons.

Suddenly, being cast into the world alone is a frightening feeling. These are the wrong reasons to date or to enter a relationship:

1. To increase your bank account

This is risky from the start. Hopefully, you learned from the death experience money is not the most important thing in the world. Good relationships do not have a price tag on them. Dating for this reason will fail to bring happiness to your life, if it is the only yardstick by which you measure the worth of a person.

2. Desperation

There is no reason to be desperate. Desperation is obvious to other people and usually attracts people who will take advantage of you. When you become secure in your own person and have confidence in yourself, you will develop healthier relationships. You are worthwhile and worthy of the right kind of relationship.

3. Finding a father/mother for the children

If you are widowed with children, you certainly want someone who will be loving and good to the children. However, you must find the person who is right for you first; then see if it is a good fit for the children. Having children may rule out many relationships, but it will not rule out the right relationship.

4. Maintenance

One of the things you miss about your spouse is the amount of maintenance he did for you in daily life. If this is the only reason for dating someone, you would be wiser to hire someone from an employment agency. It is much easier to fire someone than to divorce him. Doing acts of service is a gift from one spouse to another, but it comes because of love and commitment. Looking for someone to date because he can maintain you is certainly a poor reason for dating.

5. Fear of being alone

Earlier, the difference between being alone and being lonely was discussed. If you fear being alone, get a dog. It will be a lot less trouble than getting involved with someone you do not love. There are many positive actions you can take to stave off loneliness. Learning to like yourself and to enjoy your own company is an important step for someone who fears being alone.

6. Looking for the fairy tale fantasy

When our life is in the pits, we often daydream of happily ever after. If a widowed person's reason for dating is looking for Mr. or Ms. Perfect, it is indeed a poor reason. Hoping this enchanting person will come along and sweep you off your feet, bringing happiness and a wonderful lifestyle back into your life, is a pipe dream. It can only end in disaster because it is not realistic. No one can assure you of a problem-free life. You must get your own house in order and your life back on track. When you are healthy emotionally, you are more likely to find the right relationship. You may find a wonderful person out there somewhere, but he will not be perfect. The search for the fairy tale ideal keeps you from finding a real person.

Self-care

Self-care was discussed previously, but it cannot be stressed enough. Before considering reentering society by social gatherings or dating, it is important to take care of yourself. Eating right, exercising, taking care of your grooming, and getting enough rest are important in creating a better feeling about oneself. Good self-care improves your life view and strengthens your ability to make long-range decisions. When you take care of yourself and begin to feel better, your libido will return, and you will be ready for an intimate relationship again.

Take your time.

Take your time before reentering society. There is no rush and no reason to panic about how long you should take before becoming social again. It is up to you, and you will decide to become more social when you feel ready. You suffered a grievous wound and need time to heal. If you broke your leg, you would need time to heal before you could walk again. Grief is convalescence. It is not to be hurried. You do not need to rush to recapture a lifestyle. Do not give in to pressure from well-meaning people urging you to recouple before you are ready.

Go out with friends first.

It helps to overcome the fear of reentering society if you have friends to help you break the ice. Either going out with a group or dating a friend is a more comfortable way to socialize. Friends will be able to nurture you as you make this step forward and ease the path for you. If you date someone who is a friend, you can experience companionship without sexual pressure. This will help you to build your confidence in being able to socialize without your life partner.

Be honest.

From the beginning of a dating relationship, set boundaries and expectations with the new partner. Your goal is to make social contact again. If you want companionship without the pressure of sex, make this clear from the beginning. Do not feel embarrassed to clarify this point. If you want nurturing with some physical contact, you can indicate it to your partner. Always be willing to talk. It is much better to talk about things than to assume. Assuming leads to misunderstanding and embarrassing situations.

Most importantly, keep your sense of humor. Christian writer Barbara Johnson says a sense of humor can help you through many of life's toughest times. She describes a sense of humor this way:

> A sense of humor, involves more than just telling jokes. As
> sense of humor is connected to the way you look at life, the

way you can chuckle over what is absurd and ridiculous, the way you put your problems in perspective and the way you can feel joy because you know that: ANY DAY ABOVE GROUND IS A GOOD ONE!

If it has been a long time since you dated, there can be some pretty humorous things about going out again at fifty, sixty, seventy, or eighty! Keep your sense of humor, have a good laugh, and enjoy life.

Leave the past in the past.

Your partner left this life. You are still here. What you did when he was alive is one thing. What you choose to do today is quite another. When you are married to one person for a long time, you develop routines and habits you both follow. It takes time after he is gone to change your habits. Keep in mind you do not have to do everything just as he wanted. Being dead does not make him right. If it is time to change, change.

Dating is a change you are making without your spouse. If and when you have a new sexual relationship, do not feel guilty about it. Your obligation to your spouse ended with death. I will respect and remember my husband the rest of my life, but I do not have to deny myself happiness because he was once my life partner. When he lived, I was the best wife I could possibly be to him. I loved him deeply and missed him more than words could express. In my heart, I know he is living a new life and enjoying it thoroughly. I am doing the same. Leaving the past in the past is a must if you want to go forward.

Remarriage

After dating for a while, some widowed people find new relationships and decide to remarry. Studies show men remarry faster than women. Widows who remarry do so in a little over four years after the partner's death, but men who remarry do so within two years.

There are several reasons for this, and none of them has anything to do with the depth of the love for the deceased. The availability of more women for men is one factor. The other is the indication from women of being satisfied with their new life and their reluctance to give up the independence widowhood brings. The other social outlets mentioned earlier, which women have before the loss, provide social activity for widowed females. Independence of more women and financial security allow more women the option of remaining single.

Statistics show women outlive men by several years. Therefore, as the population ages, there are more women without partners than men. This is another factor impacting the possibility of remarriage for women. The older the woman is when she is widowed, the less chance she has to remarry. Under the age of twenty-four, most women remarry within one year. Under the age of thirty, widowed women have the best opportunity to remarry. In the thirty-five to fifty-four age bracket, the majority of widowed women remarry, but the numbers drop considerably. Over the age of fifty-five, there is a major drop in the remarriage of women. The availability of males in this age bracket is one factor. Another factor is single men in this age bracket often marry younger women. While women in our society do marry younger men, this is the exception rather than the norm.

The decision to remarry or not presents a plethora of issues to consider. Most importantly, it must be for the right reason. That reason being you found someone with whom you want to spend your life—to plan, hope, and dream together. You found someone who will be the companion you sorely need. This person is a good fit for your family, and you are with theirs.

If this is the right person, you can work out all the technical details of wills, marriage prenuptials, property, living arrangements, the children (minor or grown), and finances. All these things should be discussed and decisions made before the marriage.

You loved once and lost that person to death. You are daring to love again and risk great sorrow, but it is definitely worth the risk. People ask me, since I remarried, if I had a conflict with my feelings for my first husband and my feelings for my second husband. My answer is this is a comparison of apples to oranges. The two relationships have nothing to do with each other. Each man's personality is unique, and each one possessed qualities I admire in a mate. I have enough love in my heart for both. My first husband is no longer of this world. I am still here. I know he would want me to be happy. I never abandoned him during the hard times or let him down during our life together. We were a partnership—a true team. I gave him my complete love and devotion. I can no longer do anything for him in this life, except keep his memory in my heart. I met someone who means the world to me, and I am happy with him. My heart is big enough to hold all that love.

Parent Loss

> You never really feel alone in the world until you stand on your parents' graves.
>
> —Gary Small
> Center on Aging

Losing a parent is one of the greatest sorrows, which can befall a person. As Mr. Small stated, one of the loneliest feelings in your life is when your parents die. Barbara Bartocci, author of *Nobody's Child Anymore*, said,

> Losing a parent is a profound loss. No matter the age, circumstances of your rearing, how loving or lethal the relationship, it is such a primal connection it is impossible to ignore. The ultimate tie-genetic inheritance—entwines us no matter how hard we try to disconnect.

As parents age and their health becomes more fragile, you expect death. If your parents are healthy, you logically expect they will die before you do. However, when death comes, your knowledge of these rational things does not matter. Even if they were ill and suffering, you find you are not truly prepared for the hole their loss creates in your life.

My dad died of pancreatic cancer after only a brief illness. Until the time of diagnosis, he was an active, vital person, busy working and making future plans. As my family reeled from his loss and tried to restructure our lives without him, my indomitable mother became suddenly ill. She died following surgery three months after the first year anniversary of my dad's death. Suddenly, I felt alone in the world without the two people who knew me the longest and the best.

Since both of them were active until the last two months of their lives, it was very difficult to see them quickly become frail and helpless. James Atlas, writer for the *New Yorker*, said in one of his articles:

> To see your parents so vulnerable is hard. At the same time, you feel sorry for yourself. It's like having two sets of children instead of one.

Although my sister and I did not have a lengthy time of caregiving with my parents, it was emotionally painful to experience the changing of the roles from the adult interactions we were used to having with them. Suddenly, we became the "parents," and they became the "children." They abdicated decision making to us and told us they knew we would do what was best for them. This is a momentous time in your life when you are no longer the child.

It is sad to be an orphan. Your age does not matter. It is impossible to prepare yourself for the solitary feeling. If your parents lived a long full life, the deaths may be justified with statements such as, "They had a good life." "They were ready to go on." "They were in pain, and now they are at rest." While good intentioned, justifications are irrelevant. You do not care about all the reasoning and logic in the world. You miss them. Becoming an orphan is a lonely, painful experience.

The Meaning of the Loss

One reason losing the parental relationship hurts so intensely is because there is no other relationship longer lasting than parent-and-child. None is so special. Parents figure daily in your life whether you live close to them or not. Even if you cannot see them every day, you carry them with you. You were formed in your mother's womb by your parents' love for each other. When you were born, your parents began building your foundation. That foundation determined much of who you are today. Because they knew you so long, losing them is losing part of your history. Parents provide a connection to your past. Your parents formed your image of yourself. Losing a parent is losing a part of you.

Secondly, the loss of your parents is the loss of the most influential and powerful figures in your life. Parents serve as your earliest role models. Your parents gave you not only roots, but they gave you wings to go into the world and live on your own. They taught you how to *be*. This is especially true of the mother.

Generally, the mother spends so much time with the child her teachings lay the groundwork for how to be human in the world. The father role is important too, but there is a bond between mother and child, which is quite different than the one between father and child.

A mother often serves as guide, critic, and refuge for the child. One of her major roles is as the communicator, translator, or confidant. Death of the mother takes away the family buffer. If the father survives, children sometimes find it difficult to communicate with him because mothers usually do most of the family communicating.

An example is seen in the interaction, which takes place when a child calls home and the father answers the phone. He may say a few words, but invariably, he will say, "Here's your mother." This does not mean fathers have little interest in the child. He sees his role as different from hers. The role of gathering and dispensing the information and communication falls to the mother.

I loved both my parents dearly, and we were a close family. However, I was more comfortable talking to my mother about problems than I was with my father. I knew, as close as they were, she would relay information to him, and he would give input on the situation; but I did not often go directly to him.

Each parent's influence on the child is different. The bond with your father and mother is different. Your mother carried you in her body. It was she who first counted your fingers and toes, kissed the fluff on the top of your head, and snuggled you to her breast in a loving embrace. You came from her. Although the umbilical cord was cut, there is an emotional cord, which is always there. You are bound by mother love.

Fathers contribute greatly to who we are too. Some fathers are not as emotional nor do they show love in open ways as mothers often do, but this does not mean the father does not love deeply. Fathers teach about respect, honor, duty, the importance of your word, and how to be a responsible person. Fathers are often problem-solvers, fixers, and a source of all types of know-how. Fathers provide a sense of safety to the child.

Many of the differences in the way a mother relates to a child and the way a father relates has to do it with the differences in the way males and females think, act, and react in general. In discussing gender differences in grief patterns between men and women on previous pages, it was mentioned the feminine modality was affective (emotional), and the male modality was cognitive (thinking, problem solving).

An interesting example of this is looking at the things males and females select to keep as mementos of their parents. Staudacher, in her writings, noted men most often selected mementos from their fathers, which were work-related. For example, articles such as tools, toolboxes, or objects made by their fathers were important. Males are more apt to select furniture or some useful object. Females, as a rule, select items of more emotional or sentimental value to keep. Usually the females select personal items such as articles of clothing or pieces of jewelry.

The third reason the loss of your parents is so difficult is mothers and fathers are the first authority figures in your life. They were important in shaping your reactions to authority as you moved into society. Knowing how to use your authority and how to function under the authority of others is an important life skill. It begins with the parental role of authority and, to a great extent, determines the success the child experiences in life. To lose the authority figure, which had such an impact on your life, is indeed a profound loss.

Understanding the impact of parental authority requires you to consider the roles filled by the parents. The family roles filled by the father frequently take his physical presence away from the children. In most families, even if the mother works outside the home, she spends more time one-on-one with the children. The larger amount of daily time together contributes to the closer bond for mothers. She becomes the first line authority figure influencing the child's life. This constant daily interaction makes the mother role very influential. It also often designates the father's authority to a level one step away from the daily fray of activity. Therefore, sometimes the father appears to be more influential when he steps in to situations of discipline.

In my family, my mother did most of the disciplining of my sister and me. Our father was a farmer and worked long hours away from the house. By the time he came home, most issues were resolved. However, when he spoke, we, the children, were much more attentive than we were to our mother. We obeyed our mother, but our father's words seemed to carry a great deal of weight because he rarely had to correct us. Not all families follow these lines of authority, but whatever the pattern of authority established in the family for the children has a lasting impact on the life of the child.

Another significant loss with the death of your parents is the loss of the people who nurtured and comforted you the most. Not only in your childhood and formative years but, as you took your place in the world, home was always a place you knew as a sanctuary. Throughout your life, your parents provided guidance, acceptance, opinions (when you asked for them), and unwavering support. Even when the roles are reversed, and you become the nurturer and comforter for frail elderly parents, the memory of their nurturing role sustains you.

When you lose your parents, another secondary loss is the loss of the people you most want to impress. Parents provide a type of love like no other in your life. Parents are your cheerleaders. They validate your accomplishments. They are someone to whom you can prove yourself. They are someone to give you praise and recognition. They are proud of you and brag on you. To them, you are the best. If you cannot be a star anywhere else in the world, you can be a star in your parents' minds and hearts.

Notice the number of famous people who will, when receiving an award, attribute their success to their parents. Even if the parents are deceased, recipients will acknowledge their parents' part in their success and regret the parents not knowing about it.

Another secondary loss from the death of parents is the loss of the primary source of unconditional love in your life. From the earliest of days, unconditional parental love has been one of the most treasured gifts from parent to child. In the Bible, the story of the prodigal son who failed at all he tried exemplifies the depth of unconditional parental love. When the son returned home, totally defeated in life, his father welcomed him with open arms. The father did not approve of the things the son did, but his love for the son was unwavering.

No matter your failings, parents love you. They may criticize you or chastise you, but they still love you. You know you can always go home, if not physically, at least emotionally. Home becomes synonymous with your parents. Home is a place where you are loved.

There are many secondary losses brought about by the loss of your parents. These are a few of the most obvious ones. Each mourner may add to the list due to the very personal relationship of parent to child. Just as there are many losses to grieve because of the death, there are many factors that affect the child's grief.

Factors Affecting Grief:

1. The Quality of the Relationship

If you were close to your parents, saw them often, and participated in many activities together, naturally, the grief will be more intense. Children who do not live close enough to the parents to visit daily may stay in close contact by phone, e-mail, and frequent visits. A deep emotional attachment makes the loss more difficult.

Unfortunately, not all parent-child relationships are good. If the relationship is not a positive one, the child may not feel the secondary losses described in the previous section. If parent-child relationship is strained, it can be fraught with misunderstanding and resentment. When the relationship is strained, there is always a possibility of relating at some future point, as long as the parent is alive. When the parent dies, this opportunity is lost forever. So even strained relationships carry a load of pain when the parents die. This shocks survivors when it happens. If the relationship was estranged or strained, the child often thinks the death will not be difficult to handle. Surprisingly, it can be more difficult because of the regrets and self-recriminations.

Another reaction to parent loss children may experience when the relationship is poor is relief. A conflicted relationship can be a constant source of pain for the child. Death brings relief from the stress and turmoil. If relief is the emotion you feel, do not feel guilty about it. Sometimes parents have their own serious problems. Therefore, they may not be capable of being good parents. If a parent is neglectful, abusive, suffers drug or alcohol addiction, or has serious mental health issues, the child may have so many unpleasant memories that it is not possible to feel sadness over the parent's death.

2. The Parent Role

The more roles a parent plays in the life of a child, the more the loss hurts. The literature in the previous section discussed the many secondary losses suffered in parent loss. The younger the child, the more important those roles are to the development of the child. Thus, losing a parent at an early age can have a huge impact on the child's life, depending on the circumstances. The older child, who is living on his own and not as dependent on the parent, will perhaps suffer fewer traumas from the death.

If the parent was a confidant and friend as well as a parent, the loss will be compounded. Parents who filled the roles of organizing the family activities, rituals, holidays, and planning the reunions leave many roles to fill. The roles of chief cook, social planner, and family CEO left unfilled by the death leaves the family in chaos until these roles can be reassigned.

Again, it is easy to see the strong effect the loss of these roles have on younger children. Adult children struggle in realignment of the roles, but it is overwhelming for the young because they have to wait for an adult to assume those roles.

3. The Personality of the Parent

The personality of the parent is another factor impacting the child's grief. If the parent was generally a pleasant person, being around the parent was enjoyable. It is only natural to enjoy pleasant people. A difficult personality presents a constant barrage of negative interactions. Depression, extreme anxiety, a pessimistic attitude, a critical personality, controlling behaviors, and the tendency to be overbearing are some negative personalities, which make it difficult to be with people. When your parents have these personalities, you may experience relief to be away from them since their company was burdensome for you.

Parents who regularly interfere with the child's life become tiresome. This type of parent personality usually is accompanied by intense critical scrutiny of everything the child does, thus, putting a wedge in the parent-child relationship. Personality has a great deal to do with the grieving process—both the child personality and the parent personality.

4. Unfinished Business

Some bereaved children feel there is unfinished business with the parent. This is most often seen when the relationship was estranged or conflicted. However, it can also happen in very good relationships. Perhaps, the unfinished business is sins of omission. This means the child worries about things he did not do for the parent. It could be worrying you did not say I love you. An often-mentioned item of unfinished business is not getting to say good-bye to the parent. If unfinished business keeps you from processing your grief, a professional can help you resolve these issues.

5. Your Perception of Your Parent's Fulfillment in Life

If your parent lived to old age, this usually is not a factor in your grief. Knowing your parents did the things they wanted to do, accomplished what they wanted to accomplish, and enjoyed life is comforting after death.

When a parent dies young, perhaps, this comfort is not there. The death of a parent at a young age means a lot of hopes and dreams went unfulfilled. One important unfulfilled goal is living to see the child reach adulthood. However, young children suffering the loss of a parent may not have the maturity to understand the impact of this factor.

6. Age and Specific Circumstances of the Death

The circumstances of the death and the age of the parent and child have a major impact on the intensity of your grief. The location of the death, type of death, reason for the death, and your preparation for it all determine how you process the loss.

The timeliness of the death deals with your perception of how acceptable the death was for this person at this specific time. It is one thing to lose a seventy-five-year-old parent due to cancer. It is quite another to lose a thirty-nine-year-old father due to cancer. If the parent lives a long, fulfilling life, you may not necessarily want to let him go, but it is easier to deal with than losing your parent when you are fifteen and the parent is forty-five.

Research by Thompson and associates into loss of a parent by natural causes versus loss of a parent due to violent causes studied the impact of such losses on children ages nine through seventeen. The research found the death of a parent during childhood was related to a higher occurrence of secondary stressors. For young children, it was found the death is not an isolated event but a series of events. These secondary stressors were family disruption, change in economic status, a decrease in positive family events, and daily life changes.

Caretakers of the children in this study also reported more internalizing behavior problems in the child. These internalizing behavior problems consisted of poorer academic performance, more health problems, lower self-esteem, and more psychological adversities.

The research also showed the children who lost a parent to a violent death more often manifested externalizing behavior problems than the children who experienced the natural death of a parent. The externalizing behavior problems consisted of peer difficulties, difficulties with authority figures, disruptive behaviors at school, and some criminal behaviors.

The results of this study strongly suggest the method of death of the parent strongly influences the child's response to the death. The children whose parent died of natural causes processed the death better than those whose parent died by violent means. The act of violence, which took the parent, challenges the youth's trust in the benevolence of the world in general. It also challenges the adults' capabilities of restraint, specifically.

While the children whose parent died of natural causes experience difficult adjustment too, if adequate family resources are in place, these youth adjust better. Adequate resources include competent substitute care and emotional support. When resources are in place, the youth is better able to return to the previous levels of functioning before death of the parent.

Losing parents when you are in transitional stages of your life, such as the twenties and thirties, presents additional issues particular to this developmental stage of life. As you are becoming independent from your parents—building your own identity, career, and family—you may still be relying on parents for advice and guidance. Losing a parent at this vital time presents a complicating factor to your grief.

6.   The Preventability of the Death

The preventability of the death is another factor affecting your grief. Knowing everything was done, which could be done, is easier to handle than thinking there was something left undone. This is one reason accidental and/or violent deaths are extremely difficult for the mourner. In these types of deaths, you can think of many things you believe would prevent the death. It is important to note the determination of preventability can be unreasonable as well as reasonable. The perception of preventability lies in the thinking of the survivor.

7.   Health of the Parent

Any child, who must see a parent slowly deteriorate physically or mentally, knows death is sometimes a blessed release for the parent and the child. If the quality of the parent's life is no longer good, it is easier to let him go. If the parent is suffering great pain with no hope for recovery, death is merciful.

On the other hand, a parent who dies suddenly, with few or no previous health problems, creates difficult loss adjustments. One client, in expressing her feelings over losing her father suddenly to a heart attack at fifty, explained she wasn't finished with him yet. Her sense of frustration stemming from his death was the death coming before she was prepared to do without him.

Realizations

The death of a parent brings adult children face-to-face with some sobering realizations. This type of loss makes you more aware of where you came from and where you are. These realizations open your eyes to some truths you may never have considered.

First, you just experienced a tremendous role shift if your last parent died. You are now the older generation. I never thought about the position of the older generation much until both parents died. I remember the great-aunts and great-uncles, the great-grandmothers and the great-grandfathers. Now, as the comic strip character Pogo said, "We have met the enemy and he are us!" After the death of my parents, it suddenly struck me: I am the top of the living family tree!

That is an awesome and sobering thought. I never felt old, and still do not, but the fact is I have moved into my parents' place. There is no generation above me to depend on as I depended on my parents. Becoming the elder in the family is a gigantic step. As the younger adults in the family begin to look to my sister and me for guidance and advice, we can see the shift is taking place. Life is moving forward.

Another realization is the awareness with the death of your parents, your home is gone. Your parents may have long ago moved from the house you lived in, but as long as they were alive, the sense of home existed in your mind. Parents are home. They are the hub around which the family gathers, communicates, and socializes.

My father came from a family of seven. As long as his parents were alive, we all knew what went on with the many different families. There was a great familiarity about the daily lives of the aunts, uncles, and cousins. Why? We were familiar because my grandmother weekly called everyone. She kept us informed as to the family news. As long as she was alive, all of us gathered faithfully several times a year to eat together, share stories together, play games, and stay in touch with each other. When she died, unfortunately, so did the family nucleus. The hub was gone. A few times, different family members tried to arrange reunions or family dinners, but most were failures. The family lost the glue, which held us together. The home was gone.

Another realization when your parents die is how vulnerable you are. Not only have you moved to the elder position in the family, you are positioned closer to death. Unconsciously, you think of your parents as being the buffer between you and death. In the natural order of things, they should die before you do. Now they have died, and you have moved a step closer. It brings home the mortality of your own life. This may cause you to take stock and make some readjustments in your life.

A surprising realization is the longing, which follows the death of your parents. This longing surfaces at different times throughout the rest of your life. It has to do with the sense of discontinuity. You want your parents to see how life turned out. There are many things, which happen to you through the years, you would like to share with them. You long for help when things go bad, and you long to share the fun when things are good.

My parents had only grandsons. This was fun since they had only daughters. But as the grandsons reached adulthood and married, the chance for great-grandchildren came along. My father lived to see the first great-grandson. That was a blessing. Just before my mother died, there was a second great-grandchild expected. She really wanted a great-granddaughter. She talked about the dresses she would buy. She made a hand-sewn quilt for the baby. She died two months before her first great-granddaughter was born. Now two great-granddaughters and another great-grandson have been added to the family. At times, I think about how much I would love for my parents to see these beautiful children. This is sustained longing.

The realization of how much your parents truly meant to you does not come until they are gone. As an adult, you have your own life to live and often do not expect to grieve so hard for your parents. The expectation is since you have strong attachments to other people in your life, the feeling of pain will be less when you lose a parent. This is proved to be far from the truth when the reality of the loss hits you. Yes, you have others to turn to for support; but no matter how old you are, you were always your parents' child. Being nobody's child is a devastating truth.

Loss of a Child

The death of your child is the most horrifying tragedy a parent can face. Words are not sufficient to describe the kaleidoscope of feelings sweeping you into an unending sea of sorrow. Just as this loss is difficult to describe, words fail to identify the bereaved parent. Bernstein, in *When the Bough Breaks*, says when a parent dies, the child is an orphan. She adds when a spouse dies, the survivor is a widow. However, she points out there is no word for the parent whose child dies.

For the mother, the day the child was born is a day never to be forgotten. When the newborn child was placed in her arms, love overflowed the maternal heart. Marveling at the beauty and perfection of that small being, an instant bond formed. The child was a part of the mother's body. You carried the small life for months and loved it ere you knew it. Only another mother can understand the flood of love filling the mother at first sight of the baby.

For the father, the first time you held your child in your arms, pride and love flowed forth, and you experienced a feeling unlike no other as you looked at your precious miracle. You knew this was your future. You were looking into the eyes of generations to come and seeing part of you continue through the ages.

Grieving the loss of a child is different from grieving any other loss because it has to do with excess. Everything is intensified because the loss is of such magnitude. Therefore, the grief is exaggerated and intensified beyond the grief of other losses.

Guilt and anger are emotions present in all grief but are even more excessive in parental grief. Grief professionals estimate it takes three to five years to reach a recovered state after the loss of a spouse. Parental grief might continue for ten or twenty years with difficulty processing the loss. Many believe it is a lifetime struggle for parents to deal with the loss.

Meanings of the Loss

The loss of a child has many meanings to the bereaved parent. Not only did you lose the physical presence of the child, you lost all the things the child represents to a parent.

1. The child is a representation of you.

Your child represented a vital part of you. Personality traits, physical traits, and all the things you passed to the child genetically were a part of your physical body. This was the very essence of you. The child's death was the death of a part of you.

2. The child represented your connection to the future.

Your child gave you a sense of continuity. The child was your connection to the future. Throughout the ages, parents have relied on their children to carry the family into the future generations. Not only was the child a chance to continue the genetic heritage, the child would carry on the values, rituals, and customs of your family. With the child's death, the bridge to the future is taken from you.

3. The child was a primary source of love.

There is no other love like the love of a child for a parent. The child's love is based on need, dependence, admiration, and appreciation. To the small child, you are a god. You are the ideal. Your child looks up to you and trusts you to make things right for him. Children give an innocent and unconditional love. This is powerful. Even when you are not at your best, your child loves you. When the child dies, you miss this open admiration and love.

4. The child is a representation of your own treasured traits and talents.

Parents often see in the child reflections of their own talents and personality traits. You received their love not only physically but also by the way the child emulated your behaviors. Parents often brag. "He's a chip off the old block." Some parents say, "She's just like her mom." The child's patterns of behavior replicating the parent's behaviors are heartwarming sources of pride and love.

5. The child represents your future expectations.

Secondary losses were mentioned earlier in this material. These losses are major in grieving the death of your child. The child's death ended the many future expectations you held for your child. Your hopes, dreams, and goals are turned to dust with the child's death. There are so many nevers to mourn.

Depending on the age of the child, the death may leave more nevers than others. Losing a child at a young age means the life was snuffed out before it had a chance to mature and blossom into adulthood. Irregardless of the age of the child, the death signifies to the parent an uncompleted life.

There are numerous milestone events the child did not live to celebrate; therefore, the parents are also denied the celebration of these events.

Reactions to Child Loss

As in other grieving circumstances, people react differently when losing a child. Each parent grieves in his own way, but there are some common threads to parent grief. Understanding the many reactions and the impact these reactions have on grieving parents is important to the healing process.

Grief Blocks

Grief blocks are reactions to child loss, which impede the grieving process. There are as many blocks as there are unique personalities, but discussion here will focus on five common ones.

1. Guilt

The parent's main responsibility is to take care of the child. When your child dies, although it was out of your control, you might feel guilty because you think there was something you should have done. This is not logical, but grief does not produce logical thinking. You cannot fully process your grief when you get bogged down with the shoulda, woulda, and oughta kind of thinking. This is not productive and only brings you down lower, filling you with senseless blame and guilt.

2. Obsession with Revenge

Parents who become obsessed with getting revenge for the death exhibit great anger. This reaction is observed most often in accidental or violent deaths. The unfairness of the death and the possible preventability of it fill the parent with rage. In the parent's mind, someone must shoulder the blame and pay the price for the death. It is important when suffering this reaction to be able to channel it into positive actions. One action may be to pursue legal action or to work toward enactment of legislation to prevent future similar deaths.

3. Stuck on Instant Replay

This reaction is the replaying of the scene of the death or the last viewing of the child in the parent's mind. Over and over these pictures play through the mind as though they are on rewind/replay. This reaction brings continuous pain with no forward progress. It also interferes with the grief process in several ways. One, it freezes an unpleasant image of the child in your mind. Second, it interferes with your sorting and storing the pleasant memories you want to keep. It takes cognitive imaging of your child in happier times to replace the unwanted scenes playing repetitiously in your head. Every time you do this instant replay, you relive the death. Therefore, the focus is on the death, not the life of the child.

4. Not Talking about the Death

This reaction is considered a grief block because it keeps you from healthy processing of the loss. Recognizing the differences in the way males and females grieve, as well as the difference in personal grief patterns, it is still important to talk about and express feelings concerning the loss of your child. Keeping intense emotions inside is asking for mental distress. While you may prefer private grief, you can still achieve this by sharing your feelings with someone you trust. Be that a professional, family member, friend, or clergy, finding a setting to put the emotions into words is a step in ending this particular grief block.

5. I'll Never Be Happy Again

Thinking you will never be happy again is a normal reaction in the early days of your loss. At the time of the loss, it does seem ridiculous to think you will ever be happy at some date in the future. Certainly, happiness will be a stranger to you for a long time. It will not return soon, and when it does return, it will come in small doses.

Interviews by Finkbeiner with numerous bereaved parents who lost their children through a variety of circumstances revealed happiness did return to their lives eventually. She noted the parents who found happiness again were able to do so because at some point, they made a conscious choice to be happy. Bereaved parents, in her interviews, reported being more cognizant of daily living with death. They said this awareness made them more appreciative of the simple pleasures. After the death of the child, these parents found happiness in small things, which occurred daily in their lives. Finkbeiner also found experiencing happiness again took much longer for bereaved parents than for mourners of other losses. The encouraging finding in the work of Finkbeiner is the fact happiness did not disappear forever from the mourners' lives.

Suicidal Thoughts

Another reaction to the loss of a child, which is as common as the grief blocks, is the thoughts of suicide. Finkbeiner found, when working with grieving parents, many admitted to considering suicide after the death of the child. Accepting the loss is such a difficult task; many parents confided it took at least a year for them to fully realize the child was dead. Groups from The Compassionate Friends revealed they thought in many ways the second year after the death was worse than the first. This seemed to be when the finality of the loss fully struck the parents. As discussed previously in the chapter on the phases of grief, the acceptance of the death in any type of loss is often the lowest point for the mourner. This is validated by the comments made by the parents in The Compassionate Friends groups.

During this period of time, thoughts of suicide were expressed as common with bereaved parents. However, various reasons were given for not acting on the thought. One parent said she considered suicide for two or three months; then instead of thinking "I'm going to kill myself," her thought changed to "I wish I'd been killed too." She described a period of not actively thinking she would kill herself or wanting to, but simply not caring whether she lived or died.

The main reason given by bereaved parents for not committing suicide was concern for other family members. For some, it was a spouse; and for others, it was other children in the family. One parent said she felt the message she would send to her other children was she loved the child who died more than she loved them. That was not true, so she decided to live. Many expressed this sentiment of not wanting others to think they cared for the deceased person more than they cared for the rest of the family.

Grief research has not specifically studied suicide in bereaved parents as opposed to suicides in other types of loss. There is little data on whether or not bereaved parents are more likely to commit suicide than parents who are not bereaved. Finkbeiner noted, in working with bereaved parents: "Parents did not so much choose to live; they just didn't choose to die."

Loss of an Adult Child

Losing a child is losing a child no matter the age of the child. However, there are some differences in the reactions to the loss of an adult child, which are different from the loss of a young child. By the time a child reaches adulthood, the parent has invested a lifetime of work into rearing, teaching, educating, and loving the child. The adult child represents a culmination of the parent's hard work. When the child dies, the life's work is gone.

The sacrifices you made, the education you helped the child obtain, the life journey you traveled together is obliterated. The child's death brings the empty feeling all the parent's work was for naught. The death negates something you spent your life creating. This adult child was your masterpiece, your opus. Now it is gone.

More importantly, if the relationship with your adult child was healthy, it grew from parent-child to an adult-adult relationship. Your grown child became a friend to you as well as your child. You shared activities and interests and often had a social life revolving around the adult child. Perhaps you shared vacation times together and participated in many life celebrations as friends as well as family.

Although you had time with the adult child to make special memories and to celebrate many milestones, you are still cheated of future celebrations. Just as the bereaved parents of young children suffer the many nevers, the bereaved parents of adult children suffer their own nevers. Having a child for thirty or forty years does not lessen the amount of grief when the child dies. The length of time is never enough, and you are never ready to be separated from them.

The death of an adult child is still a death out of the natural order. No parent wants to or expects to outlive his child. When you lose an adult child, you still have many unanswered questions. "Why did my child die before me?" "Why am I still here?" You expect to live a full life with your child, then precede him in death—leaving him to carry on the family name, values, and traditions. This is the way it is supposed to be. The child preceding you in death is against nature.

Some bereaved parents believe the death of their adult child is a punishment visited upon them in their older years. Losing a child in the late stage of the parent's life seems to be a cruel twist of fate. Some parents rely on the adult child for care or assistance with daily life. Losing the child brings fear, anxiety, and a feeling of being unjustly punished. In the parent's mind, the help and security the child provided to the parent has been unfairly taken away, so it must be to punish the parent for some wrong.

The circumstance of the adult child's death is another factor impacting the bereaved parents. Suicide, homicide, accidental deaths, or deaths due to substance abuse are common types of deaths, which can cause the parent to suffer unfounded guilt. Feeling the death was preventable in some way brings forth feelings of failing the child. Also, if the death was due to problems with alcohol, drugs, legal issues, or other negative circumstances, the parent may feel failure in parenting the child. This brings unfounded feelings of guilt because the parent mistakenly thinks the death was within the parent's control.

Some bereaved parents of adult children are not able to fully express their grief at the time of the loss due to responsibilities for the child's family, which now fall on their shoulders. The parent may have to put parental grief in second place to the grief of the child's spouse and/or children's grief. In some instances, the grandparents have to assume the role of parent to the grandchildren. These issues bring such drastic change the grief gets pushed aside in order for the adults to take care of the pressing immediate responsibilities.

Adult children sometimes die leaving money to the parents. This is difficult for the parents because it brings uncertain feelings about accepting the money. Of course, there is no amount of money to compensate for the loss of your child. Some parents find it difficult to take the money from insurance or an inheritance. They often find it even harder to spend the money because it creates feelings of guilt.

An older widow in one of my groups talked to me after group discussion about a similar issue. Her unmarried son was killed in an automobile accident. He had quite a bit of insurance, and she was the sole beneficiary. Therefore, she came into a rather large sum of money. She had enough for her needs, but she did not live an extravagant lifestyle and pinched pennies most of the time. There were several repairs needed at her home, and she considered using some of the money for renovation. Also, there were some opportunities to do more socially if she had extra income. However, she said she felt so guilty thinking she would be enjoying the money from her dead son. This is a good example of the dilemma money from a deceased child can bring to the bereaved parent.

Losing a child as an adult is no easier than losing a child at any age. The feelings are devastating. It is impossible to know why one person dies and another person lives. We do know survivors are left to live a life changed forevermore. Healing and going forward with life are the tasks to be completed by the survivor. Surviving parents can take comfort in the words of Nancy O'Connor: "Though death may take your child, the love never goes away."

Changed Relationships

Bereaved parents experience changes in two areas of relationships. One is in the friendships they had before the death. The other relationship changes occur in the marital relationship. Both of these relationships included the interactions with the child. With the child taken out of these primary relationships, there is a hole to fill and adjustments to be made.

Friendships built around the child and child-related activities lose the common thread that created them—the child. One parent describing the result of losing a son who was a school athlete said she missed the other parents. The parents in the booster club—working together in the concessions stand and participating together for fund-raising events—provided a social world, which was lost to her with her son's death.

Other parents reported a loss of interest in friendships with people the parents now viewed as shallow or spending too much time and effort on trivial things. The bereaved parents' shift in perspective as to priorities distanced them from some of their former friendships.

Some parents reported missing the presence of the child's friends. Parents of teenagers often have their child's friends hanging around the house, sleeping over or visiting on a regular basis. One mother commented she lost not only her son, but she lost his group of friends. She said cooking for extra kids, the blaring music, and the constantly ringing phones were some of the things she missed the most. In her words, when her son died, the house died.

The other relationship impacted by the loss of a child is the marital relationship. There is disagreement among professionals as to how devastating the child's death is to the couple's marriage. Staudacher, in *Beyond Grief*, states 90% of all couples who lose a child are confronted with serious marital problems within the first year after the death. She also adds many marriages end in divorce after the death. However, it appears the marriages most likely to fail are those that were stressed previous to the death. Thus, the child's death proved to be the last straw for the marital union.

The divorce rate is exceptionally high, according to Staudacher, in marriages where the child who died was an only child. Evidence points to the parents' focus being solely on the child in these situations. Without other bonding activities between the marriage partners, when the child dies, their common interest is gone from the relationship. If the only relationship they had to begin with was the child, there is no relationship when the child dies to sustain them through the mourning process. Therefore, the marriage ends.

Marital stress is often created following the death of the child because of the different ways in which people deal with loss. Compounding this is the major differences between male grief and female grief. Generally, male grief is expressed in more silent, private ways with discussion of facts being the focus of talking about the loss. Female grief, in generality, is a more public expression of the grief, accompanied by expression of feelings in open communications. If these different grief patterns exist between the marriage partners, misunderstanding takes place, and the marital relationship suffers.

A lack of pleasure and intimacy in the marriage after the death is another stress factor affecting the marital relationship. Grieving is draining. One or both partners may lack the energy for intimacy. In the early days of loss, putting together coherent thoughts is difficult and taxing. The stress is at an all-time level. All of these factors affect not only each partner's libido but also the desire for any physical contact. Failure to maintain physical closeness leaves the couple unable to comfort each other.

The couple's sense of morality can compound the problem because they might feel it is wrong to feel any pleasure at this terrible time in their lives. As the couple distances themselves from each other intimately, they lose the connectedness needed to sustain the marriage. Staudacher's view on the importance of not letting this happen in the marriage is well stated when she said,

> It is important to understand that experiencing pleasure is not the same as renouncing your dead child. Pleasure must not be associated with disloyalty.

Research by Murphy and associates examined the influence of three types of violent death of children on marital satisfaction between the surviving parents. The types of death were homicide, suicide, and accidental death. Their finding was marital satisfaction decreased significantly over time and reached the lowest level five years past death. However, the *cause* of the child's death did not significantly influence marital satisfaction. This study substantiates the fact a child's death directly impacts the marriage but emphasizes it is the death itself, rather than the way the child died, which is the marital stressor. The results also emphasize processing a child's death is a very lengthy process.

A study by Kamm and Vandenberg of the impact of grief reactions and communication on marital relationships indicated the importance of grief communication between bereaved partners. Couples with greater positive attitudes about communication demonstrated greater marital satisfaction over a period of time than those couples with negative grief communication styles. Open communication was related to higher grief in early stages of the loss, but in later stages of the bereavement, the open communication style lowered the grief reactions.

Studies of the impact of a child's death on marriages often give conflicting reports. One reason is the studies report on two different things: (1) negative changes in the marriage and (2) the rate of divorce. Another reason for the conflicting results has to do with the measurement tools. Studies measuring changes in the marriage or changes in marriage satisfaction measure those changes in different ways. Therefore, the results may be contradictory. When researchers look for clear-cut data, such as the divorce rate, it is easier to get consistent agreement on the results. However, when researchers try to measure how a person feels about his marriage, depending on how the questions are asked and the mood of the subjects on any given day, the results may vary.

We do know the death of a child is one of the highest stressors for a marriage. The unique process of grief complicates the study of its impact on people, relationships, and families. Evaluating something as uniquely individualistic as emotions, human interactions and reactions, and the impact of experiences on human life produces a plethora of variables to affect the outcomes. Do we know child loss stresses a marriage? Yes. Is it the cause of marital problems? Maybe. Does it cause divorce? We are not sure. It is hard to be definite about an outcome, which can be affected by so many different variables.

Some couples lose a child and become even closer. They draw on each other's strength and comfort each other in their deep sorrow. Other couples grow apart, each retreating into his own private world. Some couples find they only communicated through and because of the child. So when the child dies, they are two strangers, not knowing what to do with each other. Determining the success or failure rate of marriages due to the loss of a child is difficult because of the unique human factors, which make up the family and the marital relationship.

Changed Perspectives

The death of a child changes the parents' perspectives on life in many ways. After such a devastating loss, parents find their reference point is changed forever. Priorities shift, and as the parents work through the loss, they find some valuable life lessons emerge from the pain.

1. Changed Reference Point

> The child's death becomes the zero point, the reference point, against which everything else is compared.
>
> Anne K. Finkbeiner

When you lost your child, everything started from that point forward. Compared to the loss of your child, what does it matter if someone cuts in line at the post office? At work you see people complaining about this task or that responsibility, and you think, "Big deal." It no longer seems important to keep up with the Joneses. Belonging to the right club is a farce. It does not matter if you get the corner office or not. The routine, mundane things, which take up 70% of your daily life, pale in importance to the zero point of your child's death. This leaves you with little patience for whining, complaining, and worrying about what you now see as unimportant things.

2. Priority Shift

When comparing everything else in life to the zero point of reference, you are able to sort the trivial from the truly important. This causes you to make changes in your life. These changes involve relationships, activities, and goals.

You may find people who focus on inconsequential things are irritating to you. Therefore, you begin to distance yourself from people caught up in unimportant, superficial activities. As you realign relationships and activities, you readjust goals.

You may become more sensitive to the pain of others, having suffered great pain too. You can often see pain in the eyes of others once the pain has been in your eyes. Before the loss, you probably sailed unaware through life and did not see the walking wounded. You may find yourself developing goals and activities, which involve doing for others. You begin to avoid people you view as insensitive.

A priority shift, which occurs, is living in the moment more than the distant future. Parents commented about letting go of many materialistic goals and enjoying what they have now. Noticing and appreciating the simple things in life was mentioned by several parents in the bereavement interviews by Finkbeiner.

3. Life Lessons

Two of the hardest lessons for parents are (1) understanding the death is final and (2) learning life goes on. Neither of these two things happens anytime soon after the death. Most bereaved parents indicate it is at least a year for the finality of the loss to sink in to their consciousness.

Until the parent accepts the death as final, it proves difficult to go forward. At some point in time, and this is different for different people, a breakpoint is reached. A breakpoint is when you begin to have some energy for people and do things outside yourself. Something happens to symbolize the end of preoccupation and despair. This can take up to four or five years for some parents to reach this breakpoint.

Research validates this time span, reporting few differences in general functioning of parents four years or thirteen years after the loss of their child. The conclusion of this research was stabilization from the loss was reached around four years postdeath. The impact of the loss from that point up to thirteen years postdeath remained about the same. One parent said, "Letting go of the child is impossible. Your child is of your blood, and the bond does not break."

The child is gone, but the parent is still here. Life slowly and painfully continues. This brings the parent to the realization a choice must be made. You, the parent, make the choice to get better. It is a conscious decision to go on with your life. Your choice now is to *live* or to merely *exist*. Most parents indicated this was the breakpoint for them—when they made that choice. This is when you learn to do things to help get you through the bad times. When this happens, you are able to adjust the relationship with your child from the physical to the spiritual. As one mother said, "My son is not gone. His soul is still alive in another world and in my heart."

Many bereaved parents find the loss causes them to develop great emotional strength. Surviving the tragedy of losing your child gives you greater courage to face other fears. There is absolutely nothing you could be asked to face that could be worse than the loss of your child. Other fears pale in comparison. Many parents expressed much less fear of failure from the zero point forward. Therefore, they tried new approaches to life and pursued dreams or goals they previously were fearful to try. This inner strength, which developed, led them onto different paths than the ones they followed before the zero point.

Different View of Death

After the death of a child, many parents feel death loses its macabre, emotional overtones. It loses its fearful grip. Knapp, in *Beyond Endurance*, interviewed scores of bereaved parents. He found at five or more years, the parents no longer saw death as an enemy. They saw death as the place their child resided. These parents felt there was the prospect of a reunion with the child when the parent's time came.

Parents viewed subsequent deaths in the family differently after the loss of the child. For example, one mother who lost her father after her son saw this as a reunion of the grandfather with her deceased son. She took comfort in thinking of a family reunion in another place and in the fact her son would have family with him.

Losing a child at any age leaves the surviving parents feeling their child's life was a life unfinished. Coming to terms with this view and thinking about life purpose both for you and the child who died is a huge task in the mourning process. Referring to the death of a child, Viktor Frankl helped put this in perspective when he said,

> We cannot, after all, judge a biography by the length, by the number of pages in it; we must judge by the richness of its content.... Sometimes the "unfinisheds" are the most beautiful symphonies.

Sudden/Traumatic Death

> There are always two parties to death; the person who dies and the survivor who is bereaved.... And in the apportionment of suffering, the survivor takes the brunt.
>
> —Arnold Toynbee

This statement is especially true when the death is totally unexpected. The sudden loss of a loved one is so incomprehensible the mourner is left in a totally bewildered state. Nothing prepares you for this sudden devastation. One moment you have a normal life, and the next, your life is turned upside down. In the blink of an eye, a vital part of your daily life is obliterated. The reaction to such a loss is numbness, shock, and disbelief. A confusing sense of unreality envelops you. Your first thought may be, "This is not possible. I'll wake up any minute, and this will be a bad dream." You desperately hope a mistake was made, confusing your loved one with someone else. Shaking the sense of unreality is one of the most difficult steps in adjusting to a sudden death.

The first several days, or even weeks, may pass with you in a state of numbness. You may not be able to fully comprehend the finality of your changed world during this time. The drastic alterations in your present and future life are incomprehensible while you are in this state of unreality.

The initial days following the loss are filled with funeral arrangements, visitation, and the whole series of events surrounding the death of your loved one. These may pass in a blur to you, and you probably function in a haze throughout this activity. You may have a period of time before you can hold the funeral if an autopsy needs to be performed or other legal issues need to be resolved. This puts you in a holding pattern for a while but also complicates the responsibilities you are asked to carry out while in this dazed state.

The day of the death is permanently frozen in your mind. Years later, you will most likely remember minute details of the day you found out your loved one had died. It is common to remember where you were, what you were doing, and many other unimportant activities, which normally would not be worthy of remembrance.

For example, the day my late husband was injured in his near-fatal accident is still, many years later, imprinted in my mind. The trauma froze every detail in my memory. I not only remember the ordinary events of that day, I remember the particular food I was preparing for dinner when I received the news of his injury.

Almost thirteen years later, when he died suddenly of a heart attack, it was déjàvu for me. The events of the day of his death are indelibly imprinted in my mind. Trauma of such magnitude etches lasting images in absolute clarity in your psyche.

Types of Traumatic Death

There are several types of sudden, traumatic deaths, which create difficult mourning for survivors. Sudden death due to physical illnesses is one type. Accidental deaths are another. The last two types, and perhaps the most complicated for the mourner, are the violent deaths of homicide and suicide.

1. Accidental Death

Accidental deaths are the number 1 cause of death among people in the group of fifteen to thirty-four years of age. One reason is these years are the time of highest risk-taking behaviors for most people. When you are young, you do not think about death. Death seems far removed from your life, so you may make decisions, which endanger you. As you age, risk-taking behavior lessens.

There are many deaths in this category. Traffic accidents rank high in the cause of accidental deaths. Other causes are work accidents, hunting accidents, drowning accidents, and falls. Falls are especially dangerous in the elderly population. Accidental drug or alcohol overdoses are other causes of accidental deaths.

Accidental death of a loved one takes the survivor completely by surprise. It is the dreaded phone call or the appearance of a police officer at your door, which first alerts many survivors to the tragedy. Sometimes a relative or close friend will appear to deliver the bad news. No matter how you are notified, it is a terrifying experience for which you are totally unprepared.

Survivors in my bereavement groups through the years, who lost loved ones in accidents, expressed the perplexity and confusion felt when the death occurred. Most survivors echoed the thought it was impossible to believe because they just said good-bye to the loved one or talked to them on the phone. Some were waiting for them to arrive home for dinner. The general feelings seemed to be, "How can this happen when they were perfectly fine a short while ago?"

Other common feelings expressed by these survivors were feeling the initial report of death was a mistake and being sure the loved one would come in the door any minute. This magical thinking helped the family deal with the shock and was a sign of the denial of the death.

Research by Barry and associates to evaluate the role of preparedness for the death and the effect on bereaved persons determined feeling a lack of preparedness by the mourner contributed significantly to their acceptance of the death. The mourners in the study indicated the lack of preparedness caused difficulty in accepting the permanent separation from the loved one. This study also found a higher incidence of complicated grief issues when the mourners felt unprepared for the death. A significant likelihood of major depressive disorder among these mourners was also observed.

The preventability factor in accidental death causes more stress on the mourners. Replaying the accident over and over in one's mind opens the door to many what-ifs and if onlys. Often, this brings guilt feeling because you begin to second-guess your actions, leading up to the accident. You try to be a Monday morning quarterback to an event over which you had no control. The randomness of the accident negates a prevention plan.

On more than one occasion in my groups, parents expressed this type of regret. In each of these instances, the child was killed in an automobile accident. Some parents expressed regret for giving the child a car. Others rued giving the child the keys to their car for the particular time of the accident. Others spoke of wishing they had refused permission for the child to go out that particular night or to go to a certain event. Each situation is an example of mourners' suffering the angst of the preventability of an accident.

Sudden Physical Illness

Another traumatic death is the death of someone who suddenly becomes ill and dies. In some cases, the loved one had some medical history, but it was not considered life-threatening. Other times, a person who appears to be perfectly healthy suffers a massive heart attack, stroke, or aneurysm and is dead in an instant. Whatever the reason for the death, the loss of the person strikes the survivor like a bolt of lightening.

The question of preventability again arises in the mind of the survivor. You question whether or not there were signs and symptoms you should have noticed. You chastise yourself for not making your loved one eat healthy, go to the doctor, exercise, or live a healthier lifestyle in general. There are a million ways to blame oneself for the death.

Questioning your own actions is assuming you have control over the situation. If that were true, your loved one would still be alive. You did not have control. Accepting the death of your loved one was beyond your control is the only way to put guilt aside.

If you were with your loved one when he suffered the fatal illness, you may have negative images of the final moments, which replay in your mind. The feelings of terror, helplessness, and powerlessness can be overwhelming. The trauma of seeing the death complicates your mourning and interferes with your ability to remember more pleasant times with the loved one.

If you were not with your loved one, your inability to say good-bye presents another challenge. You wonder if the loved one knew this was his final time on earth. Did he suffer? Did he think of you? Was it a peaceful death? Did he know you loved him?

Although my husband suffered many medical problems throughout the years following his work-related injury, I was not expecting his death at the time he suffered the heart attack. We both knew he had serious health issues but did not see death as imminent. He was home, recovering from a recent hospitalization, and I had returned to work. Someone was with him until thirty minutes before I came home from work. During those thirty minutes, he suffered a heart attack and died. I know, firsthand, the question you ask yourself when you did not get to say good-bye.

I asked myself all the questions, and the answers I arrived at in order to process my grief were the answers it is important for all survivors to believe. Yes, when our final moment comes, we know it. Yes, when our final moment comes, we hold those we love in our hearts. Yes, when death comes, no matter the circumstance, it is peaceful. The process of dying may be painful, but the death is peaceful. Most important is the answer to the question of whether or not the loved one knew you loved him. A most definite yes to that question. Love transcends the bonds of death. Whether you are physically with your loved one or not, your love warmly enfolds him just as his love enfolds you. Love is boundless and timeless. Love never dies.

Suicide

In Nancy O'Connor's book *Letting Go with Love*, she says, "Suicide is the most hostile rejection a person can make of another person." Most survivors of a victim of suicide would probably agree with this statement. The sense of rejection, the feelings of powerlessness and helplessness, coupled with the intense feelings of anger and guilt, make suicide one of the most devastating kinds of loss.

Myths about Suicide

Myths about suicide continue to complicate the mourning process for the survivors. One myth is suicide is rare. Statistics on suicides in the United States show it is not an uncommon kind of violent death. Figures from the Centers for Disease Control and Prevention (CDC) and the National Institute of Mental Health (NIMH) rate suicide as the ninth cause of death in the United States. The suicide rate for teenagers has increased at an alarming rate in the past forty years. Suicide is the third leading cause of death for fifteen- to twenty-four-year-olds in the United States.

The ripple effect of one person's suicide is tremendous. The CDC estimates thirty thousand people die by suicide annually in the United States alone. Worldwide it is estimated eight hundred thousand people kill themselves each year. For every individual who takes his own life, it is estimated at least seven to ten people are intimately affected. Approximately five million survivors are left behind every year. This is a staggering number of people who are left to deal with the aftermath of such a tragedy.

As researchers study these figures for suicide, several risk factors become apparent. There appears to be a high risk for single white males. Males are three times more likely to commit suicide than females. White males over fifty years of age make up only 10% of the population, but they account for 28% of the suicides.

There is a higher incidence of suicide among older men for several reasons. For males, aging often means ending their lifework and entering retirement. With the ensuing decline in feeling useful, productive, and capable of working, self-esteem and feelings of self-worth take a downward turn. For some older males, the inability to exercise control and to function independently diminishes purpose in life. Add to this the difficulty some males always had in the way they viewed their own performance, and these males become more prone to despair in their later years.

The male self-identity is closely related to occupation. Retirement takes this away. If you are no longer a teacher, plumber, carpenter, or doctor, what are you? Finding other avenues to use your talents, skills, and intellect is important for all older people, but especially so for males.

Suicide of seniors is also impacted by the death of a close person. A study of senior citizens who attempted suicide showed the group experienced a recent close loss twice as often as the members of the nonsuicidal group. The impact of losing a spouse, parent, or child raised the risk factor significantly in the group participating in this study.

The identification of high-risk individuals is a key to prevention. Besides the high-risk populations previously mentioned, four definitive factors appear to predispose a person to suicide. These are alcohol, drugs, violence, and homosexuality.

Drugs and alcohol are involved in two out of three suicides. Alcoholics have higher rates of suicides than drug addicts and homosexuals. As in other suicides, it is believed the proclivity for suicide began developing at an early age. It grows from emotional characteristics as well as social and cultural integration. Therefore, the suicides in these groups were not because of alcohol, drugs, or homosexuality per se but due to the individual's lifelong patterns of dealing with life, relationships, and self-image. Not only the individual's coping styles but his worldview and his perception of how others view him have a tremendous impact.

Factors affecting drug and alcohol suicides reflect the impact emotional, social, and cultural integration has on the person. In reviewing the personal history of suicide victims with substance abuse problems, two issues are apparent. One is the victim's inability to maintain a rewarding, long-lasting, and loving relationship. Second is the inability on the part of the individual to commit to the personal responsibilities, which come with a long-standing relationship. Commitment and responsibility contribute to feelings of self-worth and success. Succeeding at these two things provides a close human connection. Having someone to share intimate feelings with stems feelings of being isolated. Substance abusers, especially alcoholics, fail even more than others to succeed with these two relationship builders. Isolation is a symptom of the disease of alcoholism, and it is also a contributor to suicidal tendencies.

The higher risk factor for homosexuals is strongly connected to the underlying restrictions and condemnations of a cultural, societal, and religious nature. Being ostracized, shamed, and blamed for being who you are can demolish your sense of self-worth and self-esteem. Many homosexuals face the scorn of not only the outside world but the condemnation of their own families. This is the ultimate rejection of you, as a person, when your own family sees you as an abomination.

Providing therapy for homosexuals was an eye-opening experience for me. The abuses suffered by this segment of our population are indescribable. The courage to face daily rejection, anger, and disrespect for being who you are would be a challenge to anyone. Working with this population, it became obvious why suicide is a high-risk factor for this group.

Many of the patients I worked with were HIV-positive, which was an added burden for them to bear. Not all families turned their backs on these patients, but many did. The issues the patients dealt with were major enough, but when families withdrew their support, the struggle was magnified. Man's inhumanity to man is a terrible thing, but this population sees it and lives through it on a daily basis. For many, the struggle is too hard, and suicide seems to be the only way out of the pain.

A second myth about suicide is the person usually displays obvious behavioral symptoms before the suicide. Thus, the self-destruction could be prevented. Suicide is not a single act. The final act of suicide was set in process long before the sudden impulse to end one's life. In Staudacher's writing about suicide, she says, "It is a coalition of forces, both external and internal, which makes suicide possible."

The death itself is not the major factor. Death is the accompanying act to a painful state, which has become all consuming and overpowering. Because humans are so complicated, and each person's worldview differs, it is impossible to pin down a definitive answer as to why a person decided to take his own life. However, people who take their own lives apparently feel trapped by what they see as a hopeless situation.

These feelings spring from great despair and unhappiness. The unhappiness is due to multiple forces. *Who* the person is and *where* the person is in life is an important force. It is important to understand this is not who you think he is or where you think he is in life. It is solely determined from the viewpoint of the person.

If a young man is unhappy and views himself as a failure, whether or not he truly is, he may develop low self-esteem. Since he sets certain needs and expectations for himself, he sees his life as not fulfilling these needs or meeting the expectations. This may or may not be apparent to those around him, but it is very much a part of his internal mind-set. When his life does not measure up in his eyes, the result is a feeling of chaos and despair.

Once the young man has this perception of his life, external forces validate his opinion of himself. If he is experiencing this thinking process, problems in a relationship, at school, or on the job reinforce even more the feeling of despair. Each event in a series of events produces more negative emotions. Thus, suicide becomes a *release* from the pain, chaos, and despair. *Taking* one's life is not so much the focus as *controlling* one's life. In the victim's mind, life stopped before it stopped.

When this state is reached, people around the person may not observe any unusual behavior. As the situation appears more hopeless to the person, he may isolate emotionally from family relationships, friendships, and the reality of life. After the suicide, family and friends pour over the days and weeks leading up to the death—seeking clues, signs, or reasons. Sometimes clues are found and sometimes not. Usually, if there were clues, they were so obscure they were not discernible to family or friends.

A third myth, which has distressed families of suicide victims and brought undue stigma, is that suicide is an act of insanity. It is not necessarily the act of an insane person. While some suicides have a diagnosed mental illness, the majority of them do not. Suicide is an act committed by a person who felt intense, unbearable anguish and hopelessness. John Hewitt, author of *After Suicide*, says,

> He or she probably wasn't choosing death as much as choosing
> to end the unbearable pain.

Families of suicide victims are frequently embarrassed to tell the cause of the loved one's death because of the stigma attached to it. Thinking the suicide was due to insanity on the part of the victim creates difficulty for the survivors and deprives them of the support they need at this time of loss. Many families feel the death is a negative reflection on the family, and their own mental state may be in question.

Cultural and religious interpretations of an earlier era are also responsible for the stigma associated with suicide. It is important for families to see these as biased interpretations and refuse to feel embarrassment and shame. You have suffered a devastating loss. It is important to confront it. It is important to confront the word *suicide*. Keeping it a secret deprives you of the pleasure and joy of speaking about your loved one. This isolates you. Isolation keeps you from the contact you need to help you grieve.

Surviving the Suicide of a Loved One

As a survivor of a loved one's death by suicide, you are given an enormous task of mourning. Suicide mourning is like no other. First, you have the added burden of understanding the motivation for the death. This is elusive and quite often impossible to ascertain. Second, you face a grieving process, which will be of longer duration than many other grief processes. This is in part due to the quest to understand the motivation behind the death. There really is no definitive answer, but it takes a while for the survivor to accept this.

As long as the survivors of suicide victims relentlessly continue the quest for the why of the suicide, they are able to disguise or ignore the feelings of anger, guilt, and shame inside. By refusing to acknowledge there is not a rational reason for the suicide, the search for reason becomes a shield.

Along with the frustration of the pointless search for why the suicide happened come other problems for the survivor. Silence becomes a mask the survivor wears. Many refuse to talk about the death because it is so painful. Not only will survivors refuse to talk to outsiders, but also often, family members fail to discuss the loss within the family. This leaves everyone in the room with a very large elephant, which cannot be mentioned.

Just as silence creates great internal stress for the survivors, negative realizations add to the distress. One of the negative realizations is the suicide removed all possibility of the survivor being able to help the victim. Whatever the victim's issues were, the survivors were not given an opportunity to help with a resolution. In the survivor's mind, this is the ultimate rejection. This can create powerful feelings of worthlessness and helplessness in the survivor. The survivor questions his own behaviors and approachability. Did I listen carefully enough? Did I pay enough attention to him? Did I appear too busy to deal with problems? Being able to talk with other family members, who may have similar feelings, is an important release for the survivors.

Surviving the death requires the survivors to gain some new perceptions. First, you must understand your anger in order to process it. What is your perception of the anger you feel? Some of the anger arises from the rejection just mentioned. Another source of the anger is the pain you inherited from the loved one when he died. Pain and confusion were dumped on you with no time for preparation. This seems very unfair and produces anger and great frustration. Added to this anger is the speculation about the normalcy of you and your family due to the suicide. Being put in the position of having to make sense of something so senseless, and putting the death into some kind of context, is not only difficult but accelerates your anger over the entire event. Understanding your anger does not prevent it, but it does help you diffuse and express it in positive ways.

A second perception change forced on you is the change in how you view your relationship to the suicide victim. The death left you to deal with your damaged self-image and your damaged image of the loved one. You cared for this person deeply and felt him worth the investment of time, energy, love, and devotion you gave him. You felt just as valuable to him as he was to you. The death brings this perception of the relationship into question. How much did you mean to him? Where did you really stand with him?

Third, you must change your perception of guilt. How do you look at guilt? Suicide is a complex issue consisting of many major influences. You do not have control over everything. You keep trying to see the death as within your power or control. It is not. When you can abdicate your power over the life or death of this loved one, you are able to walk away from the guilt. The death was in the realm of the victim's control, not yours.

A monumental task for the survivor is to come to terms with past issues, stresses, and problems remaining from the relationship. These items of unfinished business, if not put to rest, keep a sense of guilt alive in the survivor. Guilt prolongs recovery.

The suicide of a family member is a triple threat to your emotional health. First, it is a sudden death with no time to prepare. Second, it is the loss of a significant person in your life. Third, it is an action loaded with emotional content. Your task to survive this is quite a challenge. However, you have a right to survive, and you can survive. You do it by putting to rest the search for a reason, letting go of guilt and blame, and releasing the person.

Uppermost in the survivor's mind must be the thought *you are not responsible for someone else's suicide*. In the final moment, he made a choice. He chose to end the pain of life by dying. It was not your decision. For whatever reason, and no reason will ever be good enough for you, the person chose to die. It does not make sense to you, and it may never make sense. There is no reason good enough to relieve your pain of separation.

Eventually, being able to release the person from your life will bring peace. Releasing does not mean erasing. It is important to understand the difference. Releasing him means not being preoccupied with the memory of the suicide to the point it continues to interfere with you living life again. It takes time for you to reach this point. Sometimes it takes two years or more. Take the time you need. Slowly, you begin to realize you are making progress forward in life. It may be on teetering legs with infinitely small steps, but progress will be made if you dedicate yourself to it.

Suicide survivor Carla Fine summed up the release of guilt, recriminations, and the suicide itself by her comment:

> Gradually, I came to realize that while it may be possible to help someone whose fear is death, there are no guarantees for a person whose fear is life.

Homicides

Homicides, like suicides, affect the survivors in many similar ways. The disbelief, shock, and numbness due to the total lack of preparation for the death are common to both types of death. The additional feelings of terror, vulnerability, and victimization compound the loss of a loved one to murder. A basic need for humans in Maslow's hierarchy of needs is the need for safety. Murder is the ultimate violation of that need.

The issue of the preventability of the murder is a huge problem for the survivor just as it is in a suicide death. The act of murder is totally senseless. It is impossible for the survivor to fathom any good purpose or reason for the death. If the homicide was a random act perpetrated by a stranger, it is even more bewildering to the survivors. The age-old questions of "Why my loved one?" "Why at that time or in that place?" and "Why couldn't someone stop it?" echo inside the heads of the surviving families and friends.

The anger felt by the survivors is intense when the death is a homicide. Revenge and retribution come to mind immediately. Someone must be held accountable. Someone must pay for this horrible act. The compulsion to establish responsibility for the crime is a driving force in the lives of the survivors.

Some survivors are shocked at the murderous thoughts they have of the killer. Venting these murderous impulses by discussing them with a therapist helps to diffuse these intense emotions and bring some relief to the mourner. The intensity of the violent thoughts of retribution upsets many of the survivors because they have never felt this way before or thought they could feel so vindictive toward another human being.

Considering the fact it may take a while, if ever, to apprehend the killer, the family has a period of intensified anticipation of justice being meted out to the offender. Sometimes the offender is never caught, which compounds the family grief. Even when the offender is caught, the wheels of justice grind slowly, so the family may face months or years of trials and appeals. During this process, the surviving family members must relive the horrible events of the murder over and over. This is a constant drain on the family's emotional reserves. It can be compared to picking a scab, never letting a wound heal.

Homicide produces an overpowering sense of victimization. First, the killer victimizes the family. Then they are victimized by the legal system. Third, the media victimizes them. Although the victimization by the legal system is not intentional, it is difficult just the same. Interrogations, which must be done, are disturbing to family members at this emotional time. Detachment and perceived lack of empathy from law enforcement officials adds to the feeling of being victimized. Others often perceive the professional detachment required for officials to do a difficult job, such as theirs, as being cold and unfeeling. Added to this is the fact the first to inform the family of the death is usually law enforcement. No matter how compassionately they try to do this, the family remembers this terrible moment forever. Unfortunately, humans have a tendency to respond negatively to the bearers of bad news.

Feeling stigmatized by others is common in violent deaths such as murder. The news coverage of the event, the questions by the curious, and the accompanying notoriety of all events up to and including the murder leave the family feeling violated. Their privacy is invaded, and there is little opportunity to be left to grieve in private with close family and friends.

This stigma is even worse if the perpetrator of the crime was another family member or close friend. Just as the survivors of suicides torture themselves with the idea that they should have prevented the death, these survivors sometimes feel they are to blame for not seeing danger signs. Having someone you loved and trusted violate that trust in such a despicable way—as to kill someone else you loved too—is the ultimate betrayal. Outsiders are often prying and unsympathetic with the survivors because they mistakenly believe the family should have known about this danger within their midst.

The feelings of guilt and self-blame are intensified when the murder was committed by an acquaintance or fellow family member. Feeling responsible for not observing signs of instability in someone close to you is common in survivors. Feeling great anger at such violation of the sanctity of the family bond leaves the survivors feeling helpless and frustrated as to how to deal with this intense emotion.

Murder of your loved one is a personal violation of your belief and value system. Murder violates everything you believe to be right, fair, honest, and good in the world. An act such as murder strikes at the very core of your belief system. If this horrendous act can take a life with so little compunction and treat life with so little value, what other beliefs do I have, which are perhaps false? Loss of trust in the world as you always believed it to be is a secondary loss for the survivor of a murder victim.

Homicide represents a tremendous loss of control of your life. Someone took command of your life by taking the life of someone you loved. Then you lost control to the system. You were forced to deal with coroners, autopsies, law enforcement, the judicial process, and the media. Everyone appeared to be running your life but you. The intrusion of the outside world into your world and the consequent chaos often pushes you to withdraw until you have the strength to reenter the world of the living.

How do you get over a loss such as homicide? The answer is you don't. Madeleine L'Engle said,

> We don't get over the deepest pains of life, nor should we. During an average lifetime there are many pains, many grieves to be borne. We don't "get over" them; we learn to live with them, to go on growing and deepening, and understanding.

Issues Complicating Traumatic Grief

The survivors of traumatic deaths begin their journeys of grief with additional baggage than survivors of other types of grief. As you read about the different types of loss and their impact on survivors, you may notice there are some similar reactions; but also, each type carries with it its own brand of misery for the survivors. Research into the impact of traumatic death on survivors hold few surprises to clinicians working with bereaved clients because the results most likely validate what is seen in therapy with these survivors. Research by Harwood to study grief reactions in survivors to older people dying by suicide showed significant differences in the reactions of survivors of suicides compared to reactions by survivors of death by natural causes.

The age group studied in this research was sixty years or older with a mean age of seventy-two. The composition of the groups was 68% male, 80% white, 35% married, and 49% living alone. The suicide survivors of this group reported significantly more problems with law enforcement, the coroner's office, the delay between the death and the inquest, and distress over what to put in the newspaper than as reported in the control group of nonsuicide survivors.

The moods assessment of the two groups found survivors of suicide victims scored 49% compared to 39% on the depressed range in the control group. There was also noted a 14% increase in alcohol intake in the suicide survivor group compared to the control group. On the grief expression questionnaire (GEQ), the unique reactions of stigmatization, shame, and rejection were higher in the survivors of suicide. Comparing children of the deceased in both groups, the children of suicide victims scored higher on rejection than the control group. With the age of the suicide victims being sixty years and above, these were adult children.

Research, mentioned previously by Murphy, examined the influence of three types of violent death (accident, suicide, homicide) and time since the death upon four parent outcomes. The four outcomes were mental distress, posttraumatic stress disorder (PTSD), acceptance of the death, and marital satisfaction.

The traumatic experience scale (TES) measured PTSD. While all groups of parents scored high on this outcome, the parents of homicide victims had the highest scores for PTSD. The study covered a time period of four- to sixty-month intervals. Evaluations were done on the fourth, sixth, twelveth, twenty-fourth, and sixtieth months. Acceptance of the death took a significant amount of time. The acceptance showed no significant difference among the three types of loss. (The marital satisfaction outcome results are discussed in the section on suicide. Therefore, discussion will not be repeated about that particular outcome here.) However, it is important to note the study reported the change over time in all four outcomes was highly significant. On the average, over time, there was improvement shown in the four outcomes for the three types of traumatic death.

Based on the results of research and the writings of many professionals in the field of bereavement, there are some specific issues in sudden death to be aware of due to complications in the mourning, which may be caused by these deaths:

1. Diminished Coping Ability
    The surprise of the death, and the ensuing shock on the part of the survivor, puts coping mechanisms into neutral for a time.

2. Shattered Worldview
    Everything the survivors believed about order, predictability, and safety is destroyed. The result is anxiety and feelings of vulnerability.

3. The Senselessness of the Loss
    The randomness of the event brings home to the mourner how impossible it is to be really sure about anything in life. There is no

rhyme or reason to such an illogical act. The death makes no sense and does not fit any way into the context of the survivor's previously held beliefs and views about people or the world.

4. Unfinished Business
There may be a feeling of incompleteness. Sometimes survivors feel some things needed to be said, which were left unsaid. A quarrel may have needed to be resolved, and now it is too late. There was no chance to say good-bye.

5. Length of Acute Grief and Shock
The death is so unimaginable reality cannot set in for a long time. Shock lasts longer in this type of loss. The initial pain may be more intense. Many survivors and others around them do not understand the longer time needed and the depth of the pain.

6. Instant Replays
The survivors play over and over the events surrounding the loss. Sometimes to the point of obsession, these scenes run over in their minds. This is done for the comprehension of the loss to sink in and become real. The unreality of it lasts for a long period of time.

7. Fear
The mourner's sense of safety in daily life may be challenged. This is especially true if the traumatic death was a homicide. Fear of intruders, fear of attack out in public, fear of the night, and many other phobias may surface. Traumatic automobile accidents may make it unbearable for a survivor to ride in a car or drive one. Traffic may be unnerving. These fear reactions are due to the trauma of the loss.

Fear of trusting loved ones is a fear that surfaces if the murderer was another relative or acquaintance. The mourner's whole system of establishing trust and feeling safe in close relationships is shattered. This severely impacts family ties and friendships.

8. Distorted Relationship
The loss abruptly severs the relationship with the loved one. The survivor may highlight in his mind interactions with the loved

one, particularly the events surrounding the time of the death. Realistic recollections may be replaced with intensified problems or remembering things out of proportion to the reality of the interactions. This can cause the survivor to mentally increase a sense of guilt because of imagined negative communications or actions on his part with the deceased.

9. Intensity of Emotions
    The wound is raw. The pain is severe. The hurt is deep. The anger is hot. The frustrations are unbearable. All emotions are magnified in intensity. On a scale of one to ten, with ten being the highest, your emotions are a twelve!

10. Secondary Losses
    Many nevers are to be mourned. Life was snuffed out before so much could be completed. Dreams may be left unfulfilled. Milestones cannot be celebrated with the loved one. Companionship, roles, hopes, and plans are all lost as far as having the loved one to do those things with you. These secondary losses will haunt the survivors throughout the rest of their lives. Just as the eternal question asked by so many mourners is why? In the loss of someone to sudden, traumatic death, it seems especially an affront. Rabbi Kushner writes,

    > Laws of nature do not make exceptions for nice people. A bullet has no conscience; neither does a malignant tumor or an automobile gone out of control. That is why good people get sick and hurt as much as anyone.

Grief is the price you pay for loving the special people in your lives. There are no guarantees. Nothing lasts forever. When you lose someone you love, you understand completely the importance of fully living each and every day. None of us would give up the opportunity to love these special people. The loss makes them more precious. Just as there is no answer to why they entered your life, there is no answer to why they were taken away. The loss has nothing to do with how good you are nor is it a punishment. It is what it is. We have been blessed by their presence and will continue to be blessed by their memory.

Death after a Prolonged Illness

If a loved one died after being ill for a long period of time, your grief will be different in many ways from the grief following a sudden death. With a long illness, the survivor does some anticipatory grief. Simply put, anticipatory grief is the psychological reorganization and coping, which takes place in response to the awareness of a loved one's impending death.

It is misleading to think anticipatory grief is undertaken between hearing the fatal diagnosis and the actual death. Anticipatory is more complicated than that description of it. There are three foci in time for anticipatory grief: the past, the present, and the future.

The span of time covered by this type of grief is not confined to one segment in the time continuum. For example, you experience anticipatory grief in the past when you grieve losses you had due to the illness. When the loved one became ill, secondary losses began. Perhaps it was the loss of your once vibrant, healthy spouse. Your grief may have focused on the loss of the possibility of future children. Maybe you lost the physical side of your relationship with your spouse. Another past loss is altered lifestyle of the couple or the family. You cannot do the things you did before the illness. You no longer see the people you saw socially due to limitations imposed by the illness. Thus, your pattern of socializing altered from the one you had before the illness.

There are also changes in your physical environment, which produce grief due to the changes you must make. Rooms in your home may have to be rearranged to accommodate a hospital bed. Additional room must be made for medical equipment. Some of your possessions may be displaced to accommodate the needs of the person with the debilitating illness. Health care people are in and out of your home on a regular basis. Your sanctuary is invaded, and you lose privacy. Your grieving process begins as you grieve all these changes to your world.

In the present time of the illness, there are more losses to grieve. It is heartbreaking to see your loved one's health deteriorate. As debilitation increases and their independence decreases, it is painful to watch the process. Because worry is your constant companion, you lose your peace of mind. As control over the life of your loved one and oneself slip away, you grieve the loss of something precious—a sense of independence. If any opportunities come along during this time, which you normally would pursue, there is no time to take advantage of them, so you grieve lost opportunities.

Along with grieving the past and present losses in anticipatory grief, you also grieve the future losses you realize are ahead of you. When you know death is the final outcome of the progression of the illness, you know future hopes, dreams, expectations, and plans with your loved one are lost to you. You dread and grieve the point of lost mobility for the patient. You dread that moment in the future when you will lose him to death. You grieve the loss of the future milestones you will not reach together. You grieve the fact this loved one will not be present to witness any success you may have or any joys, which may come to the family in future years.

Variables Affecting Anticipatory Grief

Just as grief is unique for each mourner, there are many variables, which affect the survivor's anticipatory grief. The first is the nature and meaning of the role the loved one plays in the lives of the family members. The perception of the loved one's role includes the sense of his fulfillment in life. Thus, a person with a dying child may find the grieving more difficult than the grieving for his dying eighty-five-year-old mother. This does not mean one loss is more important than another. It simply means the mourner may perceive the eighty-five-year-old loved one lived a full life and accomplished many of her goals, thus, completing her life. On the other hand, the child had so much life ahead and had great promise, which will not be fulfilled.

The quality of your relationship with the dying loved one also impacts your anticipatory grief. The personality of the loved one and the interactions you had with him strongly affect the feelings you have surrounding the death. It is much harder to think of losing someone who brought joy and happiness than to accept losing someone with whom you experienced a strained relationship. If there was little love and closeness in the relationship, or if the person was always difficult to be around as opposed to enjoyable to be with, that will have a strong impact on your grief.

Another variable influencing anticipatory grief is the personal characteristics of you, the mourner. Your maturity and intelligence levels impact the grief because you may have developed better coping skills than other mourners. Due to maturity, you might have previous experience with illness, death, and loss. Intelligence might help you better understand the illness, treatments, and projected outcomes of the illness; so you had a clearer idea from the beginning of what you and the patient were facing. Your age will have an impact too. Young children and teens do not fully understand the dying process and/or death. However, there are many adults who do not understand this either; but generally speaking, adults are capable of gaining insights, which are harder for young children to grasp. Your sense of self, your confidence level, your ability to be your own person, your flexibility, and your ability to adapt to change all affect your grieving process.

The type of death is another variable affecting the grief. At the time of diagnosis, it is of vital importance to acquire all the information you can about your loved one's illness. You will be his strongest medical advocate, securing the best treatments for him if you know what to do. In order to control your anxiety level as much as possible, it is most helpful to know what to expect. While you can never be completely prepared for the death of your loved one, you can mentally prepare yourself much better if you are knowledgeable about the situation.

Depending on the type of illness your loved one suffered, long-term caregiving may have been required. The availability of help with caregiving makes a huge difference in the impact the death has on the survivor. If the patient remained at home, with little outside support for the main family caregiver, exhaustion and total depletion of the caregiver's energy will take its toll and affect the immediate impact of the loss. Being at home with the patient and having assistance with adequate care can often be the best situation since the family members can do other household chores along with caring for the patient. Traveling back and forth to a care facility can be taxing, and it may deprive the patient of seeing the whole family. Therefore, the patient's location and care for the patient are two large issues impacting impending grief.

My personal situation with my husband's health problems had an unusual combination of many of the situations discussed. Since he lived almost thirteen years after his serious accident and had so many medical complications and surgeries during that time, we experienced many of the emotional distresses talked about in this book. While he did not get to the point of being bedridden during the thirteen years, fifty-five surgeries and too many hospitalizations to count took its toll on both of us. Compounding the problem was the out-of-state traveling involved to secure his medical treatments. Numerous convalescent times at home, with light nursing care from me, was a regular pattern for us. Having a small child and a full-time job along with these responsibilities proved to be quite challenging as a caregiver.

When he died, I found my physical and emotional resources were nearly depleted. I was at the point of exhaustion in both of those areas. The last year of his life, I had numerous health problems, which were related to the high stress levels. I can speak with some authority as to how weary to the bone a caregiver can be when the loved one dies. This is why it is so important to secure as much outside help as possible when faced with a long illness.

A positive, which may come during anticipatory grief, is the chance to talk to your loved one about the impending loss. If you both are open to talking about the illness, you have an opportunity to finish all business between you. You have the opportunity to say all the "I love yous" and the chance to let him know how deeply you care.

When death finally comes, knowledge about it ahead of time does not make the loss any easier. You probably will not be shocked as those experiencing sudden death are, but the pain of separation is still there. In knowing your loved one was at the terminal moment of his life, you had to face him every day with that knowledge. This is a difficult task, and it takes great courage. That courage will now help you as you grieve.

If your loved one had a particularly difficult illness with great suffering, the death may be a welcomed release for you and your loved one. It is excruciating to watch anyone suffer, especially someone you love. However, the relief felt at the death may bring with it guilt for having those feelings. You should not feel guilty. You loved this person and gave unselfishly of yourself to make his last time on earth the best it could be under the circumstances. Feeling relieved his suffering is over does not diminish your love. Who among us wants our loved ones to suffer when hope for recovery is gone?

After a long illness, you are probably exhausted before you even start to face the death, arrangements, visitation, funeral, and grieving process. It takes time to get our own body and mind rested enough to grieve. Some mourners describe it as being tired in spirit. It is an exhaustion of the soul. Allow yourself the time to rest, and take time with your grief. There is no hurry and no time constraint on grief.

Another issue for the survivor following death of this nature is the perception of unfilled time. After things settle down from the initial activities surrounding the loss, you may suddenly find yourself with time on your hands. You may feel as though you do not have enough to do. If you kept a bedside vigil, or were a daily caregiver, a great deal of your time was absorbed with the care of the loved one. When everyone else returns to normal daily activities, you may feel disrupted by your change in routine.

It does not matter if you have a job or not; now the reason for the extra duties you performed daily is gone, so there is a hole in your schedule. If you do have a job, going back to work does take up some of your time; but your extra responsibilities at home no longer exist, leaving spare time for you to fill. It takes a while to adjust to a less rigorous schedule.

The most important goal for healing loss after a long illness to death is to accept all the feeling you have and feel no guilt. You successfully completed a final act of love for your loved one. Now it is time for you to heal yourself physically and mentally. The days ahead may be frightening and challenging. You will feel hopeless, helpless, and full of despair; but that is normal. You are grieving. You are lost and seeking your way. Believe you will eventually find your way. Believe you will once again discover purpose.

In the present time, devote yourself to self-care. Allow yourself the time you need to heal. No marathon runner completes the race in a fast dash. He paces himself, for he knows the race is long and difficult. Pace yourself.

Chapter 6 References

1. Balaswamy, Shantha, Virginia Richardson, and Christine A. Price. 2004. Investigating Patterns of Social Support Use by Widowers during Bereavement. *The Journal of Men's Studies* 13, no. 1 (January): 67-76.
2. Barry, Lisa, M. P. H., Kasl, Stanislav V., PhD., and Holly Prigerson PhD. 2002. Psychiatric Disorders among Bereaved Persons: The Role of Perceived Circumstance of Death and Preparedness for Death. *American Journal of Geriatric Psychiatry* 10, no. August (August): 447-448-457.
3. Bartocci, Barbara. 2000. *Nobody's Child Anymore: Grieving, Caring, and Comforting When Parents Die.* Notre Dame, IN: Sorin Books.
4. Bernstein, Judith R., PhD. 1980. *When the Bough Breaks: Forever after the Death of a Son or Daughter.* Kansas City: MO: Andrews McMeel Publishing.
5. Blair, Pamela, PhD, and Brook Noel. 2000. *I Wasn't Ready to Say Goodbye: Surviving, Coping and Healing after the Sudden Death of a Loved One.* Milwaukee, WI: Champion Press LTD.
6. Bowlby, John. 1982. Attachment and Loss: Retrospective Prospect. *American Journal of Orthopsychiatry* 52 (1980): 664-664-678.
7. Caine, Lynn. 1990. *A Compassionate, Practical Guide to Being a Widow.* New York:NY: Penguin Putnam Inc.
8. Campbell, Scott, and Phyllis R. Silverman. 1996. *Widower: When Men Are Left Alone.* Amityville, NY: Baywood Publishing Co.
9. Carr, Deborah, James S. House, Ronald C. Kessler, Randolph M. Nesse, John Sonnega, and Camille Wortman. 2000. Marital Quality and Psychological Adjustment to Widowhood among Older Adults: A Longitudinal Analysis. *The Journals of Gerontology Series B* 55B, no. 4 (April): 447-446-457.
10. Finkbeiner, Ann K. 1996. *After the Death of a Child: Living with Loss through the Years.* Baltimore, MD: The John Hopkins University Press.
11. Grollman, Earl A. 1974. *Concerning Death: A Practical Guide for the Living.* Boston, MA: Beacon Press.
12. Harwood, Daniel, Keith Hawton, Tony Hope, and Robin Jacoby. 2002. The Grief Experiences and Needs of Bereaved Relatives and Friends of Older People Dying through Suicide: A descriptive and case-control study. *Journal of Affective Disorders* 72, no. 2 (November): 185-184-194.
13. Henderson, John M., Bert Hayslip Jr., and Jennifer K. King. 2004. The Relationship between Adjustment and Bereavement-Related Distress: A Longitudinal Study. *The Journal of Mental Health Counseling* 26, no. 2 (February): 98-105.

14. Johnson, Barbara. 1994. *Mama, Get the Hammer! There's a Fly on Papa's Head: Using Humor to Flatten out Your Pain.* Dallas, TX: Word Publishing.
15. Kamm, Sherrie, Brian Vandenberg. 2001. Grief Communication, Grief Reactions, and Marital Satisfaction in Bereaved Parents. *Death Studies* 25, no. 7 (October): 569-570-582.
16. Kushner, Harold. 2002. *When All You've Ever Wanted Isn't Enough: The Search for a Life That Matters.* New York, New York: Simon and Schuster.
17. Lukas, Christopher, and Henry M. Seiden. 1987. *Silent Grief: Living in the Wake of Suicide.* New York, NY: Macmillan Publishing Company.
18. Meyer, Charles. 1997. *Surviving Death: A Practical Guide to Caring for the Dying and Bereaved.* Mystic, Conn: Twenty-Third Publications.
19. Murphy, Shirley, Clark L. Johnson, Lang Wu, Juan Fan, and Janet Lohan. 2003. Bereaved Parents' Outcomes 4 to 60 Months After Their Children's Deaths by Accident, Suicide, or Homicide: A Comparative Study Demonstrating Differences. *Death Studies* 27, no. 1 (January): 39-40-61.
20. Neeld, Elizabeth Harper, PhD. 2003. *Seven Choices: Finding Daylight after Loss Shatters Your World.* New York, NY: Time Warner.
21. O'Connor, Nancy, PhD. 1984. *Letting Go with Love: The Grieving Process.* Tuscon, AZ: La Mariposa Press.
22. Rando, Therese A. 1996. Complications in Mourning Traumatic Death. In *Living with Grief after Sudden Loss: Suicide, Homicide, Accident, Heart Attack, Stroke.* Bristol, PA: Taylor and Francis.
23. Rando, Therese A. 1986. *Loss and Anticipatory Grief.* Lexington, Mass: Lexington Books.
24. Schiff, Harriet S. 1977. *The Bereaved Parent.* New York, NY: Crown Publishers.
25. Shuchter, Stephen R. 1986. *Dimensions of Grief: Adjusting to the Death of a Spouse.* San Francisco, CA: Jossey-Bass.
26. Staudacher, Carol. 1991. *Men and Grief: A Guide for Men Surviving the Death of a Loved One.* Oakland, CA: New Harbinger Publications.
27. Staudacher, Carol. 1987. *Beyond Grief: A Guide for Recovering from the Death of a Loved One.* Oakland, CA: New Harbinger Publications.
28. Tatelbaum, Judy. 1980. *The Courage to Grieve: Creative Living, Recovery, and Growth through Grief.* New York, New York: Harper Row.
29. Wolfelt, Alan D., PhD. 1992. *Understanding Grief: Helping Yourself Heal.* Muncie: IN: Accelerated Development Inc.

Chapter 7

RESTRUCTURING LIFE AFTER LOSS

The life-restructuring process began with the death of your loved one. You did not notice it because it was not obvious. However, in many subtle ways, every breath you breathed, every step you took, and every decision you made following the death began the process. A familiar life, a life you enjoyed—a life filled with the many ups and downs, joys and sorrows, worries and smiles—ended with the death of such a vital part of it. The scope of the tragedy was not immediately apparent to you and the other survivors. A new beginning started in your life cycle without the sounding of trumpets but with the sigh of a last breath.

Hubert Humphrey, presidential candidate, once said,

> Some people look on any set back as the end. They're always looking for the *benediction* rather than the *invocation*. But you can't quit.

Losing a loved one narrows your focus on the ending. When faced with this ending, or benediction as Humphrey says, you cannot help wanting to quit on life. Society looks at death as the ultimate ending, so it is difficult for survivors to understand, in the early days of loss, a new life chapter is beginning in their lives. The invocation goes unnoticed. With feelings of despair, the reaction most commonly is, "Enough! I quit!"

All sense of normalcy is lost in the early days and weeks of restructure. Well-being becomes a thing of the past. Melancholy sucks you into a mire of despair. The future seems nonexistent, and the contented life you once lived is a dim blur in memory.

Grief is a road trip with no alternative routes. This is a long, tedious trip full of potholes. The pathway to hope for a better life appears to be impossible to find. In the early days of the trip, chaos reigns. Each day is a struggle to gain footing in foreign territory. The only way to get from *where you are* to *where you want to* go is to keep *moving*!

"Exactly where am I?" you may ask. You are in the tri-city area of Depression, Sorrow, and Disappointment. Where do you want to be? During hard times like this, you want to be in Peace Valley. Temporarily, you are lost. What you need are *directions*. That is the purpose of this chapter—to give you directions for restructuring your life after loss. You cannot quit on life because an invocation has been given, and there is much work to do to move forward.

How long will this road trip take? There is no time limit for it. Author Karen Linamen says a watch is useless on a trip such as this. She encourages mourners to use a calendar. Minutes and hours are too infinitesimal to measure progress. It can best be measured in weeks, months, and years.

When discussing adversity and other life experiences, you often hear life compared to a lovely tapestry. The threads form a beautiful picture. It takes many colored threads, bright and dark, to complete the finished pattern. It is the same with your life tapestry. Good times, sad times, happy times, and bad times are patterns woven into the life tapestry. This grief road trip is only one pattern in the tapestry.

When death comes, it rips the fabric of your life tapestry. Just as tears in the artistic tapestries can be repaired, so can the tears in the fabric of your life. It takes tedious work over time to repair the artistic tapestry, and it also takes laborious work to repair the tear in your fabric of life.

Even when rewoven, traces of the tear remain in the tapestry. So it is with the repair of your life. It can be rewoven, but a scar remains. Because of the length of time required and the delicacy of the work, the work of restructuring your life is a job, which will be a work in progress for years to come.

Most people do not realize the inordinate amount of time required for the restructuring process. Studies of bereavement and the time needed for processing the loss show it takes much longer than many professionals previously thought or allowed for normal grief.

Research of the Cocoanut Grove fire in 1942 indicated a serious effect on mourners for six weeks. By the 1960s, studies indicated six months were needed for the effects of loss to diminish. Parke's model in the 1970s gave the process one year. Recent hospice guidelines estimate the process takes two to three years.

Other research indicates traumatic loss such as murder, suicide, and loss of a child requires five to ten years for integration of the loss and restructure. In some cases, more than ten years are required. Also, as indicated by participants in these studies, the pain never totally disappears. It simply becomes more bearable.

Goals of Restructure

As you seek directions on this journey of restructuring, there are three main goals to complete in the process. One is the reorganization of self. Second is integration of the loss. Third is the successful transition to your new life.

Reorganization of Self

The loss of your loved one struck a debilitating blow to your sense of self. Perception of your roles, self-image, purpose, and belief system suddenly seems skewed. Your loved one, to a certain extent, validated your defining qualities. Now that person is gone; and you are left to question your own worth, what you believe, why you are here, and your own mortality. Actions, thoughts, and processes you previously felt very sure about are called into question as you work on this reorganization.

The certainty of the relationship between you and the one who died may be questioned in your mind. Were you as competent as you thought? Did you do all you should have done for the person? Did you show the love you felt? Did you express your feelings to the loved one? Did your loved one trust you? Were you thoughtful enough? Many questions and doubts arise during this period of reevaluating your sense of self and the relationship you shared with your loved one.

Another task in the reorganization of self is to redefine your roles. When the loved one was living, your roles were established and familiar. A comfortable routine developed between the two of you. After the death, the comfortable routine is gone, and chaos rules. Perhaps you have to learn to be single again. Maybe your role as a parent is changed forever.

Even roles, which did not change, are affected by the role changes directly connected to the loss. It is as though you learned a part in a play, only to have the drama changed. You now have a new part and feel you are starting over in learning your lines.

Dealing with the changing roles is a challenge for my clients struggling with bereavement issues. Clients often ask the following question in sessions: "If I am not a _____ (spouse, parent, child, brother, sister, or friend), who am I?" These clients struggle with the transition from a known, comfortable role to defining new roles. A lengthy period of time is required before you change your role with the deceased from a physical to a spiritual placement in your life. The change in placement for your loved one is a major shift in your mind-set.

Self-reorganization requires adjustments in your life purpose. For many mourners, this is the first time life purpose comes under intensive scrutiny. Normally, people do not spend much time thinking about the purpose of life—where man fits into the scheme of things and the reasons for the mysteries of the universe. Death brings the hustle and bustle of daily life to a screeching halt and forces survivors to consider these philosophical matters. Thoughts of this nature require serious soul-searching to determine why you are on this earth, what you are doing with your life, and what you feel you need to do with your life.

As long as you breathe, there is a purpose for your life. After loss, one of the biggest tasks is determining why you must rebuild a new life, even though you may not want to participate in such a building project. Seeking a new direction in life is never easy. It means coming out of your comfort zone and making changes. As the captain of your ship, you normally plot a route and stay the course. But any good sea captain knows there has to be changes in the course at times in order to weather the storms. Life is like that too. You hit a major storm with the death of your loved one. Your course in life requires adjustment in order to weather the storm. Finding purpose is finding hope for the future and resetting your course.

Your belief system is questioned too after a loss. It is normal to have doubts about beliefs you previously held without question. The chapter on spirituality discussed at length finding your purpose and gaining a better understanding of your beliefs. It is important to touch on it again in this chapter because it is such a vital part of self-reorganization. As you reorganize, many of the old patterns will not fit your new life. In order to determine the ones to keep and the ones to change, you must examine and question all the parts of yourself, including your beliefs.

Scrutinizing and questioning your belief system does not mean you turn away from the truths and faith you always held dear. Far from it! Questioning helps you to clarify what you truly believe and to identify how this belief system can be the bedrock upon which you build your new life.

Some people falsely hold the belief if they are good enough, harm will not befall them. Others believe their faith protects them from all evil. Some believe hard work will be rewarded. Many believe success, money, and prestige bring happiness. There are many beliefs of this nature, which are challenged by loss.

Out of this close examination, hopefully, comes the acceptance of some "inevitables" in life. Faith is not a protection from evil. Safety has little to do with being good. Rewards are not always based on hard work. Happiness is often elusive. Life is not fair. It rains on the just and the unjust alike.

Accepting the inevitables in life does not diminish your faith. In fact, it is quite the opposite. It enables you to fully use your belief system to handle these inevitables. Bad things happen in life. When they do, it is important to have faith to sustain you and a system of beliefs and values to give you the tools you need to go forward with your life.

Examination and questioning of your belief system allows you to identify the parts of it, which help you the most in times of trouble. It also encourages you to drop beliefs, which prove to be incorrect or not helpful to you when you put them to the test. Faith is often reconfirmed, but your worldview and the context in which you used your faith may undergo some modifications. You may find your old system was incomplete in some manner, so modifications may include additions to your belief system. Clarifying your beliefs is sustaining when you face difficult times.

Dr. John Bowlby believes it is necessary to discard old patterns of thinking, feeling, and acting before new ones can be established. During the process of selecting and discarding, a redefinition of self occurs. Until the redefining occurs, no plans for the future can be made. You must know yourself—what you need, what you want, and what you want to do with your life—before you can make a blueprint for the future.

Integration of the Loss

Just as the loved one's presence was integrated into your life, his absence must be integrated too. As previously stated, there is no time constraint because this integration is a long process requiring laborious emotional, psychological, and spiritual adjustments.

During the integration process, you are charged with four tasks. First, you have to psychologically reassign the relationship. Second, recognition of the continuity of life helps move you forward. Third, the restoration of order out of chaos gives you a sense of regaining control. Finally, you must change your mind-set from a focus on the past to a forward-thinking focus.

It takes a great deal of time for you to psychologically reassign the relationship. Eventually, a day comes when you realize you survived and your loved one did not. Logically you knew this. It is not a news flash. But for some time after the death, you operated in a temporary living arrangement. Temporary living keeps you from full acceptance of the death. In temporary living, you continue to live as though the loved one is simply away and will return. This prevents you from moving your loved one from the what is to the what was.

Temporary living does not mean you think the loved one is still alive. You know he is dead. Good-byes were said. In your rational mind he is dead. But psychologically, the loved one is still with you. As quoted earlier from Dr. Alan Wolfelt, "You said goodbye in your head. It takes longer to say goodbye in your heart."

When you successfully move the loved one to memories of the past, you take a giant step. When you are able to change your relationship with him from the physical to the spiritual, you take another giant step.

As you successfully reassign the relationship, it brings to you a sense of the continuity of life. This is a peaceful, soothing realization. Realizing the impact of lives lived before you—your loved one's impact and, eventually, the impact of your own life—enables you to see the continuation of life before, during, and after death.

When you are able to make the connection of the meaning of your loved one's life to the continuity of life, you acquire the understanding of how important it is to live life to create meaning for those you will someday leave behind.

Sherwin Nuland, author of *How We Die*, says rabbis often end a memorial service with the sentence *May his memory be for a blessing.* This not only gives dignity to the life lived by the loved one because it emphasizes the lasting impact of his life, but it also provides the mourner with hope. The hope is for the mourner to also achieve such a state of dignity before death. So therein lies hope for the future.

Reassignment of the loved one's life to the past, but understanding the blessing of the life as well as the lasting impact, gives you a reason to go forward with a sense of hope. A life of dignity requires you to live in a manner that creates a legacy for those you will leave behind. Thus, understanding the continuity of life enables you to restructure a new, positive life based on hope.

As integration of the loss progresses, you struggle to bring order to chaos. Chapter 4 discussed the transition between disorganization and reorganization as being one of the most unsettling processes for the mourner. Everything seems out of control and chaotic at this time. It is impossible to believe you will ever feel better or get your life back together.

It is important, when handling chaos, to put margins around your life. When there are no margins, everything is an emergency. When everything is an emergency, your stress level builds, and you become overwhelmed. Putting margins around your life means blocking off areas of your life over which you do have some control and focusing on those areas.

An example of the living in *emergency state* is what happens after most deaths. Your whole routine is disrupted. Not only your routine, but also the routines of your children, family, friends, and coworkers are disrupted. There is no daily schedule. The familiar sameness of your days is gone. There is no peace and solitude in your own home because family and friends are everywhere. Your children are with other people while you take care of pressing obligations. You must deal with details pertaining to the death. Adding to the chaos is the bombardment of questions and requests and people asking you for decisions.

After the funeral, things settle down, but you still do not get your routine back. Putting margins around your life means you start putting boundaries and routines back into your daily living, thus, taking control of the things in your power. You may make a daily plan. If that is too daunting, you might consider a first-hour-of-the-day plan. You zero in on some things you can accomplish each day. You also set boundaries concerning things you do not want to do. This prevents you from being pushed into taking unwanted advice from others by preparing you with action plans ahead of time.

Putting margins around your life by setting a routine and establishing boundaries gives you some breathing space. Perhaps you want an hour a day as alone time. Let everyone know this is when you will not be available to visitors. You will not answer the phone, the door, or deal with intrusions because this is time you need to accomplish grief work. If everyone knows you are okay, but working on yourself by doing something positive, they are likely to honor your request.

When this happens, you have earned a breathing space. You may want to use this time to think, pray, meditate, cry, go for a walk, write in your journal, or sit in your chair and stare at the wall. The important thing is you made a decision to do something positive for yourself.

When chaos seems to be all you see, take a "blessing break." Yes, most of your world does seem to be in utter chaos, but not everything in your world is *terrible*. Consciously taking a break to consider the good things, which you still have, can do a lot to push the smothering feeling of chaos and despair away.

Organizing the chaos is like cleaning a messy house. You have to start somewhere. You cannot do it all at once. You pick one room to start cleaning. In that room, choose one job to complete first. Then you move to the next task, the next, and the next. Soon you have one clean room. If you are tired, you can sit down in the one clean room and feel good about your accomplishment. When you are rested, you tackle the next room. This is the same way you organize the chaos in your life. Take on one task at a time. Rest when you need to rest. Pat yourself on the back for each accomplishment; then tackle the next task.

When you take positive steps to organize the chaos of your life, you are doing something to take responsibility for putting your life back together. The ability to successfully go on with life lies within you, but only you can choose to use that ability. It is a conscious decision.

Another important part of integrating the loss involves looking at another direction. At the time of the loss, and in the early weeks of bereavement, you stand facing the past. Like Moses looking at the Promised Land, you see where you want to be, but you cannot go there. What you must do, which is so difficult, is to turn your back on the past in order to face forward. Naturally, it is not as simple to make this turn as it sounds.

Turning your back on the past does not mean forgetting. It means letting go of the past as a place of permanent residency. You can visit occasionally through memories, but you cannot successfully live for today if you keep yourself focused on the past.

You have the opportunity to travel an exciting journey on the sea of life. However, you cannot set sail if you have one foot in the boat and one foot on the dock. The dock is your past. The boat is your chance to live today and reach for tomorrow. Which one are you choosing?

Letting go means you will always love the one who died. It also means you reassigned him to your past life. He forever lives in your heart, mind, and memory; but that is the only existence he can have in your present and future life. Letting go means you found the appropriate placement for the relationship.

The memories are the opportunities you have to visit your loved one. Just as you go to see family members, friends, and neighbors for a social visit, you can always have a visit with your loved one through memory. Fitting the memories into the appropriate place in your present life is another forward-looking activity.

In *After Goodbye* by Ted Menten, he emphasized the importance of memories. He tells the story of a widow in one of his groups. She attended group meetings a few times but remained detached and did not participate.

One night, the topic was remembering and honoring the loved ones who died. As the discussion progressed, she became agitated and finally broke into the discussion to voice her frustration. She said remembering was a shallow and empty activity. Her words were, "I don't want memories! I want my husband!"

After a stunned silence in the group, another woman answered her. She said to the distressed lady,

> **Not one of us wants to settle for less than the real thing, but the real thing is gone. Margarine isn't the real thing. Butter is. But if there is no butter, then you make do with the next best thing. I don't want my life to be dry toast. I want it covered with rich golden butter. But my butter is gone, and all I have left is the memory of its richness, its pure golden quality, its sweet taste. The margarine of memory will never replace or even approximate the real thing. But it is better than dry toast.**

Looking forward requires you to use margarine when you prefer butter. Looking forward keeps the rest of your life from being dry toast.

Looking forward, instead of backward, includes seeing opportunities in your life. The death closed the door on the past, but when that door closed, another opened. Your dilemma is finding the courage to walk through the new door. Opportunity means a choice has to be made. Refusing to cross over the threshold of opportunity is to wither in spirit and to become bitter. Crossing the threshold is choosing to live.

Every opportunity means saying good-bye to something familiar and saying hello to something new. I have the advantage of looking back twenty-six years since the death of my husband. It was a terrible loss. So much was lost forever. However, hindsight shows me the reality of the doors, which opened for me each and every time another door closed in my life. Relocation, losing friends, losing loved ones, educational pursuits, career changes, and the ever-changing family circle not only brought pain and sad good-byes but also opportunities for growth. I found, as you will too, life is one long series of good-byes and hellos. You can deal with the good-byes by retreating into bitterness and despair, or you can focus on the hellos by walking forward into the future.

Successful Transition to New Life

The ultimate goal of restructure is to successfully transition into the new life, which started for you upon the death of your loved one. Whether you suffer the death of someone you love or some other loss, you soon learn transition is the norm rather than the exception. Life is full of give-and-take. You constantly have things come into your life, which enrich it with their presence. You also lose many things for which you mourn.

The things that enrich your life are cherished gifts. They are precious because even when they are gone, the memory of their richness lingers to bring memories of beauty and joy to your waking moments.

Chaim Potok says of these cherished gifts: "Something that is yours forever is never precious."

This is one reason losing your loved one hurts so much. You lost something precious. It was precious because it was never meant to be forever. Now you are called to make the transition into a new life without this cherished gift. This is a monumental hurdle for the mourner. It is understandable to find so many people struggling with this process.

Life constantly tests each of us for perseverance and endurance. Adversity makes some people better and causes others to crumble. This can be observed throughout history in the struggles of man over adversity. What is it that creates strength in some people but is sorely lacking in others?

Observe in nature the way extreme pressure on coal produces a diamond but on sandstone produces pebbles. What makes the difference between producing a diamond and producing a pebble? In nature, it has to do with the substance and strength of the mineral. In life, it has to do with the substance and strength of the person. In life, it is courage. Life is constantly a test of courage.

After experiencing tragedy, reentering the mainstream of life as a fully functioning person requires courage and the changing of maladaptive behaviors. These two actions intertwine because changing behaviors is such a monumental task. It requires all the strength and courage you possess to make the changes required.

You may think you do not possess the courage to make this life transition. Perhaps you consider courage as something unattainable for the average person. When difficult times come, courage to face them simply means giving your best effort to do something even though it may seem impossible. Your first inclination may be to run away—to hide from life. The problem with this choice is the less action you take, the more you feel controlled by the situation. Feeling controlled produces fear, anxiety, and feelings of helplessness. Giving your best effort to actually *do* something lessens these negative feelings. This is courage.

Courage is needed to restore your functioning ability. Others may offer a helping hand, but you have to exert the courage to reach out to take it. There are many steps to take before functioning normally again, but you must have the courage to take the first step. Courage helps you regain your balance. Slowly but surely, your topsy-turvy world begins to right itself because you summon the courage to stand up and begin work on the chaos.

Courage gives you the ability to change your focus. Gradually, your focus turns from the loved one's death to his life. Courage turns the constant thoughts of loss and sadness to memories of pleasurable times with the loved one. Courage gives you back the joy of sharing his life.

As you think about the joy of your loved one's life and the impact he left, you come to the realization of the part you played in the relationship and how much time you spent on it. The time you devoted to the relationship weighs heavily on your hands. For a period of time after the death, this surplus of time brings restlessness and the feeling you need to be doing more with your hours. Courage gives you the ability to reinvest the time to make the most positive impact you can on your own life and the life of others.

Tremendous strength and courage are needed to change maladaptive behaviors. In the face of death, you do not suddenly develop a whole new mode of behavior. You react the way you learned to react to earlier losses in your life. Starting with small losses and moving to bigger disappointments in life, you learn ways to cope with loss.

Think about the way you reacted to previous traumas in your life. Did you withdraw and isolate yourself? Did you seek the help of others? Did you turn to negative behaviors such as excessive drinking, taking needless medications, using drugs, excessive shopping, or overeating? The coping skills you relied on to deal with past traumas will surface again with the biggest loss in your life—the death of someone you love.

If you developed positive coping skills, you will most likely use positive actions to deal with your loss. Unfortunately, if you have negative coping skills, you may slide into using those negative behaviors again. This is where great courage comes into the picture. It takes courage to change from maladaptive behaviors to positive behaviors.

If you ever needed courage in your life, this is the time for it. Your reactions to the loss are magnified because the loss is so huge. Developing positive ways to deal with these magnified reactions takes determination, courage, and perseverance on your part to be successful in this transition.

The first negative behavior to overcome is your ambivalent attitude toward living. Eventually, there will come a day for you to make a decision to heal. As stated earlier, there is no exact time to say when this will happen. It will happen when you *choose* to live.

Some bereaved parents said they did not exactly choose to live in the beginning of their loss. They simply chose not to die. However, in this part of the restructuring of your life, a *conscious* choice to live has to be made, and only you can do this. You said the physical good-bye at the time of death. Now it is time to say the emotional good-bye. Making a decision to live gives you permission to heal. Choosing to heal avoids living a lifetime of grief.

The second maladaptive behavior to change is the persistent questioning. This was covered in the discussion on the phases of grief. While questioning is a normal phase of the grieving process, as you reach the transition into fully functioning again in life, you have to give up the questioning behavior.

It is important for you to ask all the questions you need to ask about the facts of the death. The how, when, where, and any other important data you can gather to help you understand exactly what happened can be helpful. If you do not know all there is to know about the death, these questions may haunt you for years. These are the easy questions because you are seeking factual information about the death.

The hard questions are those that have no answers. These questions must be dropped. Carrying them throughout the rest of your life is like carrying a heavy suitcase 24/7. These unanswerable questions weigh you down and bring on exhaustion. These questions are not searching for the factual answers of how, where, and what but ask the eternal question, why?

Why was my loved one taken? Why didn't he take another way home? Why did I allow him to go on the trip? Why didn't I kiss him good-bye? Why do such awful things happen? Why didn't he go to the doctor sooner? Why are we being punished? These are questions about the life experience. Even if there were an answer to the why question, it would not help you with the deep hurt of separation.

A beautiful poem, which illustrates the uselessness of this eternal question asked by legions of mourners, is called "The Weaving."

The Weaving

My life is but a weaving between my Lord and me,
I cannot choose the colors, He weaveth steadily.
Sometimes, He weaveth sorrow, and I in foolish pride,
Forget He sees the upper and I the underside.
Not 'til the loom is silent, and the shuttle cease to fly,
Shall God unroll the canvas and explain the reason why.
The dark threads are as needful in the weaver's skillful hands,
As the ones of gold and silver in the path that He has planned.

The question of why is unanswerable at this point. You cannot see the whole picture. Looking at it from the underside merely presents a one-sided view. The dark threads, which hurt so deeply at the time of loss, cannot fit into your perception of life.

As the poem points out, you see the weaving of your life from the vantage point of *this* world. Warren Wiersbe, in his book *God Isn't in a Hurry*, admonishes each person to remember this is the vantage point from which you view the world and your life. You can only live life one world at a time. God views your life from kingdom come. You are based in the here and now, but God is based in eternity.

The lines in the poem, "Not 'til the loom is silent and the shuttle cease to fly, Shall God unroll the canvas and explain the reason why," tell you the day you arrive at kingdom come, answers to the many why questions will be given.

My thought is, "Will it really be so important at that point?" When you arrive in kingdom come, you will view the pattern from the upper side, and the weaving will make perfect sense. Looking at the weaving from this world and looking at it from eternity are two very different vantage points.

A third type of maladaptive behavior exhibited by some mourners is victimization and/or martyrdom behaviors. Fortunately, not all mourners fall into this pattern of behavior; but for those who do, this behavior becomes a major roadblock to the restructuring process.

Falling into the victim role during bereavement and staying there creates intense feelings of helplessness. This behavior is not referring to the feeling of being a victim if your loved one died a violent death. This behavior is exhibited by mourners who see the adversity of death as an affront to them personally and react by wallowing beyond normal bounds of grieving. The victim mentality does not allow the mourner to make any choices to take action for improvement. It can lead to self-pity and neediness on the part of the mourner, which eventually pushes other people away.

Victim behavior is often seen in mourners who previously used this behavioral reaction during other crisis periods of life. The payoff for this behavior pattern is it allows the mourner to continue to make others responsible for the victim's life. The victim avoids self-responsibility by drawing into the comfortable cocoon of helplessness and letting others carry the load. Victim behavior aids the mourner in remaining lost in the maze of grief. If there were an exit sign for the maze, these mourners would not follow it.

Martyred behavior shares some patterns with the victim behavior. Martyrs enjoy the attention of others. They too do not look for the exit from their suffering. Both of these maladaptive behaviors are difficult to change because the people exhibiting them are adept at deflecting any and all suggestions or plans to assist them in moving forward. These are the "yes, but" people in help groups and therapy. Any solution presented is met with a "yes, but" reason for why it will not work.

There are some differences in these negative behavior patterns. Martyrs are the people who are not happy unless they are unhappy. Yes, they are suffering, but suffering is one thing they know because they are adept at creating suffering scenarios in their lives. This is not to say the initial loss did not bring true suffering to them. The loss to them is devastating, but it also provides them the opportunity to turn grieving into their lifework.

A martyred mourner will not give up grief without intensive help. Suffering is worn as a badge of honor. A martyr in support group will practice one-upmanship with everyone else in the group. The martyr's grief is more intense, harder to cope with, and worse than anyone else's pain—according to the martyr. You can never suffer enough to top his suffering.

Unlike the victims, who make others responsible for them, the martyrs make others *think* they are responsible for them; but in reality, the martyr is in control. This is seen in the deflection of any solutions, which would resolve the situation. I frequently observed this behavior while working with spouses of alcoholics.

Another example of the underlying control issues with martyrs came from working with these alcohol-related groups. When I worked with family groups dealing with addiction issues, I observed some couples divorced when the spouse became sober. At first, this was surprising and puzzling to me. It did not make sense to leave the marriage once the issue of alcohol was resolved by recovery.

As I continued to work in this area of counseling, I began to realize the impact the alcoholic's recovery had on the spouse and other family members. There were major control issues at work in these relationships once the alcoholic entered recovery. The martyred nondrinking spouse had tremendous control of the family during the drinking days of the alcoholic. Although the load of responsibility was heavy, it also put the responsible spouse in control of the household. The nonaddicted spouse and the children controlled the home environment. Sobriety caused the recovering alcoholic to be able to assume leadership roles in the family again, and this created problems with not only the spouse but with the children. No one wanted to give up control. I found martyrs could be intense *control freaks.*

Martyrs are often *repeat offenders.* By this I mean if a martyr is relieved of the difficult situation, which brings so much suffering, he will sooner or later become enmeshed in another situation fraught with chaos, problems, and suffering. Working with spouses of alcoholics in my practice provided good examples of this behavior. On several different occasions, I had the opportunity to work with women married to alcoholics who suffered this maladaptive behavior. A few of them divorced, and one experienced the death of her husband. Sometime later, these women appeared in family group again, having remarried another alcoholic.

Some caregivers exhibit this martyr behavior also. After caring for a spouse with a debilitating illness and spending years in the demanding role, some caregivers end up in another caregiving situation after the spouse's death.

I observed this firsthand while visiting support groups for caregivers sponsored by a religious organization. The group of fifteen people had four who were in a second round of rigorous caregiving due to remarriage. This is not to say every person who ends up in more than one caregiving situation is a martyr. However, in talking to some of these people, I observed the tendency to dwell on their own problems more than offering help for others.

One woman, in particular, seemed to relish talking incessantly about her situation without regard to the feelings and needs of the others in the group. She gave many reasons for not accepting help from community resources and appeared to relish how much she was required to do for her patient. She also referred several times to her past experience in taking care of a loved one. She seemed to get great satisfaction from being needed so much in the caregiving role.

Behaving as a victim and/or a martyr is a seductive behavior. It pulls you into an emotional trap. Once in the trap, it is hard to pull yourself loose. You cannot allow yourself to wallow in the negativity of the trap. Consciously reminding yourself you do not have to stay in this trap is one way of pulling loose. Taking an action, making a step, refusing to feel sorry for yourself, and reaching outside yourself to help someone else are all positives ways to pull loose from the trap of this maladaptive behavior.

The final maladaptive behavior, which must be changed in order to restructure your life, is the attitude of negativity. Negativity contributes to the helplessness of the victim behavior. Negativity produces a give-up attitude, which undermines your ability to take control of your life. This attitude fosters learned helplessness. No forward thinking takes place because the continued focus is on how helpless you are in your particular situation. As long as you have the behavior pattern of negativity, you will never be able to develop the courage needed to reassert a degree of control over your destiny.

Not only does negativity interfere with the development of courage, it neutralizes hope. Negativity tells you all is lost. Your life is over. You will never be happy again. Cherry Harlman said,

> If your dreams fall apart, sweep up the pieces and save them. Slivers of hope can be found in the debris of shattered dreams.

Negativity encourages you to throw away the pieces of your broken dreams because dreams are a part of the past, never to be recaptured. If you throw the pieces away, you are withdrawing from the world, saying the joy in life is over and will never return. Taking the slivers of the dreams and using the hope in them enables you to dream new dreams. If you dreamed once, you can dream again. As long as you have life, you can have dreams. Joy is not a one-time event in your life. The behavior of negativity convinces you it is.

Changing from negativity to positivity is seizing the initiative. When you make this change, you resolve to do something about your life. This is the remedy to negativity. The remedy is not in the success but in taking the steps.

Change and the Restructure of Life

Great changes in your life must be made in order to meet the goals of restructure. Change is one process humans universally dislike. We are creatures of habit. We become familiar with certain patterns of behavior and intensely dislike the suggestion to change any of them. There is great comfort in familiar patterns and routines. Examples of resistance to change can be found in the workplace, in houses of worship, in social activities, in marriages, and in families. If you want to upset a group of people, enter the room and announce, "There are going to be some changes made."

Immediately, the response whether it is spoken or not is, "How will this change affect me?" The challenge change presents to most people can be frightening and overwhelming. It brings forth the words *different*, *new*, and *adjustment*. Hearing these words, each person considers first and foremost the impact the change will have on his functioning. Replacing old ways of doing things with new methods creates anxiety.

What Change Represents

Using the word *change* as an acronym helps to better understand why it is such a frightening word. As I dealt with the change in my life after the death of my husband, I found change brought me *challenge, heartache, anxiety, new life, grief, and endings.* These six components of change encapsulate the variety of stressors brought about by change.

Death is a tremendous disruptive change in the life of the survivor. It poses a threat to your stability. Therein lies the *challenge.* Death brings a tragedy, which twists and disrupts your entire life. You have not only the death to resolve but also the many other disruptions rippling from the death like falling dominoes. As though losing an important person in your life is not enough of a change to make, you also must deal with changing relationships, different family schedules, changing finances, and, often, changing your location.

The challenge to you is to garner the strength and the wisdom to enable you to rise to meet the demands of change. Tragedy strikes in the life of each person sooner or later. How you deal with your particular tragedy, and the changes brought about by it, determines your outcome. The death itself presents a major challenge. However, many more challenges spring forth from the death. You can no longer function in the old routine. Your schedule is not predictable. Some old parts of the routine are gone, and in their place are new routines. This puts you in the position of *learning* new behaviors, rituals, and patterns.

Learning and implementing new concepts presents everyone with a challenge. During my teaching career, I observed students liked doing the things they did well. They felt confident and sure in the processes and felt in control of their success. Their attitude was one of progressive confidence.

However, when a new concept was presented, no matter the intelligence level of the students, the reaction was universal across groups. The students became distressed and less sure of their abilities. They became anxious and needy, requiring much more assistance. When the new concepts were implemented, the students were challenged to do something different; thus, stress and distress rose to a higher level. This was the time the most complaints were registered about not liking the class. This was the time I could count on a great deal of moaning and groaning to ensue when work began on that particular concept.

The insight I tried to instill in the students was when they were doing a task repeatedly, and doing it well, they were not learning. Once they attained the skill of performing well on a particular concept, they were merely practicing the skill. When a new concept was presented, they could no longer stay in the comfort zone of practice but had to step into a new zone of learning. That was new territory. In order to learn the new information, they were required to try alternative solutions numerous times until they integrated the new learning into their database.

After the concept was learned, the students practiced it until they felt comfortable with it and could use it with ease. The transition between learning and practice was the challenging part of the process for them. It was also the time there was growth in their education.

This is like the challenge brought by grief. You, like the students, are asked to stop doing the daily familiar routines. The major life change requires you to enter new territory and learn new behaviors, routines, and interactions. This is the time you feel the least confident and the most vulnerable. This is the time you may stumble and not perform well. This is the testing time of trial and error until you find what works for you. This is the challenge of change. When you met the challenge and master the new ways, you have experienced growth.

Because change means letting go of some or all of the old in order to successfully integrate the new, there is *heartache*. No one knows this better than the mourner. The change brought by death brings heartache so intense you think your heart is broken, never to heal. The many types of death discussed in chapter 6 bring their own special brand of heartache. The heartache in loss is due to the death of someone precious and the many changes the loss brings.

Many behaviors described in the grieving process fit the description of heartache, as it relates to change. There is heartache in saying good-bye. There is heartache in the empty place at the table. There is heartache in the changed family celebrations. There is heartache in the changed goals and dreams you had together. Your changed life, due to death, begins with heartache.

As you think about the challenges and heartaches you face, you can readily see why there is so much *anxiety* attached to change. Facing the unknown is daunting. Few people like to live on the edge. Most people like for their daily routines to be predictable in order to know ahead of time how to act and react. Although you may feel you are in a rut, your rut is a comfort zone.

Anxiety is the residue of fear. Fear commonly accompanies change. Not knowing whether or not you can handle the tasks ahead of you creates fear of your competence. From this fear comes anxiety. Change pushes you into new areas of unexplored territory. You will be forced to make new plans, perform new tasks, and realign your direction. You may be required to think outside the box. Change pushes you to find solutions to new problems. You cannot stay in your comfortable rut. New track must be laid! This in unknown territory, and it brings with it fear of failure. Therefore, you become anxious.

Change of any type brings with it *new life*. This is exactly what the death of your loved one did. This new life is the very reason you are in the restructuring process. As any mother who experienced labor can tell you, the birth of new life comes with a great deal of pain. Just as the mother looks at the child and considers it worth the pain to have the new life in her presence, it is hoped you will someday look at your restructured life and realize you once again have joy.

Your new life is not immediately joyful. That is what the restructuring process is about. Change is moving you from the painful beginning of your new life through a long and difficult process to reach reorganization and normal functioning ability. This new life must first gain some stability, then establish new patterns and relationships, realign old relationships, and, eventually, reach a return of the sense of normalcy. Progress in becoming more comfortable in the new life is slow and gradual.

This new life is like coming home with a new pair of shoes. At first, they do not seem to fit as well as the old ones. They feel stiff, awkward, and unfamiliar. It takes a great deal of walking around in the shoes before they begin to feel right. New shoes require you to break them in before they feel right on your feet. This is the way the new life brought by change affects you. It is stiff, awkward, and unfamiliar. It takes a great deal of walking around in the new life before you gain a sense of comfort and normalcy.

The change in restructuring your life also brings *grief.* The grief is for the many good-byes you are required to say. Good-bye to the physical presence of your loved one. Good-bye to the old life. Good-bye to some friends. Good-bye to many hopes, plans, and dreams. Any change means something becomes different. If it is different, obviously, some things with which you are familiar no longer exist. Because these things and/ or people were important to you, grief comes with the change brought with good-bye.

The final letter in change represents the *endings*, which accompany all changes. You are restructuring your life because an ending occurred. This ending changed everything for you. There is an old saying, "All good things must come to an end." This is true with life, but you are never ready for good things to be over. Life being as it is, it is unrealistic to think good things will last forever. However, it is important to understand two things about endings. The first is just as good times end, so do bad times. There is great hope in that thought. While this seems to be the most terrible unending pain ever, someday it will lessen. Someday it will get better. The second thing to understand about endings is with every ending, a beginning follows.

Life has a way of moving us on, whether or not we want to move. What we find as we make the journey is what seems to be the benediction turns out to also bring an invocation. Endings are not really endings but new beginnings. New beginnings always take great courage.

Reactions to Change

Life is full of changes. Change is one constant. The essence of life itself means change is an ongoing process. From the day you are born, you begin to move toward death. No matter the length of the journey, you will go through many changes along the way. Change is a normal life process. Since it is such a normal life process, many of the changes occurring on a daily basis are so subtle you do not notice them taking place.

You do not become aware of the changing of life until you are caught up in a major change. Suddenly, a child is old enough to drive. Children leave home and go away to school. Perhaps the children marry and establish their own homes, leaving you with an empty nest. Jobs change. Maybe your partner asks for a divorce. The house burns, destroying everything you own. You or a loved one becomes seriously ill. It is these changes that bring forth feelings of worry and distress. These are changes that make us stand up and take notice. These type of changes give *change* a bad name. You feel threatened in some way. You feel fearful; therefore; change takes on a negative connotation.

Change is upsetting because most people have the erroneous belief life is fairly stable. They ignore what is right before their eyes—the ever-changing world. When a tragedy strikes, it destroys this belief in a stable world, as well as the person's sense of equilibrium.

Several years ago, my minister preached on the subject of life changes. One of the illustrations he used stuck in my mind all these years. He spoke about being prepared for death and how people ignore the daily signs of fleeting time and increasing frailty. This is the story he told:

> Death came to a man's door to take him away. The man answered the knock and saw it was Death. Death told the man it was time for him to go. The man told Death it couldn't be time yet. He added he couldn't go with Death because he was not ready. Death, arriving so unexpectedly, gave him no time to prepare himself to leave.

> Death saw a mirror on the wall in the foyer and led the man to it. Death said, "You did not know I was coming? Look in the mirror. Did you not notice the thinning of your hair? What about the white streaks? Did you not notice they began to outnumber the dark? See how you lean forward to closely look into the mirror? I notice you are wearing very strong glasses. Did you not notice your failing eyesight? Look at your skin. Is it not beginning to wrinkle? As you walked toward the mirror, I noticed a shuffle in your step. Look at your hands. See the swollen joints?

> You say this is sudden, and you did not know I was coming. I say to you, I have been on my way for some time. You were given many signs I was getting closer to your door. The changes were in front of you all the time. You simply chose to ignore them.

This story stuck with me because it illustrates the many changes taking place in us and around us on a daily basis. It also illustrates the finiteness of life. Life does not last forever. Things do not stay the same. Change is a daily part of life, and man's task is to continue with life after change takes place. You have no choice about whether or not change will take place. You do have a choice as to how you will react to it.

Nancy O'Connor, in *Letting Go with Love*, discusses four possible responses to change. When death enters your life, you respond in one or more of these ways. As you go through the phases of grief, you may respond in one way at one point, then later exhibit another response.

Hopefully, you will restructure your life to integrate changes due to loss in positive ways.

1. Conservation

Responding to change by practicing conservation is to be resistant to the change. You struggle to maintain the old lifestyle and try to live in the past, which is seen as safe territory. The more time passes after the death, the more perfect your past life appears to you. You begin to idealize the past and the person who no longer is with you. There is a tendency to isolate from others because to interact with people would require you to step away from the past.

It becomes increasingly difficult to understand the death. The need to blame someone else becomes strong. If there is someone to blame, there is a reason the death occurred. You stay focused on the death instead of focusing on life. This reaction keeps you stuck in the past, which cannot exist in the present. It keeps you from moving forward with the restructuring process.

2. Revolution

This reaction to change manifests itself in a sudden rejection of former values and beliefs. The mourner revolts against the familiar and denies the present pain. Former providers of stability may be shunned because deep down, the mourner feels these were a sham. The reaction to change in this manner indicates the mourner is disappointed in the values, beliefs, and other stabilizing factors he relied on before the loss. In his mind, these things let him down. "What's the use?" may be the attitude of the revolution response.

While the revolution response is not one of talking about or expressing feelings, the feelings are exhibited through various ways. The mourner may exhibit bursts of energy and throw himself into work or some project with energy and zeal. He may develop a frantic social whirl. He may stay on the go constantly. He does nothing in moderation and goes overboard investing time in various pursuits.

Repressing feelings, he denies the pain he feels. He may react to others in angry and aggressive ways. He may be short-tempered, impatient, and irritable. He may express negative views about the future and develop a cynical "live for the moment" attitude.

The rejection of former beliefs and values brings about drastic changes in personality. The mourner who was normally a quiet worship-attending person may develop a party hardy demeanor. He may quit attending worship, go on the party circuit, and become involved in risky behaviors.

Reacting to change by revolution means the mourner feels the change challenges everything he believed. He is angry, fearful, and ready to throw caution to the wind. Unlike in conservation—which seeks safety in the past—in revolution, the mourner turns outward, but with a "damn the future" attitude. The sense of being betrayed by the stabilizing factors of his life causes him to turn away from them in rebellion. Without the security of these stabilizing beliefs, and the inability to establish new ones, the mourner is isolated with his pain and cannot restructure in a healthy manner.

3. Escape

The escape reaction to change is an avoidance behavior. The mourner who responds with this reaction turns to either chemical or behavioral alternatives. The goal is to withdraw from the present existence. The mourner wants someone else to take over the responsibility of his life. He does not want to deal with the changes.

Some of the addictive patterns, which may emerge in escape, are alcohol, drugs, food, sleep, sex, gambling, and/or shopping. The addiction provides the mourner with escape from directly dealing with the issues at hand. The addiction provides a temporary sense of comfort.

If the mourner does not exhibit addictive behavior, he may exhibit other alternative escape behaviors. One of these behaviors is joining a cult or a cultlike organization. While not a cult, some rigid religions have a strict organization, which rules all aspects of the followers' lives. These religions may appeal to the mourner in the escape mode. Feeling insecure and needy, the mourner wants someone to take over the responsibility about how to live life. A cult or rigidly structured religious organization meets that need.

Another alternative behavior seen in mourners who deal with change by using the escape response is hypochondria. One physical illness after another meets the mourner's need for attention and the need to have someone else be responsible for his life. Basking in the attention, care, and concern focused on him provides comfort for the mourner and allows him to continue to be dependent on others.

The behaviors discussed earlier in this chapter concerning victims and martyrs fall into the escape method of handling change. These behaviors are negative responses to the changes required in new life. The central theme for both of these is for attention to be focused on the mourner. The mourner enjoys the rescue attempts made by others but will reject all solutions. People using these behaviors are adept in deflecting responsibility.

The escape mourner needs professional help to develop more positive coping skills. What is needed is self-discipline and self-control. While these goals require the mourner's commitment, he may not be able to achieve these two goals on his own. If the practice of escape is a lifelong established coping method for the mourner, he will need help in learning to be a survivor.

4. Transcendence

Transcendence is a healthy way to respond to change. This requires the mourner to be open to change and willing to be more flexible. The commitment is to the here and now. The past is the past. It is over and cannot be changed. If the mourner can see the past from this viewpoint, a great deal of angst is avoided because he is not tied to the "shoulda, oughta, woulda" mentality.

With this reaction to change, the mourner does not dwell on the future to the point of constant worry. Just as the mourner realizes he cannot change the past, he realizes he has no way of knowing the future, so he chooses to live in the present. With this focus, the mourner becomes involved in life as it unfolds. This requires confidence and trust in your own capabilities.

Transcendence requires the mourner to drop fear of failure and the unknown and replace it with confidence in his ability to survive. People who are able to do this developed positive coping skills early on in life. Positive coping skills are strengthened with each crisis arising in life. Since mourners learn to mourn, beginning as children with small losses, if positive coping skills are learned along the way, the ability to withstand what life dishes out is greatly improved.

When you suffer loss and are faced with the changes you must put in place in order to restructure, you may jump back and forth among these four reactions. Hopefully, you will not remain in the first three. Most people use some of the first three before they can hope to move into the fourth reaction.

Resistance to Change

Fear is a very strong emotion associated with change. Author Barbara Johnson says of fear:

> "Fear is the darkroom where negatives are developed." When you fear, you are not joyful. Fear gives birth to negativity. Negativity takes the joy from life.

Resistance to change is an extremely negative behavior. It is responsible for much of the stress and unhappiness in daily life. Surviving adversity depends on your ability to adapt. If you cannot adapt to changing situations, you are at a distinct disadvantage. The rewards in life do not go to the strong and the brave but to the *adaptable*. If you are resistant to change, you greatly diminish your chance to survive adversity.

The three horsemen of resistance are fear, impatience, and inflexibility. These three can and will create havoc in your life by preventing you from seeking solutions to your problems. Forms of these three behaviors are seen in the change reactions of conservation, revolt, and escape.

The fear of change makes many people dig in their heels and refuse to move forward. Fear is paralyzing and prevents you from taking positive action. It undermines your self-esteem, your feelings of self-worth, and your confidence.

Wearing blinders of fear keeps you focused on the dangers of the unknown. They also block out the view of the many possibilities, which reside in the new life ahead of you. If you resist change out of fear, you are relegating your life to mere existence when you could be fully living.

Impatience is another form of resistance to change. When actions are familiar to you, you can complete tasks much quicker than you can when you are changing your procedure. Lacking the patience to make the adaptations needed is one reason for people to be so resistant to change. This goes back to the difference between learning and practicing. Once you learn something, it is easier and faster to accomplish the task because in reality, you are practicing a learned procedure. It is the learning with the starts and stops and trials and errors that is tedious, lengthy, time-consuming, and annoying. During the learning period, patience is required.

Patience is very important when implementing changes. Being impatient is a detriment to the process of change. The hardest place to be patient is in the furnace of suffering. You have questions. You demand explanations. You cannot wait to see the fulfilled promise of life. You want to get through this grief thing, get past it, and get on with life; but you find it is not quite that simple.

Restructuring your life after loss can be compared to rebuilding New Orleans after hurricane Katrina. It did not happen overnight. In fact, it is still a work in progress and will be for many years to come. You will not work through all the issues relating to your loss quickly. There are so many changes, which spiral off from the loss; the restructuring project will be long and tedious. Patience helps you to stay in the moment and deal with the here and now.

In this fast-paced world, many people want quick fixes for the problems, which ail them. I call this the "McDonald's drive-through solution." Bereavement issues, addiction problems, marriage problems, family problems, and the many other issues people seek counseling to resolve take time. This is one of the hardest concepts to get patients to accept. You did not get into this problem situation overnight, and you will not resolve it overnight. It takes patience and a commitment to long-term hard work. Wolfelt says of change: "Change is not a one-time event. It is a process." Being a process, successful implementation of the changes you need in your life is not possible if you are impatient.

Inflexibility is another trait of resistance to change. There is a saying, "A tree, which does not bend in the wind, will surely break." This exemplifies what inflexibility can do to a person. If you will not bend, you will break! Inflexibility is difficult to deal with when counseling people to make changes in their lives. Not only the inflexibility on the part of the person coming to counseling, but also the inflexibility of others impacted by the issue, produces a wide range of life problems.

In Warren Wiersbe's book, he quotes A. W. Tozer in talking about inflexible people and the difficulty this rigidity brings to their lives. Tozer calls this attitude a "file card mentality." He describes it as this:

> A file card mentality is a mindset that categorizes everything in life as on neat file cards. Then, rarely are there any changes made in the file.
>
> —A. W. Tozer

The person covers this file card mentality with the cloak of responsibility and promotes the inflexibility as doing the responsible thing and not taking risks, which could endanger the status quo. Change is avoided by inflexible rigidity, which stifles growth.

Inflexibility is about control. Some call it stubbornness. Some call it tunnel vision. Some call it strong will. Some call it selfishness. Whatever label is given to it, it creates havoc, many times unnecessarily, in the lives of those who have to deal with it.

In the business world, an inflexible person in a position of leadership can stifle growth of the business and create numerous problems for those who work under his domain. Good business professionals know changes must constantly be taking place inside the business organization to meet the demand of the changing world. If an organization does not change as much on the inside as the world on the outside changes, it is doomed to become obsolete. Inflexibility to change brings death to the business. Like a successful business, you must be changing as much as the world around you, or you will become a dinosaur. You know what happened to the dinosaurs!

If you are inflexible, changing your life to integrate the loss of your loved one is a monumental task for you. Even the word *restructure* denotes change. If you refuse to change, your life stagnates. There will be no growth in your life as long as you hold inflexibly to your old life. When your loved one was alive, you were called on to make changes in your life along the way. Your ability or inability to accomplish those changes dictated whether or not life ran smoothly for you.

One of the stumbling blocks for newly married couples, which produces an influx of office visits for counseling, is the first major holiday together. You can guess what happens. Each family wants the couple at high noon on the special day to celebrate with them, and neither family will bend one inch to compromise. Inflexibility at its height of glory is the rule of the day. If working out holidays among family members is a problem, you can only imagine the difficulty of implementing the changes in life due to a death.

Somewhere early in life, rigid, inflexible people stopped growing. They reached a certain point; then exploration, creativity, and zest for life disappeared. I have counseled clients so rigid in their actions they are truly stuck trying to figure out the restructuring process. When I run across someone like this, I am reminded of a cartoon of a tombstone I once saw which said, "Died at 40. Buried at 80." This is what happens in the lives of some people. Inflexibility denies them the possibility of truly living life to its fullest and experiencing all it has to offer. Inflexibility takes the heart out of new opportunity, making it impossible to reach healing.

Benefits of Change

Although change is viewed by most people as threatening, there are benefits to changes in life. I could not see any benefits in the changes in my life after the loss of my husband. That was because I was too close to the changes to see the benefits. Now, years distant from the loss, I can look at the changes I had to make in restructuring and see there were benefits tucked away like secret gifts.

Change brings possibilities, opportunities, and growth. In the beginning of your grief journey, you are not ready to look for these nor are you ready to accept them if they present themselves to you. Pamela Blair speaks of being bogged down in the "molasses of grief." This is a good description of the difficulty of pulling yourself through the grieving process. As long as you are bogged down in the molasses, each and every step is a difficult and tiring process. As Abraham Lincoln said of General McClellan's military movements in the civil war, you have a "bad case of the slows."

Eventually, you exit the molasses bog with its accompanying "slows" and are ready to implement the changes necessary for restructure. As you do this, you begin to see windows of possibilities, doors of opportunities, and room for growth. This does not mean you lose the feeling of loss. It means you begin to focus more on the new life the loss brought to you.

Nine years after her loss, Pamela Blair said,

> I still feel the loss. I also feel the new life it gave me. In every loss there is a hidden possibility. It stays hidden until one shakes it loose—like the lost sock that ends up in the corner of the newly washed fitted sheet. It's there—you just need to ruffle up that sheet a bit and out it comes.

Personal experience taught me there were hidden possibilities in the loss of my spouse. As I struggled to restructure, I found freedom in a way I never experienced before the loss. I never had the opportunity to live on my own since I married after college and moved from my parents' home to my home with my husband.

Never had I made decisions on my own without input from others. Now I could choose what I was going to do with my life. The possibility of more education, a different career, and living in another area was an option in my life because of the loss. This is not saying I wanted those possibilities. I preferred my spouse and the life we established together. But when I arrived at the point in my grief to be able to review my options, there was a sense of freedom in knowing I actually had options.

When you reach the point in restructuring your life where you can see there are some options available to you with the changes, it is a step forward. It is not a matter of wanting those options *rather than* your loved one. You are not being required to make a choice between the two. You are facing a decision at this time as to *how you will react* to the change, which has already taken place. Will you be able to see something positive in these changes?

Once you see the possibilities in change, you recognize there are opportunities to grow. I would never wish to have the tragic experiences that happened to me, but because of those experiences, I grew in ways I never imagined I could. I became a more independent person. I gained many insights about life and how to live it. My experiences led me to further enriching experiences. I developed courage and strength of character. I grew in toughness, competence, and spirit—all of which it takes to be a survivor.

An amazing opportunity the change brought to me was the opportunity to learn how often the other side of tragedy leads to something good. I have observed people who lost their job and thought it was the worst thing ever to happen to them, only to find themselves in the position to accept a golden opportunity, which arose later. Sometimes drastic change must happen to put you in place at the right time for the right opportunity.

My tragic experience led me to another career and the opportunity to meet and help many other people. Because of those people, my life is richer and more blessed. Would I have been happy if none of the bad things happened? Yes! Would I have chosen this life over my old one? No! What I am saying, there was no choice for me to make as to which life I would be given to live. The choice was in what I did with my life once the tragic events happened. The opportunities lay within that choice.

With the possibilities and opportunities in change comes the growth. Observe in nature how growth occurs through change. Without change, the caterpillar would never become a butterfly. The seed would never become the flower. The sapling would never become the tree. Changes bring about growth. Growth is possible because of change. It is a cycle of life.

So it is with your personal life. The changes in your life bring about personal growth. Some people call this experience. People who do not grow from their experiences are destined to a life of monotonous routine. They are also destined to repeat the same mistakes over and over.

A tongue-in-cheek definition of insanity is continuing to do the same thing over and over but expecting different results. A great deal of personal pain comes from this particular mind-set. Refusing to change behaviors when you are not getting the desired results is insane. In order to grow and to get better, you must be able to roll with the punches and adapt to what comes your way. Each day you live presents the opportunity to grow. You are a work in progress and will be until you draw your final breath.

Importance of Communication

As you work through the many tasks of restructuring life after loss, the importance of communication cannot be emphasized enough. The battle is to survive as an intact, fully functioning human being. Communication offers a lifeline for survival.

When under great stress, communication is difficult for several reasons. One is the stressful event creates a feeling of disengagement from others. The tendency is to withdraw because others could not possibly understand what you feel. You feel alone in your suffering. You feel no one cares about your burden. You feel isolated.

Another reason communication is difficult at this time is your inability to put into words the despair you feel. Thinking is scattered. Forming cohesive thoughts is hard enough, much less having the ability to verbalize them. You think you must make logical sense in order to communicate, and since you cannot do that, you believe isolating yourself to be the best option.

These two kinds of thinking keep the mourner from doing what is best, which is communicating with another human being the wide range of thoughts bouncing around in your head. When you close the door to communication, you close the door to valuable help.

Sir Geoffrey Vickers, British philosopher, said of communication: "Communication makes personal experience bearable." Events from history validate this statement. After the Kennedy assassination in 1963, Lyndon Johnson kept a close friend by his side all through the first day until two o'clock in the morning. He needed the comfort and support of someone he trusted to be a confidant. This personal bond helped him to process his emotional turmoil in order to perform the difficult task before him.

Vice Admiral James B. Stockdale, who was the longest held POW of the Vietnam War, also validates the importance of communication in survival. He was a POW for 2,714 days. He suffered unbearable torture and mistreatment. He said later the only thing, which enabled him to endure such a brutal situation for so long, was the link between him and the lives of his fellow prisoners.

The POWs developed an elaborate code to communicate even though they could not see each other. When Stockdale was left in the courtyard under the sun for days, he held on because he heard the code tapped out by sweeping brooms, snapped towels, and shuffling feet—which let him know others were watching and pulling for him, supporting his efforts. These improvised methods of communication—at one of the worst times of his life—enabled him to feel reassured he was not in the struggle alone. After being released years later, he attributed the ability to communicate with fellow prisoners as being a determining factor in his survival.

Research shows a strong link between the strength of social support systems and emotional and physical resilience under severe stress. The support you receive from others helps you maintain higher morale, suffer fewer physical symptoms, and live longer than those who do not have the social support. Even doctors recognize the role emotional support plays in healing. Communication and support from others can be as effective as modern technology in promoting healing.

Research by Balaswamy of widowed males found support of family and friends served as a buffer for the negative effect of bereavement. However, the amount of support available differed with the age of the widowed. Those who were bereaved earlier in life reported less support than those experiencing loss later in life.

In early bereavement, 77% reported not having someone to talk to when feeling blue. The research suggested a couple of reasons for this. One was the man's own struggle with the loss caused him to retreat from others. The other was the feeling of intrusion on the part of his friends. Being younger, friends may not have experience with death; therefore, they did not know how to minister to the male.

The later bereaved males also reported a lack of confidants after the loss. However, the numbers were fewer in this group. Only 38% reported lack of a support system to communicate with compared to 77% of the younger bereaved. One of the strongest sources of support was the church. It appears, according to this study, the religious community offers help to those who need a place to communicate feelings of distress and despair. However, fewer functional supports for widowers during early bereavement were found.

Among the aged, communication is extremely important as a social support. In chapter 6, which discussed the loss of a spouse, it was noted the death rate was higher for the surviving spouse within the first two years following the death. Carr's study of bereaved spouses found the longer the marriage and the higher the quality of the marriage, the harder the transition was for the surviving spouse. This is another reason a strong support system to help the bereaved make the transition to life after loss is key in restructuring.

One of the basic needs for man, according to Maslow, is the need for belonging. Losing the intimate connection to your loved one—especially when older and, perhaps, experiencing a dwindling circle of close companions—strikes at the core of this basic need. Absence of human touch and communication in daily interactions contribute to the suffering. Isolation is a major roadblock in meeting this basic need.

For families who suffer loss due to traumatic circumstances, strong social support with the opportunity to communicate fears, feelings, and sufferings are of paramount importance. Studies of veterans, who suffered PTSD after returning from Vietnam, reveal the lack of social support played a key role in failure to secure adequate help with the problem. Those who had a strong system of support from family and friends, coupled with resources to provide opportunities to communicate their feelings, had a better outcome.

The role of mental health professionals, agencies, and support groups cannot be emphasized enough in promoting good communication skills for the bereaved. A safe environment in which the bereaved can express the myriad of feelings provides a catharsis for the mourner. However, most people do not go to mental health professionals for help. For some it is an issue of money. They cannot afford the services and do not have insurance to cover the treatment. For some, it is a lack of services available to them. Many people live in areas that are underserved by mental health. Also, in many areas, even if there are mental health services available, not all professionals are proficient in dealing with bereavement issues. Lastly, the idea of going to a counselor is unappealing to many people. Some see it as unacceptable because "people will think I'm crazy." Some people are opposed to talking to someone they do not know about personal problems.

The most commonly used method of communication of hurts, worries, fears, and suffering is informal. This simply means the bereaved person finds a group of fellow sufferers he trusts, feels comfortable with, and feels safe in sharing his thoughts.

There are three factors, which make this work for the individual who uses this informal communication. One is putting your feelings into words is healing in itself. Secondly, when you find a group of people who have suffered too, you form a bond. Just seeing there are others who have experienced terrible tragedy and managed someway to survive is encouraging. The third benefit to the informal communication is finding you are not weird. There are others who feel many of the things you feel. You are not abnormal, and your reactions are not unnatural. There is great comfort in that knowledge.

Staudacher, in her writings on grief, says the survivor has different levels of support systems, and the top of the tier is your own makeup. In other words, the first important factor is your own thinking, coping skills, and ability to communicate your needs to others. She diagrams your support structure in the following manner:

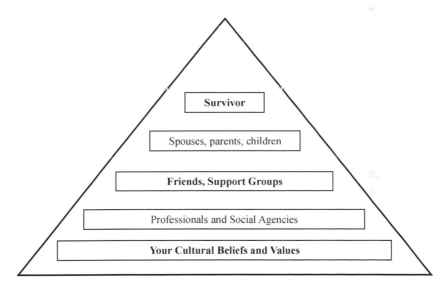

Figure 7.1 "The Grief Support System"

As this listing of supports illustrates, the professional world of mental health is far down the list of choices when people need to communicate distress over personal issues. The important communication factor is finding the right arena for you to discuss the many changes required for transitioning. Talking about your feelings, your fears, and your challenges is a huge step forward in successfully creating the restructure.

The Importance of Hope in Restructuring

A key component to healthy grief is hope. Barbara Johnson, Christian writer, talks about the importance of maintaining hope as you go through daily life trials. She says,

> It's been said man can live forty days without food, about three days without water, approximately eight minutes without air . . . but only one second with out hope.

Without hope, restructure of your life after loss is an impossible task. If you have no hope after the death of your loved one, you most likely lived a hopeless existence most of your life before the death. This is a harsh statement and demands an explanation.

People who cannot summon hope when tragedy strikes are lacking a vital skill for navigating the turbulent times throughout life. These people previously held a pessimistic, defeatist attitude, professing little hope for any good coming into their lives. The sense of hopelessness produces a sense of helplessness, creating a cycle of negativity, which undermines successful restructuring after any change in life. This doom-and-gloom attitude is a self-fulfilling prophecy. You create situations where little good comes into your life.

Hope is a major factor in your system of values and beliefs. Your worldview is impacted by whether or not you possess a hopeful spirit. In his writings, Wolfelt describes hope as an "expectation of a good that is yet to be." If you live daily with this expectation, you develop confidence and the ability to trust good things will happen to you throughout your life. Even though bad things occur as well as good things, you are able to maintain this confidence and trust. Hope gives you the ability to know no matter how terrible the present event may be, there are also some good "yet to be" experiences in store for you.

This is at the root of your will to live. If you believe there is no hope, no future joy, or no good ahead, you cannot find purpose in continuing forward with life. Without purpose, you are lost. This is the reason seeking purpose is so important in strengthening spirituality. Establishing purpose is a hopeful behavior.

Purpose, belief, and values are spiritual companions, which give you hope throughout your life. This means during bad times as well as the good. These spiritual companions give you balance in an unbalanced world. They provide you with stability.

The Psalmist, in Psalms 71, talks about the continuity of hope throughout all the days of life. This scripture stresses the importance of hope in survival. Verse 14 says, "But as for me, I will always have hope." According to the Psalmist, hope is the centerpiece of your faith. With faith and hope, you have a refuge, a rock of strength, and great confidence to use as tools for living through good and bad times. Verse 20 further states those who possess this abiding faith will be able to restructure and restore functioning after tragedies.

Psalm 71:20

> Though I've seen troubles and bitter times, you restored my
> life again.

The hope in this verse emphasizes although there were many troubled and bitter times, life was *restored*. If it was restored before, the hope is in knowing it is possible for restoration to occur again.

During this period of restructure, you are seeking peace. Happiness is fleeting. You are not hoping at this time for happiness because the circumstances prevent it. However, you are yearning for peace—peace of the spirit.

In Lamentations 3:17-18, the writer speaks of the many adversities, which have befallen him. He says,

> I have been deprived of peace; I have forgotten what prosperity
> is. My splendor is gone.

Does this not echo how you feel after the death of your loved one? Good times seem gone forever. Your thoughts are in turmoil. Great feelings of despair flood you. Definitely, your splendor is gone. This is when hope is sorely needed.

For me, this is when faith was the life preserver I clung to through these turbulent waters. In order to do the restoration work I needed to do, I needed great hope. Calling to mind the verses in Lamentations and the writer's loss of peace and prosperity, I identified with his pain. But what the writer said following the lamentation of lost splendor was the part that reminded me of the basic truth of my faith.

> Yet this I call to mind therefore I have hope. Because of the Lord's great love, we are not consumed, for his compassions never fail. They are new every day.
> —Lamentations 3:21-23

There is great comfort in these verses. First, faith provides you with hope. Second, you are loved and protected. You have a loving refuge. Third, each day you will be given what you need to meet the challenges of that day. You do not need to leap the mountain. You only need the strength for each day.

These simple truths from the scriptures are echoed in the many writings of professionals in the fields of psychology, psychotherapy, and bereavement. Resolving emotional problems, dealing with past baggage, and being healthy mentally requires the attainment of a healthy spirit. Your faith, whatever it may be, is the key to maintaining your spiritual health.

During the process of restructuring your life, your spiritual health is undergoing some adjustments too. Hope is one part of your spiritual health, which is caught in the vortex of turbulent emotions. Maintaining hope is what enables you to feel life is worth living, even though so much has changed for you. Being able to maintain this hope depends on who you are and what you value.

Discovering who you are and what you value moves you toward achievement of wisdom. The purpose of life is not to be perpetually happy. This is an unrealistic expectation. However, as you begin to establish *realistic expectations* and discover and/or *make changes* in your purpose, you acquire wisdom.

How do you acquire wisdom? The first step began before the need to restructure. You devoted attention to forming, establishing, and maintaining a cherished set of values. The restructuring process demands you take the second step toward development of wisdom, which is developing clarity in your beliefs.

As discussed previously, you carry many beliefs in life without fully testing them in the reality of your world. It is only when adverse times come that you find whether or not your belief system works for you.

This is when many questions arise. What really matters to me? What is my relationship with God? What am I willing to commit to with my time and energy?

Clarifying answers to questions about your beliefs and values gives you wisdom you did not have before the event, which precipitated this introspection. You have achieved wisdom when you discover and accept your limitations. You gain wisdom when you can be comfortable and at peace with the way life operates. With wisdom comes hope. Hope provides an anchor for the soul.

Romans 5:3-4 says,

> We know suffering produces perseverance, perseverance, character and character, hope.

What you learn from suffering is the strength of your mettle. You develop endurance. To persevere is to hold to life with tenacity. It is the quality, which drives you to work hard, learn new things, expand your circle of friends and loved ones, grow with opportunities, and never ever give up. Perseverance is the "stick-to-itness," which keeps you putting one foot before the other, day after day, as you progress forward through the turmoil. If you are never put to the test, if you never face a difficulty, if you never have to battle hard times, you do not build inner toughness and strength. Just as the heat of the crucible strengthens iron, you are strengthened by the adversities of life.

Athletes become stronger when they face tough competition. Without challenges, they would not improve performance. You are the same in your life. It is the challenges, which strengthen you. To survive suffering demands perseverance in order to meet the challenge. Every challenge met and conquered strengthens you.

The next part of the verse in Romans says perseverance builds character. Character is not an easy quality to obtain. You cannot buy it. You cannot borrow it from someone else. You cannot inherit it or pass it down to the next generation. Building character is a do-it-yourself project. Each person must develop his own character through life experience. First comes suffering (the event). Then comes perseverance (the test). Next comes character (the wisdom).

More than any other quality, your character will determine your success or failure in any endeavor, relationship, or adversity you face in life. Character is built on your ability to fight the good fight of life with courage, flexibility, strength, attitude, patience, and hope. Your character defines who you are as a person. Character encompasses your worldview, your values, your beliefs, your integrity, and your compassion for yourself and others.

Restructure of life after loss hinges a great deal on your character because character is the wellspring of hope. Hope sees possibilities in the impossible. Hope sees opportunity and growth in adversity. Hope seeks encouragement in discouraging times. Hope looks forward, not backward. Hope sees past despair and forward to joy. Hope propels you to find something to live for, a purpose for going on with life. William James said,

> Believe that life is worth living and your belief will help create the fact.

Belief signifies hope. When you believe in the worthiness of living to the fullest, adversity will not keep you down. The slivers of hope in that belief encourage you to rise to seek joy once more.

You began the restructuring process with a tremendous loss. It began with a heart-wrenching good-bye. You walked life's journey with your loved one to the station. When their train left that station, you were left with tearful good-byes. It does no good to stand at the station and wait. You must pick up your things and move on, even though you may not feel like moving onward. This chapter spent time discussing the paths you must take and the roadmaps you need to continue your journey. Like it or not, life has a way of moving you on. Learning to live once again and to enjoy the scenery along the way is the task of restructuring.

Chapter 7 References

1. Amour, Marilyn. 2003. Meaning Making in the Aftermath of Suicide. *Death Studies* 27, no. 7 (July): 519-518-540.
2. Balaswamy, Shantha, Virginia Richardson, and Christine A. Price. 2004. Investigating Patterns of Social Support Use by Widowers during Bereavement. *The Journal of Men's Studies* 13, no. 1 (January): 67-76.
3. Bernstein, Judith R., PhD. 1980. *When the Bough Breaks: Forever after the Death of a Son or Daughter.* Kansas City: MO: Andrews McMeel Publishing.
4. Blair, Pamela, PhD, and Brook Noel. 2000. *I Wasn't Ready to Say Goodbye: Surviving, Coping and Healing after the Sudden Death of a Loved One. P. 260,* Milwaukee, WI: Champion Press LTD.
5. Bowlby, John. 1982. Attachment and Loss: Retrospective Prospect. *American Journal of Orthopsychiatry* 52 (1980): 664-664-678.
6. Carr, Deborah, James S. House, Ronald C. Kessler, Randolph M. Nesse, John Sonnega, and Camille Wortman. 2000. Marital Quality and Psychological Adjustment to Widowhood among Older Adults: A Longitudinal Analysis. *The Journals of Gerontology Series B* 55B, no. 4 (April): 447-446-457.
7. Christakis, Nicholas A., Theodore J. Iwashyna. 2003. The Health Impact of Health Care on Families: A Matched Cohort Study of Hospice Use by Decedents and Mortality Outcomes in Surviving, Widowed Spouses. *Social Science and Medicine* 57: 465-466-475.
8. Coleman, Sally, and Maria Porter. 1994. *Seasons of the Spirit. P. 35,* Center City, Minn: Hazeldon Foundation.
9. Gamino, Lewis, Nancy Hogan, and Kenneth Sewell. 2002. Feeling the Absence: A Content Analysis from the Scott and White Grief Study. *Death Studies* 26, no. 10 (November): 793-794-813.
10. Henderson, John M., Bert Hayslip Jr., and Jennifer K. King. 2004. The Relationship between Adjustment and Bereavement-Related Distress: A Longitudinal Study. *The Journal of Mental Health Counseling* 26, no. 2 (February): 98-105.
11. Johnson, Barbara. 2004. *Laughter from Heaven. P. 46, 47,* Nashville, TN: W Publishing Group.
12. Klein, Allen. 1989. *The Healing Power of Humor. "The Weaving" P. 163,* New York, NY: Penguin Putman Inc.
13. Linamen, Karen S. 2001. *Sometimes I Wake Up Grumpy and Sometimes I Let Him Sleep. P 133,* Grand Rapids, MI: Fleming H Revell, Baker Books.

14. Menten, Ted. 1994. *After Goodbye: How to Begin Again after the Death of Someone You Love. P. 113-114*, Philadelphia, PA: Running Press.
15. Meyer, Charles. 1997. *Surviving Death: A Practical Guide to Caring for the Dying and Bereaved.* Mystic, Conn: Twenty-Third Publications.
16. Neeld, Elizabeth Harper, PhD. 2003. *Seven Choices: Finding Daylight after Loss Shatters Your World.* New York, NY: Tiime Warner.
17. Nuland, Sherwin, B. 1993. *How We Die: Reflections on Life's Final Chapter.* New York, NY: Random House.
18. O'Connor, Nancy, PhD. 1984. *Letting Go with Love: The Grieving Process. P. 158, 164,*Tuscon, AZ: La Mariposa Press.
19. Reilly, Marla, S. P. 1996. *Now That I Am Old: Meditations on the Meaning of Life.* Mystic, Connecticut: Twenty-Third Publications.
20. Schroeder, Joel and Ruth. 1997. *The Power of Positivity. P. 4*, Mission, KS: Skillpath Publications
21. Segal, Julius. 1986. *Winning Life's Toughest Battles: Roots of Human Resilience. P. 13, 128, 129*, New York, NY: Ivy Press.
21. Staudacher, Carol. 1991. *Men and Grief: A Guide for Men Surviving the Death of a Loved One. P. 87, 209*, Oakland, CA: New Harbinger Publications.
22. Wiersbe, Warren. 1997. *God Isn't in a Hurry: Learning to Slow Down and Live. P.113, 143*, Grand Rapids, MI: Baker Books.
23. Wolfelt, Alan D., PhD. 1992. *Understanding Grief: Helping Yourself Heal. P. 3*, Muncie: IN: Accelerated Development Inc.

Chapter 8

SPECIAL DAYS—SPECIAL PAIN

The holiest of all holidays are those kept by ourselves in silence apart; the secret anniversaries of the heart.
—Henry Wadsworth Longfellow

Birthdays, anniversaries, weddings, Mother's Day, Father's Day, and religious holidays—such as Easter, Thanksgiving, Christmas, Hanukah, Yom Kippur, New Year, and Passover—are some of the special days, which make our lives enjoyable. These are the times families come together for fellowship and sharing. These are the special occasions you look forward to throughout the year.

For the newly bereaved, special times are no longer times to enjoy but are times of special pain and renewed grief. Family celebrations, which normally gladden your heart and fill your household with excitement and cheer, bring a sense of dread. Anticipation and joy are replaced with bittersweet memories and sorrow.

The symbolism of these occasions reawakens painful feelings, which you may have successfully suppressed for several months. These celebrations are steeped in family tradition and ritual centered on the participation of all family members. When a family member is missing due to death, or absence, it produces a melancholy mood in those family members who gather together for these special observances.

After losing a loved one, all major holidays are difficult to face; but due to the unique relationship each mourner had with the loved one, there are many other special times, which bring difficulty too. As the poet Longfellow said, there are "secret anniversaries of the heart." These are not red-letter days on the calendars of others, but they are times, which mean a great deal to the bereaved. Because death brings a change in the way time is marked, survivors note more special times than the general population. The point of the death becomes the base for measuring time. "It's been two months since Susan died." "This is the first summer without Joe." "This is the first year we did not plant the garden." "This is the first winter we did not go skiing." All these firsts have meaning for the newly bereaved.

There are other examples of these anniversaries, which may not garner public notice. For a bereaved spouse, the anniversary of the first date or the day of the marriage proposal may be a difficult time. This may not necessarily be a special day to anyone else nor may others be aware of this date. The traditional family vacation may bring back memories of the last time you went to the beach or the mountains, and your loved one was there to participate. There are many such special times unique to the different relationships with loved ones. As each of these occasions arrives after the loss, grief is renewed, and the focus is returned to the loss.

People frequently say holidays in the first year after loss are the worst. This depends on you and your particular grief. While this is true for some mourners, others find the second year more difficult. Some mourners say the numbness abates during the second year, so the loss is felt more severely. The time of year your loved one died also impacts which special times will be the most difficult in the first or second year.

My husband died in early December, so the first Christmas arrived rather quickly. We were still in the earliest days of mourning. It was not a happy occasion for us by any means, but the numbness of early grief made the holiday pass with a sense of unreality. We did not have weeks and weeks to build up dread of the holiday. Our minds were not focused enough to fully absorb the impact of the loss. So the first Christmas came and went with pain but not as much pain as with the holidays a year after the initial loss. The first Christmas season passed in a blur for us as we dealt with the initial turmoil of loss.

Although in the beginning, you do not think these special occasions will ever be joyful again, the intensity of the pain does diminish with time. With the passing of time, the pain of grief lessens to the pangs of grief. The pain comes and goes, but each time it is not as intense nor does it last as long as it did during the early days of loss.

Although I have some distance from the death of my loved ones when these special times arrive, there are still moments of sadness because they are not present. As the years pass, these moments are of much shorter duration and much less intensity. Even though the pangs are there, I also am able to have joy in these occasions. Although my pain has lessened to pangs, as Dr. Wolfelt calls them, these will be with me for all the future special times because of the love I continue to hold for my loved ones.

The Reasons the Special Days Are Difficult

There are several reasons these days are difficult for the newly bereaved. The first reason seems redundant. It is because of the uniqueness or special quality of these times to you and your family. Secondly, these special times bring a renewed focus on the loss of your loved one. Add to these reasons the tendency in many families to refuse to acknowledge the impending special time. By failing to acknowledge to each other the special date is coming, these families fail to communicate about it. This builds a wall of silence and a sense of dread. The fourth reason is reassignment of the loved one's role in the special time is incomplete. Finally, the inflexibility on the part of some family members to adapt rituals to accommodate the change in the family structure creates additional stress and unhappiness on these special occasions.

Special days bring so much pain to the survivors because these are typical family times, which hold almost magical qualities for family members. The very uniqueness of the celebrations contributes to the formation of memories for a lifetime. These are the celebrations, dates, and holidays, which are filled with history for the family.

The memories of the past flood back. These are the times you gather with family members to reminisce, participate in family activities, and share information about each other's lives. You do a lot of "remembering when." Remember when we did this? Remember when we did that? Remember when we went on that special trip? Remember the surprise gift so-and-so gave? This is the time for sharing memories of when you laughed, danced, and rejoiced together. The fun times and pleasures of past special occasions are remembered, reviewed, and enjoyed. During this walk down memory lane, you remember your loved one was a part of it all. It is a time to celebrate family history together.

Now your loved one is gone. The times remembered are what you have left of that person. The realization you will no longer make more memories with him brings great pain. The loved one is now a part of the "what was." The loved one has taken his place permanently in the past family history.

The second reason special occasions are so stressful to the mourner is the returned focus on the loss. In the early days of your grief, your focus is *always* on the missing loved one. However, as you move through the grieving process, slowly you begin to focus on other things in your life. Your grief does not absorb every minute of your waking thoughts.

You begin to move into the mainstream of life and are able to function in other ways, even though you are still grieving your loss. Maybe you returned to work, began rejoining some of your social activities, returned to worship services, started to work on hobbies, and began to notice other people's sorrows. Perhaps you even started to be helpful to others.

Then the calendar brings the special day. Your focus is brought back full force on the loss you suffered. This return of focus brings renewed grief, depression, and despair. Depending on the amount of time since your loss, the pain can be quite intense.

An example, which appears to be helpful to my clients in understanding the effect the renewed focus has on their grieving process, is the comparison of the mind to a television screen. Picture a gigantic television screen with huge letters filling the screen spelling *loss*. This screen represents the view in your mind after the death of a loved one. Everything else is pushed off the screen except your tremendous loss. Other pictures pushed off your screen are previous interests, hobbies, other people, your job, activities, and the needs of others and, perhaps, even the concern about others. Your screen is uniquely reprogrammed to replace any other focus in your life with the one big picture of loss.

As time passes and you begin to process your grief, other pictures gradually creep back onto the edges of your screen. As more of these areas of focus creep back onto the screen, the *loss* letters begin to shrink in size to make room for the returning pictures. You think you are much better. You begin to feel you are getting your feet under you. The loss is there, but so are other areas of focus in your life. Suddenly the special day arrives. The *loss* looms back on the screen in huge letters, pushing away your progressive focus. This is discouraging. It brings a sense of lost progress. It also brings renewed awareness of all the things, which were lost when your loved one died.

With each passing year, the pain of the special time lessens, but it does not ever go away. However, something does happen, which is important for mourners to know, because it gives so much hope to those who are suffering in the now. As time passes and those special days arrive, there is still a returned focus on the lost loved one; but instead of intense pain, depression, and despair, it becomes a time to review and reflect on all the happy, joyous occasions shared with the loved one. At this point in the grief process, there are more smiles in remembering than tears.

There will still be some moments of sadness and, perhaps, tears, but the memories bring great comfort. If you, your family, and friends can share these memories, it puts the *special* back into these days. You find, instead of renewing your grief, a renewal of your relationship with the memory and spirit of the one you lost. This is when you begin to understand your loved one is never truly gone but lives on in your heart and memories.

Failure to acknowledge the impending arrival of the special time is another reason special days bring renewed pain. If the mourners try to pretend the special time does not exist, they are ignoring a very big elephant. When the family ignores the existence of the special day, it keeps them from planning ways to deal with the sorrow of the time. Just letting the day happen brings a return of the out-of-control feelings you had at the time of death.

This is not as likely to happen with the major holidays because there are so many people around you celebrating the big days it is hard to ignore those events. The commercialization of Christmas, Easter, Mother's Day, Father's Day, Valentine's Day, and Thanksgiving does not allow you to conveniently forget about the big day. But it does happen with those unique celebrations peculiar to your family and to the more personal celebrations you enjoyed with the loved one.

The birthday of the deceased, a wedding anniversary, and the anniversary of the loved one's death are occasions many try to ignore. People mistakenly think it is helpful to you to pretend *the day* does not exist. This thinking assumes that if the significance of the day is not mentioned, you will not remember it. Often, whole families and all the family friends carefully step around the topic of the special event. Everyone strains to pretend this is just another day, never discussing the significance of it. In the meantime, the date is uppermost in everyone's mind. It is the elephant in the room.

The anniversary of the loved one's death is an especially difficult time to mark. You may relive the trauma of the death. Vivid memories of the day are burned into your mind. Every minute detail of inconsequential things you did that particular day may resurface. Normally, some of these things would be lost to memory long ago. But that day was so traumatic and so life-changing details are etched into your mind forever. The death was such an important life marker; it is impossible to ignore the anniversary of it.

All these years after the death of my husband, I vividly recall the details of the day. Each year when the day arrives, those details replay in my mind. Even after twenty-six years, the day of his death is a sad day for me, but it is also a day for special remembering. I try to mark the day in some special way. Often, it is by doing something unbeknownst to other people. Usually, my family notes the day. It is a day of remembrance. It is a special day for me to remember the last good-bye kiss that final morning and the last time he and I existed in this world together.

Not only is it important to mark all these special anniversaries, it is important to discuss them with those family members who are affected by the loss. Putting your feelings and thoughts into words breaks the dam of silence and opens the door to family communication. It is important to discuss the significance of the impending date, the potential difficulties you see arising from the date, and possible ways the family can mark the special time. Communication allows you to put words to your thoughts. It allows the family to drop the stress of silence and openly acknowledge the importance of the person who died and the continued love for that person.

To successfully weather the crisis of these special anniversaries, communication is a valuable tool. Suffering in silence is unhealthy and nonproductive. Allowing yourself and others to share thoughts and feelings about the occasion and ideas for remembrance lightens the emotional load for everyone. Few people can endure personal suffering alone. Talking about and planning for special times gives mourners the opportunity to share the sorrow and to take some measure of control over the traumatic situation. Communication opens the door to hope. Hope lies in the sharing and planning. Hope breaches the chasm of grief. Hope enables you to survive what once seemed unsurvivable.

Another difficult issue is the reassignment of the loved one's roles in the celebrations. Every family has its own set of traditional rituals to usher in the seasons of celebration. Certain family rituals—special foods prepared by particular people, attendance at certain events of the season, familiar patterns and ways of celebrating within the family—are very much a part of the lives of the family members. The loved one played a vital role in those celebrations.

When the family circle is broken by the absence of a family member, the whole family feels the impact of the loss of that presence. The role vacated by the death of the loved one leaves a huge gap in the circle. No one can really replace that particular person. It becomes very difficult to carry on the same family rituals because a drastic change occurred in the dynamics of the family. Roles must be realigned, and adjustments must be made to the celebratory schedules. This is not quickly or easily accomplished.

No matter which family member died, he did fulfill a role in the family celebrations. Perhaps the deceased was the cook of the family or was expected to bring a special dish to the celebrations. Sometimes the deceased was the activity planner and keeper of the calendar of events. Some were the family storytellers who entertained everyone with family history or funny jokes. Some were the enthusiastic consumers of the family feasts. They could be counted on to eat heartily and give profuse compliments to the cooks. Others may have been the proverbial scrooges who "Bah! Humbugged!" the festivities but participated anyway. Some were the shoppers. Each person who attended family functions filled his own special role. Now that role is vacant, and it leaves a void.

In order to realign the roles due to the death of the family member, the mourner must deal with the fifth difficulty of special days. It is the inflexibility of the family to make needed changes in rituals. As mentioned in the previous chapter on restructuring your life, being inflexible about initiating changes prolongs and intensifies the pain of the loss. Inflexibility makes the celebration of special occasions more difficult than they need to be because the focus is on the loss, instead of making new memories and creating new family history.

Depression over the loss can become intense during these times. Families gather together, happiness and good cheer fill the air, and the whole world seems to be on a prolonged high of goodwill. Widespread festivity makes your loss seem even more unbearable. None of the usual rituals your family pursued in previous times appeal to you. You cannot even think about how to face them, much less change them.

You do not have to pretend to be happy and joyous just because the rest of the world appears festive. You do have to take control of this portion of your life and admit changes need to be made in the way your family observes these celebrations. One important fact to keep in mind is the changes you make do not have to be permanent. You are living one day at a time. You are facing one celebration at a time. What will or will not work at this point may be different in the future. Your goal is to adapt to this moment in time, and do something different as you change the celebration to accommodate the loss of the loved one's role.

Being inflexible about changing the rituals only serves to emphasize the loss. Things can never be the same because a vital role is vacant. The past rituals are now precious memories. From this time forward, new memories will be made without the loved one being a part of them. The loved one has become a part of your family history. He is not part of the family present or the family future. Being inflexible about accepting this realization only serves to intensify the pain.

Once you accept the fact you have to make changes in the roles and be flexible about new ways to celebrate the family's special times, you make a huge step forward. Just as the death causes you to reexamine your life purpose and meaning, it also causes you to reexamine your family rituals and traditions. This becomes a time of clarification, changing expectations, and restructure of the family rituals.

Family Traditions and Rituals

In order to understand the process of restructuring the family rituals after the death of a loved one, you must understand the difference between family rituals and family traditions. *The American College Dictionary* defines tradition as "the handing down of beliefs, legends, and customs from one generation to another." As pertains to religious views held by the family traditions can be a body of teachings or a body of laws. A ritual is defined as "a proceeding." Comparing these two definitions, you can readily see the restructuring process after loss will, in most cases, deal with the restructure of rituals—not traditions.

Your family traditions are the beliefs, values, and code of ethical behaviors practiced by your family for generations. The death of your loved one may cause you to reexamine these, but for the most part, these core traditions remain a part of you and your family throughout time because these traditions constitute the very fabric of your family life. Rarely does the death of a loved one change the traditional beliefs, values, and behaviors of the surviving members. Traditions give families a sense of continuity through the generations. Examining these traditions after the death reenforces the understanding that while changes of how things are done occur with the passing of time, traditions or beliefs are carried forward to the next generation. There is comfort and stability in that knowledge.

However, the family rituals practiced during the special occasions celebrated by the family may have to change because of the loved one's role in the rituals. As the bereaved family faces the many special occasions following the death, it soon becomes apparent the same routines and schedules are often inappropriate or impossible to follow. It is important for family members to identify and discuss the rituals practiced before the death. Then it is necessary for open communication among family members as to which rituals will be continued and which ones may require some changes.

After identifying the rituals, which are normal for your family, the next step is to ascertain the reason your family follows these rituals. Some rituals may have clearly understood reasoning behind them and may be closely related to the family's traditional views. Other rituals may be merely habits practiced for many years with the reason being long lost to the surviving family members. Sometimes families identify rituals, which were practiced solely for the person who died. If the ritual becomes burdensome for the family to continue, and the reason for doing it is gone, it may be a relief to discontinue this particular ritual.

One ritual in many families involves traveling great distances to the family home on special holidays to be with the parents. When the parents die, the surviving family members may decide traveling on the specific date of the holiday is too fatiguing. Even though traveling to the event was done for years, the newly restructured celebration may consist of moving the extended family gathering to a different day.

A ritual my husband, son, and I practiced on Christmas Eve was to ban television, listen to Christmas music, and play board games. Since we visited my husband's family early in the day on Christmas Eve and ate a huge meal, at dinnertime, the three of us ate sandwiches and oyster stew in the den. Looking at the lighted Christmas tree, listening to the music, and playing games were enjoyable Christmas Eve activities for the three of us.

Our ritual on Christmas Eve became obsolete. The first Christmas, only two weeks after my husband's death, my son did not want to change the routine of this ritual. Against my better judgment, we stayed home instead of going to either set of grandparents for the night. It was a huge mistake. Nothing was the same. The old ritual could not be replicated after my husband's death. My son and I both realized it and never entertained the thought of doing this ritual the next year.

Many rituals start for very good reasons, but they continue out of habit, and through the years the meaning is lost. What happens is similar to the story of the woman who always cut her pot roast into two pieces before cooking it. One day, her newly married daughter was observing her while she was preparing a Sunday dinner for the family and asked why she cut the meat in half before cooking. The mother replied that was the way her mother always cooked it, and she really did not know the reason. The mother commented she learned how to cook from her mother and never asked that question. When the grandmother arrived to eat the meal, the granddaughter asked her about the reason for cutting the pot roast into two pieces before cooking it. The grandmother replied there was no reason except that she never owned a pan large enough to hold the whole roast.

This humorous story is an example of the rituals passed down through many families, which began out of necessity at a particular time but were never discontinued when the reason became obsolete. Determining the reason behind your family rituals helps you to determine which ones are important and which ones are not.

It is important to identify the obsolete rituals well before the holidays and plan something different. One of the main roles in the ritual no longer exists, so the ritual becomes meaningless and painful to those surviving family members. The ritual no longer brings the spirit, joy, and pleasure, which caused you to originally make it a part of your celebration.

When you discuss the rituals with family members to determine the important ones and the ones that no longer fit the family structure, you may find a difference of opinion among family members. Some family members report they thought a certain ritual too time-consuming to continue but found other family members loved the ritual and wanted to continue doing it. When this happens, communication and compromise is a necessity. Brainstorming to determine ways to keep the best part of the ritual but simplify the procedure is one way to resolve this dilemma.

Restructuring Steps

As you evaluate your family rituals for holidays and all special occasions, you attempt to identify the important rituals to continue. Your goal is to weed out the obsolete rituals and the ones that will be too painful to carry out so soon after the loss. This restructuring of the family rituals is a three-step process. First, you *review* all the rituals associated with the particular family celebration. Second, you pinpoint the rituals that need to be *kept or adapted* in some way. Third, you identify those rituals you will *eliminate*.

Review

Reviewing the rituals your family practices for each special occasion helps you to clearly determine exactly what your family does to mark these occasions. This enables you to identify the activities, which will give you the most pain following the loss. It helps to make a list of all the things you and your loved ones do to prepare for and carry out the celebration. With a special day looming on the horizon, this activity brings some control to your life because you are thinking and putting your thoughts on paper. This is the first step in a planning process. This begins to stabilize the situation in your mind and gives you more confidence in facing the difficult time.

Once you complete the list of rituals, you are ready to review them. You may want to do this alone before you talk to other family members. Then you take this list to the rest of the family to determine if you left anything off the list. Also, by the time you talk to the family, you have your emotions under control and perhaps have thought about some suggestions for change.

As you and your family review the list of activities normally associated with the special event, mark the ones the deceased was responsible for doing. Look at the activities, which are left on the list, and determine who does each of the other activities. Once this is established, you are ready to move to the second step in the restructure of your family rituals. This is the *keep/adapt* step.

Keep/Adapt

You and your family are ready to make decisions about which rituals you will be able to do this year. The ones you keep may need to be adapted in some way to fit the new situation without the loved one. If the deceased accomplished an activity in the ritual, and you wish to keep it, the responsibility for the completion of the activity will need to be given to another family member. If the whole family wants to keep a ritual in which everyone participates, the timing of the activity may have to be adapted. If there are rituals you find you still must do, even though you may not feel like doing them, you may change the manner in which you do the ritual.

There are many examples of adaptations families in my groups made following the death of their loved one. One woman, who lost her husband, did not want to put up the traditional tree at Christmas. Her options were to omit the tree, do it herself, or get help putting up and trimming the tree. She said since the children and grandchildren were coming to her house, she simply had to have a Christmas tree for the little ones. Her solution was to ask her bridge club to come for coffee and cookies, assist her in putting up the tree, and to return after the holiday to take it down for storage. This was an excellent example of preevent planning.

First, she realized she did have choices about the tree. She chose to have a tree even though she was not emotionally up to the task of assembling it. Then she did another positive activity. She allowed her friends to help her. This gave her friends a chance to be useful and to companion her in her grief. The coffee and cookies added to the fellowship in completing the activity. Fellowship was emotionally good for all parties.

Even more helpful was the thought of what to do when the family visit was over and she was left alone looking at that tree. She planned another visit from her group of friends to take down and store the tree and decorations. While Christmas was not a joyful one for the family after the loss of her husband, it did have its brief moments of joy in the delight of the children enjoying the tree and the warmth of the presence of friends joining the widow for a brief while on her journey of grief.

Other adaptations families make to rituals they want to continue may involve reassignment of duties. For example, one family said Aunt Hattie made the best jam cake ever and always brought it to the Thanksgiving meal. When she died, her daughter assumed the job of providing Aunt Hattie's cake!

One family mentioned the person who died made a special candy for the family every year. At Thanksgiving, the women of the family talked about the candy and decided to gather at one daughter's house on a certain day in December and, as a group, prepare the candy so the traditional candy could still be part of their holiday celebrations. It worked well for them, and more people learned how to make the family's special candy.

My in-laws always celebrated Christmas on Christmas Eve. Everyone met at their house at noon for a huge sit-down meal. After my father-in-law's death, we still wanted to get together but realized we could not replicate the meal ritual with everyone looking at his empty chair. So we changed the meal. We met later in the afternoon and switched the formal meal to finger foods and sandwich trays served in a much less formal atmosphere. This was a new form of an old ritual.

There are many ways to adapt established rituals to new situations. The meeting place can be changed from one house to another. Some families choose to go to a restaurant for the family meal. Others opt to go out of town together. If the event involves gift-giving, many families adapt this ritual to gift certificates instead of wrapped gifts, donations to favorite charities or religious organizations, adoption of needy families for gift-giving, or exchanging special items, which did not have to be purchased.

If the family decides to keep a certain activity as it has always been, great thought must be given to the impact it will have on everyone when the special event arrives. Will it bring any joy? Will it make the time more depressing? If the decision is made to keep the activity, it is important to focus on the *reason* you are doing this ritual. Many times rituals are kept because of younger children in the family. If this is true, it is important to focus on the joy in the faces of the children and cling to that ray of hope, instead of dwelling throughout the ritual on the loss.

In determining ways to adapt old rituals to new ways, always enter into the planning with a flexible mind. Rigidly holding on to rituals—which you know will be painful and unenjoyable—simply because "we always did it this way" brings undue stress and unhappiness to an already miserable situation. Just as you must make changes in many areas of your life after a loss, you must make changes in the way you and your family celebrate all the special family holidays and milestones.

Eliminate

As you review your rituals for each special day and decide which ones you want to keep, which ones you need to adapt, and who will be responsible for these rituals, you will probably find there are some rituals that must be *eliminated.* This is the third step in the restructuring of the family rituals.

Obsolete rituals, which no longer serve any purpose, are the easiest to eliminate. I used to bake homemade goodies to take to all my neighbors during the Christmas season. When I began this ritual, I had time to do it, knew all the neighbors, and participated in more social activities with them. After a few years, neighbors moved in and out of the neighborhood. Many did not stay long, so I did not know them as well as previous neighbors. Many I only saw to speak to coming and going about our daily activities. I began to work more hours, and the baking became more of a chore.

At first, I adapted. I simply bought nice bakery goodies, arranged them on pretty holiday trays, and delivered them. After a couple of years of this, with my schedule becoming more hectic, even the adaptation became cumbersome. Finally, I asked myself, "Why are you doing this? Are you enjoying it?" I had to admit to myself my life had changed, and the initial reason behind the spirit of goodwill was no longer relevant. When an activity becomes too burdensome to do and is irrelevant, it should be eliminated! Thus, I eliminated a stressful activity and felt much better about it. This is why eliminating some of your rituals can be the right thing to do.

It is important to remember because a ritual is eliminated this year, it does not mean you will eliminate it forever. Each year, you and your family must evaluate your rituals to determine if you want to return to some you eliminated for the first year only. During the painful first year, your special events may be very streamlined and basic simply because of your emotional distress and lack of energy. As time passes, and you process the loss, gradually, your energy returns. Slowly but surely, joy creeps back into your life. As you restructure and move further along the journey of grief, you may decide to return to some of the activities you eliminated in the first year or two of loss.

If you do not feel able to have company for the special event, say so, and allow someone else to host the family. If the holiday season of Christmas is upon you, and you are not having guests, you may choose to dispense with decorations. You may visit with other family members instead of being the host/hostess. Do not feel guilty for eliminating an exhausting and painful activity while you process your grief. You can return to the rituals when and if you desire to at a later date.

Many families find they eliminate some rituals and replace them with new rituals they like better. You make new memories after the death of your loved one. These are memories with their own history minus the deceased. As these new rituals come into the family structure, they become relevant to the present life of the family and important for living in the now.

As I look back at my life and the many changes in my family dynamics due to loss and new additions, I see this review, adaptation, and elimination as a continuing process. You cannot possibly hold on to all the old rituals, refusing to adapt and eliminate, without killing the vitality of your family. Just as your family loses members to death, it adds members through marriage and birth. The same process of reviewing, adapting, and eliminating rituals must be done with each change. Inflexibility builds walls around your family, keeping it from growing emotionally and spiritually. Inflexibility also keeps you from fully enjoying the point of celebratory rituals, which is enjoyment of family and friends.

When facilitating bereavement workshops on preparation for the major holidays, the worksheet in figure 8.1 is helpful in identifying rituals and making decisions concerning change. Smaller events, while requiring some planning, may not be major enough to formalize on paper. They should however be discussed and planned with others in the family. The worksheet format can be used for these discussions.

Special Day Planning Worksheet

List below the rituals you and your family usually practice for the special day. After the ritual, write a brief reason for doing it. Then, indicate who does this activity. Finally, check the rituals you want to keep. Indicate if the ritual will need to be adapted. Last, X the ones you will eliminate for this year.

RITUALS FOR EVENT	REASON FOR RITUAL	Participant	Keep	Adapt	Eliminate

Figure 8.1

An example of an activity you might list is *sending holiday cards*. The reason could be *to stay in touch with others*. If you determine you are not up to this task this year, you might choose to eliminate it by putting an x in the *eliminate* box. If the activity is *cook the turkey*, and the reason is *my contribution to the meal*, you have to make a decision on whether or not you will keep it as is, adapt it, or eliminate it. If elimination is not a possibility because there is no one else to do it, do not mark that box. However, you do have two other choices. You can keep the ritual and provide the turkey, or you can adapt. This means you select different meat, order it from a commercial establishment, or get someone to help you with the turkey. Whatever you choose to do on each ritual, you are taking control of the demands of the event by making a decision about what you will or will not do and what you choose to do differently.

Most people feel less stressed and more at ease when there is a sense of order in their lives. Knowing what to expect and identifying the options available provides you with a sense of control of the situation. This loss of control and the ensuing chaos after the death of a loved one are two of the main reasons mourners suffer such emotional distress in coping with the loss. Restoring organization to the chaotic, disorganized lives of mourners following a loss is a complicated process. Making the transition through the many changes death brings to your life is a lengthy, painful task. Using the worksheet to review, adapt, and eliminate rituals for special occasions is only one of the planning tools to assist families making this transition.

Special Occasion Coping Strategies

There is no magical way to make the dread of special occasions evaporate, but there are coping strategies to assist the mourner in facing these events and coming through them with some measure of satisfaction. It is important to understand how well you will fare through these events depends on your own spirit of determination. While the first time for each of these occasions will probably not be the happiest for you, there can be slivers of joy found if you are determined to look. Some of the small joys may be seeing other family members, sharing food together, or seeing the sense of wonder and awe in the eyes of a child. It is in these small joys you find hope for better times to come. It is of utmost importance for you to learn ways to deal with these difficult times in order to continue the traditions and rituals of your family in the years ahead.

1. Plan ahead.

The emphasis of the last several pages is on planning ahead for the occasion. Leave nothing to chance. It will be a hard day or days for you. Accept that fact. However, you can make decisions about what you can handle and what you cannot. Make your decisions known to others. Determine how you would like to mark the special time, and tell family members and friends. You may not be able to plan for unexpected events in your life, but you can plan your reactions to the unexpected.

2. Communicate

Be vocal about your plans and wishes. This is not the time to be a shrinking violet. Others in your life cannot help you if you shut them out or refuse to give them a sense of direction. Your loved ones and friends want to help you, but you must communicate to them what you need. If you need to talk, tell them. If you do not need to talk, tell them. Do not push people away. During special times, there are many things others can help you accomplish. People want to help you. Be gracious, and let them minister to you.

3. Pace yourself.

Keeping in mind the exhaustion, which comes with grief work, you must pace yourself during special times. If the event is a major holiday with several days of activity or weeks of activity, it is even more important to set boundaries and include adequate time for rest. You will not be able to do the many things you accomplished in previous years because you are physically, emotionally, and spiritually drained. Let others pick up the mantle of responsibility for many of the rituals. Participate, but allow time for breaks and rest as you feel the need. Curtail many unnecessary activities. Keep a handle on your schedule, and learn to say no to things you are too tired to do. Keep in mind (from a previous chapter) the importance of putting margins around your life activities. Be realistic about your energy level.

4. Be realistic.

Obviously, you are not going to enjoy the holiday as in previous times. If it is a special day such as a birthday or anniversary, expect to feel sad, but plan some things to bring joy on this special day too. Do not be reluctant to enjoy parts of the day. Do not feel guilty if you find enjoyment in small increments during the special day. Do not feel guilty if you find something to smile or laugh about during this time. This is not disrespectful to your loved one. If your loved one could speak, he would wish you peace, happiness, and joy.

Do not try to hide your bad moments. Cry if you need to cry. If you feel the need to cry in privacy, excuse yourself for a short while. No one expects you to be jolly. You do not have to pretend everything is fine. If you need to leave the event early, be sure to say this, and assure others you will be okay if you get some rest.

Unrealistic holiday expectations are common even when there is no loss. Many families unrealistically expect to have holidays filled with

Kodak moments when they gather with their extended family members. Naturally, this does not often happen because families are made up of the normal range of ordinary human beings, flaws and all. Realistically knowing not all holidays in the past with the loved one were perfect gives the mourners a better perspective on the expectations for the holidays after loss.

5. Be proactive in fighting depression.

Even if you are taking medication for depression, it is not the magic bullet to cure the sense of sadness you feel. It is normal to feel sad due to the absence of your loved one. Your physician may have prescribed an antidepressant to help you. Along with the medication, you must take responsibility to implement some actions to assist you in dealing with depression. The antidepressant is not a happy pill. It will not make you feel elated, but it will enable you to feel capable of coping with your problems and using other strategies to help you.

When you are sad, think of some things you enjoy, and treat yourself by doing some of them. It does not have to be anything major. Treating yourself means finding simple pleasures, which lift your spirit. Reading a favorite scripture, watching a favorite old movie, taking a bubble bath, or buying fresh flowers could all be spirit lifters. Only you can determine the treats you enjoy. Self-care and nurturing yourself make for a healthier mental state.

You cannot, nor should you, wait for others to bring you out of the doldrums. Think of small pleasures you enjoyed during previous special occasions. Treat yourself to some of those. You must take responsibility for your own happiness and well-being. You must create your own healing. Always be good to yourself. Refuse to stay down with depression. Take actions to move forward in fighting depression by giving good self-care.

6. Manage your time.

Throughout the time of the special event—be it a day, days, or weeks—manage your time. You want to balance the time you spend with others and the time you spend alone. A good blend is most helpful in getting through special times after the death of a loved one.

During the special event, it is important to take some time to think, pray, take a walk, or get in touch with memories by oneself. You may shed a few tears at this time, but it is okay to cry. This quiet period is a time for you to visit with your loved one in memory and to reflect on your life together.

Equally important is spending time during the special day or days with other people. It helps family and friends to be with you because they feel the loss too. If you do not have family or many available friends, find other people who need company. There are many lonely people who need someone to talk to and to share a special holiday. Seek out others, and share the gift of yourself and your concern.

7. Help others.

It is difficult to think about helping others when your heart is broken. Yet suffering helps you recognize and empathize with the suffering of others. Helping to carry the burden of someone else lightens your own load of worry and pain. Feeling needed and wanted is a great antidote to despair and loneliness.

Helping others takes you outside your own world for a while. It keeps you from falling into self-pity. Self-pity is a pit of deep despair and drives away the very help you need to heal. Self-pity is a selfish act. Avoiding self-pity means to allow the joy of concern for others to shine through your tears. Barbara Johnson put it well when she said, "People will not avoid you if you cry, as long as you let your spirit shine! However, they will avoid you, if you whine!" During the special days of celebration, reaching out to others provides a much needed balm for your spirit.

8. Commemorate the life of your loved one.

As the special days come, plan ways to commemorate the life of your loved one. Commemoration means a celebration of the loved one's life, not memorializing the death. Decide ahead of time what would be a fitting and comforting ritual to perform to celebrate the life lived by your loved one. The commemoration could be as simple as lighting a special candle or placing flowers in a special place to honor the loved one. It could be as elaborate as a special service or a special dinner.

You invested a great deal of time in the life of your loved one. Perhaps you can pay tribute by giving some of your time during the special days to a charitable organization. Whatever commemoration activity you choose to do, the message is, "I loved you, and I still do. You were and are important to me."

The commemoration of celebrating the life lived is a positive perspective for the mourners. The Talmud, an ancient collection of writings, which contains Jewish law, speaks to the importance of commemorating the death as a celebration of the life in the following passage:

> Two ships sailed in a harbor: one going out on a voyage, and the other coming into port. People cheered the ship going out, but the ship sailing in was hardly noticed. Seeing this, a wise man remarked, "Do not rejoice for a ship sailing out to sea, for you do not know what terrible danger it may encounter. Rejoice rather for the ship that has reached shore, bringing its passengers safely home."

> And so it is in the world. When a child is born, all rejoice; when someone dies, all weep. But it makes just as much sense, if not more, to rejoice at the end of a life as at the beginning. For no one can tell what events await a newborn child, but when a mortal dies, he has successfully completed a journey.

Remembering your loved one and celebrating the joy he brought to your life—as well as the life of other family members, friends, and the community—is a spiritually lifting ritual, which pays homage to the imprint the loved one left on the lives of those left behind.

Following the loss of a loved one, all special days and holidays are different and call for different rituals of celebration. You are living the life of a *survivor*, and in order to do that, you have to change. Each special occasion will have its bittersweet moments and its tears, but it will have its pleasures too. You will never forget the happy times when you were all together as a complete family, but you will be able to enjoy life again after loss. You must learn although the memories of yesterday are precious, you cannot let them destroy the beauty of today. The poet Robert Frost said,

> In three words, I can sum up everything I've learned about life.
> IT GOES ON. Despite our fears and worries life continues.

So it does. Your loved one died, and you are here in the present. It is so very hard to go on, but you must. You have the legacy of the memories of yesterday, the blessings and joys of today, and the promise of better days tomorrow.

Chapter 8 References

1. Bartocci, Barbara. 2000. *Nobody's Child Anymore: Grieving, Caring, and Comforting When Parents Die.* Notre Dame, IN: Sorin Books.
2. Blair, Pamela, PhD, and Brook Noel. 2000. *I Wasn't Ready to Say Goodbye: Surviving, Coping and Healing after the Sudden Death of a Loved One.* Milwaukee, WI: Champion Press LTD.
3. Johnson, Barbara. 2004. *Laughter from Heaven.* Nashville, TN: W Publishing Group.
4. Klein, Allen. 1989. *The Healing Power of Humor. P. 156*, New York, NY: Penguin Putman Inc.
5. Manning, Doug. 1979. *Don't Take My Grief Away: What to Do When You Lose a Loved One.* San Francisco: CA: HarperCollins Publishers.
6. Segal, Julius. 1986. *Winning Life's Toughest Battles: Roots of Human Resilience.* New York, NY: Ivy Press.
7. Shuchter, Stephen R. 1986. *Dimensions of Grief: Adjusting to the Death of a Spouse.* San Francisco, CA: Jossey-Bass.
8. Stalling, Elizabeth. 1997. *Prayer Starters: To Help You Heal after Loss.* St. Meinrad, IN: Abbey Press.
9. Tatelbaum, Judy. 1980. *The Courage to Grieve: Creative Living, Recovery, and Growth through Grief.* New York, New York: Harper Row.
10. Wiersbe, Warren. 1997. *God Isn't in a Hurry: Learning to Slow Down and Live.* Grand Rapids, MI: Baker Books.
11. Wolfelt, Alan D., PhD. 2001. *Healing Your Grieving Heart.* Fort Collins, CO: Companion Press.
12. Wolfelt, Alan D., PhD. 1992. *Understanding Grief: Helping Yourself Heal.* Muncie: IN: Accelerated Development Inc.
13. York, Sara. 2000. *Remembering Well: Rituals for Celebrating Life and Mourning Death.* SanFrancisco;CA: Jossey-Bass.

Chapter 9

THE GIFTS OF LOSS

Nothing brings you more forcefully face-to-face with life than the death experience. It is because I faced death early in my life (through losses I did not think I could survive) that I came to realize what really matters in life. Life has not always been easy or pleasant, but it has been joyful despite the sad, tragic times. I feel deep gratitude for the blessings scattered throughout my life. I am confident some of these blessings might have been overlooked had it not been for my valley experiences with death. It was those valleys, which made the mountaintops even sweeter. It was those valleys, which made me take stock of the good things happening in my life as well as the bad.

All of us are guilty of taking for granted so many blessings we receive daily. It is sad to have to learn the importance of the daily blessings by enduring a major tragedy. This is the way of man. Appreciation of the things money cannot buy or station in life cannot give is a gigantic step in learning a great truth in life. Writer Warren Wiersbe said it best when he said,

> It is good to have the things that money can buy provided we don't lose the things that money can't buy. There is a vast difference between prices and values, and some people are paying too high a price for the small returns they get on their investment.

Death causes you to look at your investment and consider the returns you are receiving. Death brings introspection into your life and your actions. It makes you ask the big question, "What is truly important to me in life?"

It has been my belief from my earliest days of difficulties that every negative event brings a gift in its hand, if only one seeks it. As I read *On Life after Death*, by Dr. Elisabeth Kubler-Ross, I found I am not the first or only person to believe this. Dr. Kubler-Ross says,

> If you would only realize, nothing that comes to you is negative. I mean nothing. All the trials and tribulations, the greatest losses, things that make you say, "If I had known about this I would never have been able to make it through," are gifts to you. It's like somebody has to temper the iron. It is an opportunity that you are given to grow. This is the sole purpose of existence on this planet.

This does not lessen or negate the need for grieving. It is not making light of the suffering, which comes with loss. It does not imply the survivor should take the loss with a smile and a Pollyanna attitude. Trials of life are painful. Loss brings suffering. During these times, you will be sorrowful. However, during this time of pain, suffering, and sorrow, growth is taking place. Valuable life lessons are learned, which introduce new insights and opportunities to the survivor.

The most positive gift from the losses in my life is the growth I experienced as a person. This chapter reviews and summarizes many of the processes discussed in previous chapters. A book such as this must end on a positive note of hope for the eventual return of joy to your life. Because it is so important to be healthy with your grieving process and to learn from the loss experience, this chapter emphasizes the gifts of loss. When we see the gifts, we appreciate more the lives lived and our own life.

As time passes and you gain distance and insights from the loss, you may find several things happen to increase your personal growth. Alan Klein says,

> Seeing the advantage in the disadvantage of loss happens when you focus on the lesson (the gift) instead of the loss.

New doors may open to you. You may find yourself stronger and wiser than you were before the loss. It is likely your priorities will be quite different. You will make many positive life changes.

Researchers studying the impact of loss on survivors found a high correlation between loss and positive life changes. Calhoun and Tedeschi found the loss not only changed a person immediately after the death, it often did so in positive ways for his lifetime. Individuals reported experiencing positive transformations in goals, purpose, and perspective on life as a result of struggling with their loss.

The work of Davis and Hoeksema confirmed the majority of bereaved people in their studies reported finding something positive in their loss experiences. Specifically mentioned was a sense of growth toward full potential, increased appreciation for relationships in their lives, and improvement in their own self-esteem in regards to their performance when undergoing life-changing circumstances.

Positive Changes

After experiencing death up close and personal, you will never be the same again. While it is the most devastating and stressful experience of your life, there are positive changes occurring within you from the instant of your loved one's death. You are being reinvented. You are reinvented, not because you wanted to change but because you were forced to be a different person.

Part of your reinvention involves a self-inventory and self-evaluation. This is when you take stock of who you are, what you believe, your strengths, and your weaknesses. This is not a paper-and-pencil inventory. In fact, you may not realize you are doing it. This is when you begin to really think about what is important to you in life. Perhaps, for the first time, you question how you spent your life up to this point and think about the days ahead. You may find you are stronger than you thought you were. You may discover you can make decisions you did not know you could make. You may discover a core of courage within you to face the "unfaceable." Many people surprise themselves by dealing with the situation better than they ever dreamed they could.

Another positive change, which occurs after loss, is learning to live fully. This means living in the present. It requires stepping out of the past with all its doubts, resentments, and regrets. It means letting go of the *what was* no matter how good or how bad it was. Living fully allows you to be less demanding of yourself and others. Living fully allows you to enjoy the pleasures of the moment, without removing the joy with constant worry. Living life fully is like squeezing an orange to get every bit of juice, not wanting to miss one delicious drop. Author Stormie Omartian describes living fully as living in the present as if you do not have a past, certain that the steps you take today will determine your future.

Although Dr. Alan Wolfelt does not call this change living fully, he does describe this change in his writings. His books emphasize the importance of lightening up on the demands you put on yourself. He encourages mourners to determine what gives their life meaning and what does not. He encourages reconfiguration of your life to do more of what comforts you and makes you feel better about yourself. There is a heavy emphasis on staying in the present time, focusing on life in the moment. Dealing with small increments of time allows you to live fully in the present.

Another positive change occurs as you make the journey to wholeness. The positive change is learning to accept the reality of your life, not resisting the *what is*. When you make this change, you realize it is okay to be this changing person. To change is to live. You are ever-evolving into a new, different person in order to function in your ever-changing world. This is what this entire book discusses.

The journey to wholeness is long and treacherous. There can be many detours, delays, and setbacks. Does this not describe man's life journey itself? Naturally, after a major loss, you strive to become whole again; but is that not what life is really all about whether you suffered loss or not? Each person deals with life daily in some way to move forward to completeness. As long as you live, you will be a work in progress. This process involves being all you can be on the way to becoming who you were meant to be.

Each of us moves in a constant process of *becoming*, yet we never truly arrive because it is an ongoing process. The routes of travel on this journey to wholeness include navigating the paths of wisdom, compassion, self-nurturing, problem solving, resource seeking, courage building, gratitude, and sustained faith. As you travel the road to wholeness, you learn to soldier on through the good times and bad times of life, learning many lessons along the way. It is important to understand, in the words of author Barbara Johnson, that on this journey, "we are pilgrims, not settlers."

As you travel toward wholeness, you can never remain stationary. The goal will not be reached if you settle. This is a trip of continuous movement. There is no settling into a permanent comfort zone. The journey to wholeness calls you to be a pilgrim—marching forward, marching on, facing, and adapting to your ever-changing world.

Another positive change, which takes place as you adapt to your loss, is increased wisdom. *The American College Dictionary* defines "wisdom" as the "knowledge of what is true or right coupled with just judgment as to action." In the early days of loss, you are not sure you possess the wisdom to handle the situation you face. This is a feeling common to all mourners. Death knocks you to your knees. Your world is upside down, and you are not sure about anything at this point.

As you grieve and adapt to your loss, you begin to grow in wisdom. You begin to learn how to do things you have not done previously. You learn more about yourself than you ever thought possible. You begin to see life in a new way. You examine your beliefs, values, ideas, and relationships. You probe your outlook on life, and ask yourself some hard questions about who you are and what is important to you. You learn to deal with your problems by discovering solutions and choosing actions.

The life lessons you learn by suffering loss make you wise beyond your years. Wisdom is a positive quality to possess, and the attainment of it is a positive change brought by loss. The Bible says of wisdom in Proverbs 3:13-14,

> Blessed is the man who finds wisdom, the man who gains understanding, for she is more profitable than silver and yields better returns than gold.

This scripture speaks to the idea expressed by Wiersbe when he talked about learning to distinguish between prices and values. Money cannot buy the things that matter most in life. Wisdom is gained when you learn this through the loss of someone you love. Surviving loss with increased wisdom is a boon for the mourner. Increased wisdom improves the quality of life and your relationships in all the days ahead.

The positive changes, which come with loss, create a chain reaction. Self-inventory and self-evaluation provide you with the knowledge you need as you make the journey to wholeness. These positive changes also contribute to your ability to live fully—experiencing the joys of the now. Understanding yourself, finding the tools you need to become whole, and learning how to live fully infuses you with wisdom you did not possess before the death. As you undergo these positive changes, the way you look at your world changes. You develop new perspectives.

Changed Perspectives

Self-inventory and self-evaluation often leads to a *change in self-perception*. Death of a loved one causes you to slow down and take stock of yourself. By reviewing past hopes and dreams and comparing them to the present situation, you see the necessity for change. What qualities do you, personally, still possess? Did those change with the death? Which ones changed, and which ones did not? What will be your new direction?

When analyzing these questions and answers, your perception of self and perception of your life changes. You may find you are stronger than you thought. One discovery may be the number of people outside your own family who truly care about you. You may be surprised by the impact you have on the lives of others. You may also discover you have continued to live and function even when you never thought you were capable of such courage.

Grief teaches you there is a lot to learn about your world as well as yourself. Often the survivor is surprised to find how competent he is when times are painful. One bereaved mother said, "You do not know what you can handle until you have to." Often you are surprised about the reactions of those around you. Some people you thought would be there for you fail to deliver. Other sources of comfort, which you never considered before the loss, become invaluable. You begin to view the world in a different light. You become more observant. You become more aware of your strengths as well as weaknesses.

Many bereaved clients in my support groups admitted they struggled each day. However, most felt they were doing well to "hang in there." In fact, many commented they had fared better than they ever imagined they would. The unity of the group, and the sharing of feelings and coping techniques, seemed to give credence to their belief they were doing as well as could be expected and often better than expected. Knowing others of similar circumstances were having difficulty but surviving helped clients to feel they were as normal as one can be when grieving.

The change in self-perspective is not an immediate change. I observe it happening gradually with my clients. Chaos rules in the early days of loss. Even so, many individuals express, with the passing of time, "I don't know how I did it, but I'm surviving." A glimpse of this progress is viewed when former group participants return one or two years later with friends who recently experienced a loss. The veteran survivor shows greater strength, courage, and compassion than was exhibited in his early days of bereavement.

Some mourners indicated in private therapy the loss gave them the opportunity to see themselves in perspective to those around them. If they attended support groups, they observed how others faced loss and considered how they were faring in comparison. Again, many commented they felt they were doing as well or better than many others were. Being able to put your own actions in perspective appears to give most people a more positive self-perspective. Segal, when interviewing newly released POW troops, found that crisis and/or tragedy gave them the opportunity to see themselves in perspective. He determined this to be an important contributor to survival.

Most people put up a mask of pretense for the world to see. This creates a disparity between the way they are perceived by the world and the way they perceive themselves. The mask slips more when out of public view. In other words, only the nearest loved ones come close to knowing the real person behind the mask. Many people keep the mask in place for so long they often begin to fool even themselves. Death does not allow the mourner the luxury of pretense. The mask falls away, and the pretense is gone. The real, raw, unvarnished emotions are revealed. The playacting is over. The importance of this occurrence is it makes you look hard at yourself and discover the real you behind the mask. At this point, you are amenable to positive change. This is when your self-perception undergoes renovation.

Your *perception of life* itself changes after loss. Before loss came into your life, you probably lived as though life would never end. It seemed there would always be time later to do many things. There was always tomorrow. You know death comes to one and all eventually, but it is easy to deny this in your daily living.

Judy Tatelbaum, author of *The Courage to Grieve*, says,

> It is the denial of death that is responsible for people living empty, purposeless lives; for when you live as if you'll live forever, it becomes too easy to postpone the thing you know you must do. You live your life in preparation for tomorrow or in remembrance of yesterday; and meanwhile, each today is lost.

What a pity to use up today in living empty, shallow lives when time is fleeting and life is rapidly moving toward conclusion! Death gives you a new lease on life. A new perspective becomes clear. No one can experience a tragic loss without realizing the importance of living a life that matters. In order to do this, you have to live it moment by moment, making every minute count!

Another factor in this changed life perspective is the realization when a loved one dies, he lives on through you. There may be many dreams, projects, or hopes the loved one left unfinished. You may decide to carry on with these works the loved one cannot. Death of a loved one often brings inspiration to the mourner, establishing a purpose in life, which is a passionate, loving testimony to the impact the loved one had on the survivor's life.

The tragedy of the long illness and death of my husband left a lasting imprint on my life. My perception of life was greatly altered by it. My passion to work with people suffering emotional pain is directly attributed to the lessons learned as he and I went through the difficulty of his illness together.

His death affected me as no other event in my life ever has. Understanding the importance of intangibles over things, people over status, and gratitude over disappointment were valuable lessons, which drastically changed my perspective on life. This lesson taught me to focus on things that truly matter.

If he could come back today to see how things turned out, I know he would be proud to know although his life was shortened, his strength of character and courage in the face of death helped me to come through the pain of loss. Even more important his death was the catalyst, which propelled me into a new life career of helping others.

In finding my purpose by a change in life perspective, a purpose for his life and death continues yet today. Thousands of people have heard his story through me. Thousands of people have received encouragement due to my passion for service to others. This began with him. He left a legacy. I have used his legacy to help others. This has created my own legacy. The partnership lives on in my changed life perspective.

Another change in your life perspective is the change from such complicated existence to a simpler way of life. Death teaches you to assess the trivial ways you spend your precious time, talent, and energy. Are there better uses for it? So much of the business of your days appears unimportant in the face of death. Death makes you sift the important from the unimportant and to be selective in how you invest yourself. You begin to analyze the most productive ways to use your talent and energy. You try to determine which ways will mean the most. You ask yourself, "What do I really care about?" "What can I eliminate?" "What is really necessary?"

On the wall of my Sunday school class is this quote: "The best use of one's life is to spend it on something that will outlast it." This is the essence of the change in life perspective that takes place in determining use of your time.

One of the greatest changes in your life perspective is the *change in your values.* You discover life is really not about the cars, the house, the cash; but it is about people, relationships, love, honor, trust, and faith. Material things lose their glitter. In the face of death, they no longer seem important to achieve.

An example of this was what happened on 9/11. When those people in the planes knew they probably would not make it, when the people trapped in the towers knew they would not get out, the ones who could tried to call loved ones for one last time. Nothing was important in the face of death but a few last words with the people they loved. Relationships and love were more valuable than anything else in the face of such massive tragedy.

Your change in values or realignment of your values impacts your life forever. When your focus changes from material things to the basic values of love, honor, decency, relationships, trust, and faith, you will live your life in a much different manner from that time forth.

A changed *perspective on your faith* and your understanding of suffering also occurs after a devastating loss. At a time when suffering is intense, you begin to closely examine what you truly believe and why you believe it. You delve through the tenets of your faith and ask many hard questions.

If God is all-knowing and loves us, why does he allow such terrible things to happen to us? This is the often-asked question of wounded believers. The answer does not come quickly nor is it always the answer you accept or want to hear. Learning valuable life lessons is never painless, but valuable lessons help man to grow in wisdom and understanding.

As discussed in the chapter on spirituality, a strong faith does not protect you from suffering, disappointment, or loss. A strong faith is a support through those difficult times in life. When mourning the death of someone you love, the suffering is meaningless unless you use it as a growth process. Using suffering to strengthen your faith, your courage, and your resolve to continue life is a positive use of suffering.

Suffering is humanizing. It gives you the ability to recognize and understand pain as you never before grasped the concept. When you gain this knowledge, you become more connected to the pain and suffering of others. Your own suffering enables you to not just *sympathize* with others but to *empathize* with them. This empathy enables you to recognize the hurt in the eyes of someone else. You become a kindred spirit with the walking wounded. The example given in a previous chapter of the wounded healer refers to a person who can lovingly help others because he too has suffered and understands the pain.

As you endure the suffering after a loss, you begin to analyze your relationships, your actions, and your interactions. Through this intense analysis of your life, you come to understand some of your suffering in the past was needless. Once you are mired in a situation of despair, which was totally unavoidable by your own actions, you learn the difference between avoidable and unavoidable suffering.

Learning to discern between avoidable and unavoidable suffering requires you to ask two questions of yourself. One, what is the source of my suffering? Two, is this suffering due to something I could not prevent?

Suffering because your spouse died is one thing, but suffering because you have more debt than you can pay is another. Many tragedies befall you in life. These are unavoidable sufferings. Complications in life due to bad decisions or poor choices produce unnecessary suffering. These complications lie within your power to avoid by making better decisions. There is great wisdom in knowing the difference between these two types of suffering because that knowledge impacts your actions and reactions. Dealing with the death of a loved one certainly gives you a different perspective on suffering.

Gaining this different perspective of suffering helps to take away the anger, doubt, and disappointment you may have with God and your faith. Faith is not the protection from suffering, but faith is what you use to make sense of the pain. Faith teaches you to expect problems in life. Faith teaches you to face these problems with a positive attitude, knowing joyful times will return even though it seems impossible at this time of loss. Faith teaches you there is a gift to be found in the pain if you wisely seek it.

Dick Innes, in the following poem, talks about how important it is for people of faith to use the pain for spiritual growth and growth as a person.

Never Waste Your Pain

Dear Lord . . .
Please grant that I shall never waste my pain for . . .
To fail without learning,
To fall without getting up,
To sin without overcoming,
To be hurt without forgiving,
To be discontent without improving,
To be crushed without becoming more caring,
To suffer without growing more sensitive,
Makes of suffering a senseless, futile exercise,
A tragic loss,
And of pain, the greatest waste of all.

—Dick Innes

Understanding the place suffering has in the strengthening of your faith is a valuable life lesson. This change in perspective concerning suffering and faith is paramount in helping you to have the courage and strength to persevere. Matthew 17:20-21 says,

> If you have faith as small as a mustard seed, you can move this mountain . . . . Nothing will be impossible for you.

Believing this gives you great hope for better tomorrows and faith you will be sustained throughout all the days ahead.

I found my perception of faith broadened and deepened more in the difficult times of my life than in the good times. The difficult times were the times I had to put my faith to work. During these times, giving lip service to faith was not enough. These times were the trial by fire for what I believed and why I believed it. My belief in God and His love and protection gave me the comfort of never feeling alone. I knew I could weather the storm because I had the guidance of His hand.

I learned the answer to the question of where is God? as I changed my perspective on my faith—from one of waiting for Him to come to me to realizing all I had to do was go to Him. When you walk with God in your daily life, He is constant. If you lose Him, He is not the one who moved from the path. You did. Author Stormie Omartian said,

> We wait for Him to notice our plight; He waits for us to take
> His hand.

In the book of Matthew, the seventh chapter of the New Testament, the discussion is about the wisdom of building your house on solid rock. This analogy refers to the wisdom of building your life upon a strong faith. The scripture says in verse 25:

> When the rain descended and the floods came, and the winds
> blew, and beat upon the house, it fell not.
>
> —Matthew 7:25

This is how faith sustains you during times of suffering and loss. Note the passage does not say, "*If* the rain descended." It says, "*When* the rain descended." This is the way of life. It is not a matter of *if* there will be pain, suffering, and loss. It is *when* this happens, faith will sustain you through the storm to better times. This is a promise from God. In my life, I have found this promise to be fulfilled over and over every time I reached for His hand.

The change in attitude, which does the most to give you a positive perception of your faith during tragedy, is looking at life with gratitude to God for the many blessings you do have. Major life changes are upsetting and scary. No one wants to give up a familiar, comfortable routine. The first reaction is to feel everything has been taken away from you. You do not want to give up what you had. It is as though you fear you will never have anything good again. The gift in the terrible experience of death is twofold. First, it brings deep appreciation for what you *had*. Second, it brings great thankfulness for what you still *have*.

At the time of my husband and parents' deaths, I realized more than ever how much they blessed my life. How fortunate I was to have these people in my life for the time they were there. As I mourned their passing, I saw the many good things I still had. As I changed my life to accommodate their loss, I began to grow and change in ways I never dreamed possible. I learned to notice and appreciate the small blessings more and to put more joy and less worry in my life. I learned greater appreciation for the relationships I had with these loved ones and vowed to improve and enjoy my relationships with those people still in my life.

Living in an attitude of gratitude deepens your faith. You become aware of how very good God has been and is to you. You see while you may not have everything you *want*, you do have *enough*. The quest for attaining more and more sometimes undermines our sense of what is necessary. Death has a way of stopping you in your tracks to consider the question of what is *enough*. Although the death has taken away someone you wanted and needed, it is important at this time to focus positively on what you have left in your life.

God blesses you each day with *enough*. Being able to rise and dress being mobile—able to work, able to talk and think—there are marvelous blessings in those gifts alone. The friends, relatives, caregivers, and important other people in your life are enough in times of need. True, you *want* your loved one. The hard fact is you do not have him, but you do have enough to go on with life even though you will grieve the loss of the precious gift of his life.

As I struggled with my losses, I missed each loved one terribly. I wanted them with me, but I was blessed with *enough*. When my husband died, I wanted my husband; but I had my parents, son, friends, and faith. I had *enough*. When my parents died, I wanted my parents; but I had my husband, son, grandchildren, friends, church family, and faith. I had *enough*.

We take for granted so many of God's blessings. Focusing on the beauty left in life at the time of tragedy and loss helps to develop an attitude of gratitude. A POW from the Vietnam War commented that after his release, things he took for granted before his imprisonment, he noticed more and considered them precious. Suffering taught him the enjoyment of unnoticed treasures.

It is the discovery of the beautiful serendipities of God's universe, which can lift the spirit. The beauty of a sunset, the glistening of sun on the water, a butterfly lighting on a flower, or a cardinal pecking at the feeder fills you with the awesome wonder of God's creations. Appreciation of the gifts, often taken for granted, strengthens faith. The poet Emerson once said, "If the stars only came out once a year, everyone would notice them." Failure on the part of man to enjoy *enough* takes away appreciation for God's gifts.

Your changed perspective on time and priorities is another gift gained through loss. This change takes place slowly as you evaluate yourself, begin to live fully, work toward wholeness, and gather wisdom. The time and priority perspective is changed, just as these positive changes changed your perception of self, life in general, and your faith.

You cannot be all things to all people, but that does not stop most people from trying. Days are filled with packed schedules, e-mails, phone calls, messages, work demands, social demands, and family demands. Calendars are full of activities, and family members often meet each other, coming and going. There are too many things to do and not enough of you to go around.

Sadly, it takes a tragedy to put the brakes on this mad race of life. Death or a tragic situation calls a halt to the frantic pace and gives you time to consider, What is the most important thing in my life? It is amazing how tragedy immediately sorts the truly important from the unimportant time-consuming tasks you convince yourself you must do.

The sobering discovery of the finiteness of time makes you realize your time is limited, and wasting it on unimportant matters is beyond foolish. Maximizing your use of precious time for the top priorities in your life is a lesson of great value. This discovery resets your course for the rest of your life. It has a huge impact on future goals, actions, and choices.

Benjamin Franklin said,

> Dost thou love Life? Then do not squander Time; for that's the stuff Life is made of.

Picture in your mind a large bank, which holds nothing but time. Every person has an account at this bank. Each day you live, you make a withdrawal of time. You cannot save it. You cannot make it grow. You cannot trade it. You must use it, and when it is used, you cannot retrieve it. No one knows the balance of his account. Time is a precious commodity, and it is important to be a good steward of your account. Death brings this fact home to you as no other event can.

Being a good steward means determining those people and things in your life for which you have the most passion and putting them first in the amount of time you invest with them. Perhaps this means just tweaking your lifestyle. Maybe it means making major changes in schedules, activities, and direction in your life.

Good stewards of time make every minute count. It is as the saying goes, living today as though it were your last. It means never putting happiness off until tomorrow, next week, or next year. It means finding happiness now.

A good steward invests his time in the people and things, which contribute the most to his peace of mind, sense of wholeness, and spirit. It means enjoying life more and worrying less. It means not wasting time on trivial, unimportant things, which you really do not care about anyway. Time is more precious than any of your possessions. Understanding the value of it makes you wise in its use.

This changed perspective about time and priorities also makes you consider your hopes and dreams. Have you put off dreams until later? What have you always wanted to do? What have you put on hold because of mundane, unimportant tasks, which take priority over your dreams?

Being a good steward of time and selecting your top priorities may mean leaving a sink of dirty dishes to play ball with the kids. It sometimes means going back to school at forty, fifty, sixty, or later. It could mean traveling the country for extended months, simply to personally enjoy the beauty and grandeur of this great nation. It is making time to hug your children, love your spouse, honor your parents, and be a friend. It is sometimes disconnecting from the world of technology—the cell phones, e-mails, blackberry, laptops—and paying attention to the real people right in front of you. It is refusing to be available 24/7 to everyone in the world.

When someone you love dies, it brings home to you that time ran out for him. Perhaps for the first time, you must face you will not be here forever, so there is much left to accomplish with your remaining time. Learning to make the most of each and every day is a huge step toward returning joy to your life again.

Personal Growth

Along with the positive life changes and the changed perspectives, the mourner eventually realizes one of the greatest gifts from loss is the personal growth, which takes place in his life. This growth, like all the gains in the journey of grief, is a slow process. There are so many phases of emotions—decisions to be considered, choices to be made, and actions to take—you are totally submerged in the process. What you strive to regain is life balance. Because this growth is such a slow process, we may fail to recognize it is taking place.

The growth made in regaining life balance is not simply recapturing what was but involves the development of a new life balance. As discussed in previous chapters, you never return to your old self. That is impossible. Reaching equilibrium in your life or balance means you become acclimated to the new life you are living, and you learn to function in new ways.

312 PHYLLIS MCELWAIN, PHD, CADC

The attainment of life balance brings you closer to fulfilling your potential. You not only learn to express your feelings and thoughts, you may be able to do so without embarrassment. You grow in the ability to build better relationships with those loved ones still in your life and with new people who may come into your life along the way. The loss touches you in a way, which makes you more open to communication with others. Knowing from the lesson of loss the importance of saying what needs to be said and the shortness of time in which to say it compels you to live to the fullest. You try not to leave things undone and unsaid.

You look at your twenty-four-hour block of time and realign the allotments to those areas of most importance to your sense of peace and happiness. Knowing what matters to you helps you to reach your potential because it sets you on a clearly defined course to achieve your life purpose.

During this growth to regain a new life balance, you also grow in compassion for yourself as well as others. Self-compassion helps you meet your own needs. This is paramount in strengthening yourself to meet and deal successfully with life's difficulties. It also enables you to assume responsibility for your own peace of mind. By nurturing yourself, you not only gain independence, you learn to recognize and appreciate your own progress.

The heightened sense of compassion extends to others as well as yourself. Loss makes you more sensitive to the hurt and pain of the suffering of other people around you. Many mourners find themselves giving the service of nurturing to other sufferers, thereby, receiving the benefit of the lessening of their own pain.

Nurturing others and being nurtured in return was one of my experiences when my mother died. Her funeral was on a Sunday afternoon. The next week was the meeting of the support group I facilitated. I did not know how I would be able to lead the group with the rawness of my own grief being uppermost in my mind. I debated about finding another leader and staying home to nurse my grief. I decided that was not the right thing for me to do. I went to the group meeting as planned. During the sharing time, I shared my grief. The outpouring of compassion on the part of the group was most helpful to me. Later, I received several notes from group participants commenting on how much that particular group meeting had benefited them. This was good to hear because I knew it had benefited me with the warmth of shared compassion.

Another lesson from loss contributing greatly to personal growth is the facing of your own mortality. Living as though you will live forever leaves no room for the preparation for a most important trip. The *New York Times* columnist Jane Brody said,

> If any good came from my mother's death at age 49, it was my recognition at age 17, of my mortality and my decision . . . to live each day as though it might be my last.

What a change takes place in your life when you shift your thinking from time being endless to thinking this might be my last day on earth! Understanding your own mortality gives you a whole new outlook on life. It sharpens your focus, strengthens your resolve to accomplish your dreams, and increases your appreciation for life itself.

Growth of this magnitude brings renewal of your spirit and awareness of the opportunities around you to fulfill your dreams. Understanding your own mortality frees you to take risks to achieve those dreams. Playing it safe does not move you to reach your full potential. Knowing there are opportunities, which only come once in a lifetime, can give you the courage to reach for them.

My life is an example of how taking a risk can lead to the fulfillment of purpose. While I loved the teaching profession, after my husband's death and my subsequent remarriage, I began to consider where I wanted to go with the rest of my life.

I realized my time on earth was limited as it is for everyone. I did not know how many tomorrows lay ahead of me, so I decided to make the most of today. Through teaching, I was rewarded by the sense of touching the lives of others. This was important to me. As I considered my own mortality and what I wanted to do with my time, I was drawn to the field of counseling.

Giving up the security of a permanent, stable job and going back to school for an additional degree at almost fifty was taking a huge risk. The new venture was a daunting decision for me to make. This required courage and a leap of faith to pursue such a dream. The rewards of making that decision several years ago have definitely been worth the risk. It was not until I faced my own mortality that I was able to reach for the dream.

One of the greatest occurrences of personal growth through loss is restoration of the soul. Tragedy brings suffering. It disrupts inner peace. Your soul cries out for healing. The wound suffered is severe, and your spirit absorbs the blow. When the spirit is in agony, joy is removed from your life. The Psalmist says,

> Weeping may endure for a night,
> But joy cometh in the morning.
> —Psalm 30:56

It is during the night of grief's journey the soul suffers the most. Restoration of the soul is needed to bring a new day filled with joy. Regaining the joy happens when the soul is well nourished.

Feeding the soul requires you to nurture yourself in all ways—physically, emotionally, and spiritually. This is the purpose of the grieving process. It gives you time to review your life—to accept the ministering of others, to minister to others, and to experience a rebirth of your new self. Grief is the womb where your new identity is created. With that rebirth comes a restored soul, and with the restored soul comes the return of joy.

Self-nurturing, the development of gratitude, compassion for self and others, and gaining new inner balance bring forth the restoration needed for your ailing spirit. When you look forward again to life—knowing you have promises to keep, people to love, and places to go—you experience a return of the joy in living.

For me, feeding my soul deeply involves my faith. There is never a need for starving for nourishment of the soul when God is there to sustain you. The promise made in the New Testament, book of John 15:9, 11, renews my strength:

> John 15:9
> As the Father has loved me, so have I loved you. Now remain in my love.

> John 15:11
> I have told you this so that my joy may be in you and that your joy may be complete.

Knowing God loves me and cares about joy being in my life nourishes my soul when it needs restoration. When my soul cries out for courage and strength, again, the book of John provides the encouragement needed to enlarge my faith and feed my soul.

> John 14:27
> Peace I leave with you; my peace I give you. I do not give to you as the world gives. Do not let your heart be troubled and do not be afraid.

This is a promise of peace like no peace that can be found on earth! It is an assurance for me of sustaining encouragement and hope. This verse gives me courage when I am fearful.

The restoration of my soul was a gift for me in the personal growth I experienced after loss. While the restoration of my soul was achieved through faith, it is important to understand every individual is different. My solace came from scriptures connected to my core beliefs. You have your own belief system; thus, encouragement may come to you from different readings or even from different practices. Beliefs vary from person to person and culture to culture. It is important for you to discover the best pathway to restore your soul.

The chapter on spirituality pointed out the large array of sources of nourishment for your soul, your faith being one of them. Important nourishments for the spirit and the restoration of the soul must come from your core values. I speak from a Christian perspective because that is an integral part of my belief system and of how I choose to deal with adversity.

The lessons learned from loss contain great truths about life. The great truth I most want to impart to you, as I end our talk on loss, is in a story our minister, the Reverend John Conn, shared at my mother's funeral. He said he used the story because he knew her well and felt she discovered this truth of life early on and built her life around it.

The Great Truth of Life

A science teacher who was teaching a class on the volume of containers prepared a demonstration for the class. On the table, he placed a glass gallon jar and poured a container of large rocks into the jar.

"Is the jar full?" he asked the class.

The students looked at the jar closely and did not see how any more rocks could possibly fit into it, so they said, "Yes."
The teacher reached down to a shelf under the table and brought out another container filled with pebbles. He held them up for the class to see, then, he proceeded to pour the pebbles into the jar. The pebbles trickled into the jar, around the big rocks filling the spaces. The teacher asked the students again, "Is the jar full?"

The surprised students more carefully examined the jar this time, but after some scrutiny, they agreed, "Yes, the jar is full."

Then, the teacher reached under the table once more and pulled out another container filled with sand. He lifted the sand container and began to pour. Grains of sand fell around the pebbles and the jar held the whole container. When the last grain of sand fell, the teacher looked over the class and asked for the third time, "Is the jar full?"

Now the students were not so sure. They talked among themselves for a few minutes and finally came to an agreement. They said, "Yes, the jar is full."

"Wrong," said the teacher. The students were amazed when the teacher reached under the table again and removed a container of water. To their surprise, he poured the whole container of water into the jar and it held every drop. "Now," he said, "the jar is full."

The students were impressed with what the teacher had been able to get into one jar. "How did you do this?" they asked. "How is this possible?"

The teacher replied, "It's simple. You simply have to put the big rocks in first or the smaller items get in the way."

The jar represents your life. The greatest truth taught by loss is to put the big rocks in first because if you don't, the small stuff will get in the way. Difficult, tragic times teach us to identify our big rocks. Just as my mother knew what her big rocks were—love of family and others, her faith, compassion, honesty, and integrity—we each learn to identify our own big rocks. Once identified, we know the important truths of life.

If you gain nothing else from reading this book, I hope you will take the lesson of the jar with you throughout your life. Always put the big rocks in first! This is the greatest lesson taught by death.

Chapter 9 References

1. Bozarth, Alla Renee, PhD. 1990. *A Journey through Grief.* Center City, MO: Hazelton.
2. Calhoun, Lawrence, PhD., Richard Tedeschi PhD. 2001. Posttraumatic Growth: The Positive Lessons of Loss. *American Psychological Association* XXI, no. 4 (April): 157-158-172.
3. Coleman, Sally, and Maria Porter. 1994. *Seasons of the Spirit.* Center City, Minn: Hazeldon Foundation.
4. Davis, Chris, Susan Nolen-Hoeksema. 2001. Loss and Meaning: How Do People Make Sense of Loss? *American Behavioral Scientist* 44, no. 5 (May): 726-725-741.
5. Johnson, Barbara. 1994. *Mama, Get the Hammer! There's a Fly on Papa's Head: Using Humor to Flatten out Your Pain. P. 94, 95.*Dallas, TX: Word Publishing.
6. Klein, Allen. 1989. *The Healing Power of Humor. P. 148,* New York, NY: Penguin Putman Inc.
7. Kubler-Ross, Elisabeth, MD. 1991. *On Life after Death. P. 26,* Berkley, CA: Celestial Arts.
8. Neeld, Elizabeth Harper, PhD. 2003. *Seven Choices: Finding Daylight after Loss Shatters Your World. P. 327,* New York, NY: Tiime Warner.
9. Omartian, Stormie. 1999. *Just Enough Light for the Step I'm On: Trusting God in Tough Times. P. 171,* Eugene, Oregon: Harvest House.
10. Segal, Julius. 1986. *Winning Life's Toughest Battles: Roots of Human Resilience.* New York, NY: Ivy Press.
11. Staudacher, Carol. 1991. *Men and Grief: A Guide for Men Surviving the Death of a Loved One.* Oakland, CA: New Harbinger Publications.
12. Tatelbaum, Judy. 1980. *The Courage to Grieve: Creative Living, Recovery, and Growth through Grief. P. 13,* New York, New York: Harper Row.
13. Wiersbe, Warren. 1997. *God Isn't in a Hurry: Learning to Slow Down and Live. P. 141, 19,* Grand Rapids, MI: Baker Books.
14. Wolfelt, Alan D., PhD. 2001. *Healing Your Grieving Heart.* Fort Collins, CO: Companion Press.
15. Wolfelt, Alan D., PhD. 1992. *Understanding Grief: Helping Yourself Heal.* Muncie: IN: Accelerated Development Inc.

Index

Bonanno, George, 103
borrowed tears, 37-38
Bowlby, John, 41, 60, 84, 164, 232, 238, 273
Bozarth, Alla Renee, 17, 23, 27, 84, 131, 154, 317
Brody, Jane, 313
Burns, George, 166

C

Caine, Lynn, 46, 51, 60
Calhoun, Lawrence, 299
Campbell, Ian, 68, 84
caregiver, 68-69, 104, 229-31
Carlin, George, 95
Carr, Deborah, 170
Carter, Jimmy, 32, 44, 116-17, 144, 154
  Virtues of Aging, The, 116, 154
CDC (Centers for Disease Control and Prevention), 214
change
  benefits of, 262-64
  challenge of, 250-52
  components of, 251-54
  reactions to, 254-55
    conservation, 256
    escape, 257-58
    revolution, 256-57
    transcendence, 258
  resistance to, 259-61
  and restructuring, 250
character, 174, 271-72
Charlton, Rodger, 68, 84
Chicken Soup for the Soul, 130
Christakis, Nicholas, 84, 273
chronic insomnia, 63
chronic mourning, 102, 109-11
Claypool, John, 84, 136-37, 145, 151-52, 154
  Tracks of a Fellow Struggler, 84, 136, 154
clinical shock, 53
CLOC (Changing Lives of Older Couples), 170

closure, 20, 33, 103, 109
closure syndrome, 102, 109. *See also* syndromes
Cocoanut Grove fire, 236
cognition confusion, 6, 63
cognitive appraisal, 5, 31-32
cognitive distress, 6, 61
cognitive modality, 164-65
cognitive nurturing, 77-78
cognitive self-care, 73
Cole, Eloise, 40-41
  "Falling Apart," 40
commemoration, 294-95
communication, 264-66, 280
Compassionate Friends, 201
confidence. *See* self-confidence
conflicted grief, 102, 105, 107, 107-8
Conn, John, 14, 315
conscious reactions, 17-18
conservation, 256
cortisol, 62
counseling, 7, 22, 34, 80-81, 85, 103, 110, 232, 248, 260-61, 273, 313
courage, 16-17, 28, 244-45, 250, 302-4, 313-15
Courage to Grieve, The (Tatelbaum), 16, 27, 85, 90, 127, 155, 233, 296, 303, 317
creativity, 131, 261
crying, 36-37, 104, 142, 292
cultural/societal reactions, 20-21

D

dating
  considerations for, 180, 182-84
  wrong reasons for, 181-82
death, 112-14
  acceptance of, 8, 25, 157, 201, 212, 224, 239
  depersonalizing, 26
  preventability of the, 97, 194
  view of, 209-11
death after prolonged illness, 227-31. *See also* anticipatory grief

somatic grief, 102, 105, 109
soul, 47, 49, 116-17, 122-23, 313-15
special days, 89, 261, 292, 294-95
  coping strategies for, 11, 291-95
  and grief, 275-77
  steps in restructuring, 285
    adapt, 286-88
    eliminate, 288-91
    review, 285
spiritual health, 126, 270
spirituality
  definition of, 117-18
  and healing, 121
  ways of, 121-25
spiritual resources, 8, 121
spouse, 49, 51, 65, 68-69, 74, 84-85,
    248-49
spouse, loss of a, 158-60
  adjustment issues of
    dating, 180-84
    finances, 172-74
    psychological, 170-71
    relationship, 174-77
    remarriage, 184-86
    sexuality, 177-80
  and gender differences, 164-70
  psychological phases of, 160-64
Stalling, Elizabeth, 90
Staudacher, Carol, 164, 166-67, 171,
    188, 205, 216, 267
  Men and Grief, 85, 166, 233, 274, 317
Stockdale, James B., 264
stress, 60-63, 68-69, 75-76
suffering, 54, 67, 125, 145, 248, 280,
    306, 309
Suicidal Thoughts, 100, 201-2
suicide, 112-13, 201
  myths about, 214-18
  and the surviving loved one, 218-20
support groups, 39-40, 79-81, 248-49,
    302-3
Surviving Death (Meyer), 85, 154, 178,
    233, 274
survivor changes, 50-52

symptoms
  definition of, 98, 98
  examples of, 98-99
    See also individual symptoms
syndromes
  definition of, 102
  types of
    closure syndromes, 109
      See also closure mourning
    expression syndromes, 102-4
    skewed thinking syndromes, 104-9

T

Talmud, 295
Tatelbaum, Judy, 16, 55, 90, 303
  Courage to Grieve, The, 16, 27, 85, 90,
    127, 155, 233, 296, 303, 317
Tedeschi, Richard, 299
TES (traumatic experience scale), 224
therapy, 14, 79-80, 108-9, 111, 142-43,
    216
Thielicke, Helmut, 125
Tolle, Eckhart, 47-48, 131, 155
  Power of Now, The, 47, 131, 155
Tozer, A. W., 260
Tracks of a Fellow Struggler (Claypool),
    84, 136, 154
transcendence, 10, 258
transitional behaviors, 91
  healthy, 92-95
    See also healthy grief
  unhealthy, 95-96
    See also unhealthy grief
traumatic death, 210-11
  issues complicating, 223-26
  types of
    accidental, 211-12
    homicide, 221-23
    physical illness, 213-14
    suicide, 214-18
triggered memories, 44
Tuesdays with Morrie (Albom), 42
twenty-four-hour plan, 46-47

U

unanticipated grief, 102, 105, 105-6
unconscious reactions, 17-18
Understanding Grief (Wolfet), 27, 29,
    85, 118, 155, 233, 274, 296, 317
unfinished business, 9, 192, 225
unhealthy grief
  definition of, 95
  forms of, 98-114
    See also individual forms
  risk factors of, 96-97
  symptoms of, 98-102
unpreparedness, 25-26
up-and-down emotions, 87

V

Vail, Mary Ann, 81
values, 117-18, 270-72, 301, 305
Vickers, Geoffrey, 264
victim behavior, 247
violent deaths (*see also* homicide;
    suicide), 96, 127, 193-94, 199, 206,
    211, 214, 222, 224, 247
Virtues of Aging, The (Carter), 116, 154

W

"Weaving, The," 246
wellness, 67
  expression, 78-83
  physical care, 68
When the Bough Breaks (Bernstein),
    154, 157, 197, 232, 273
wholeness, 12, 300-301, 309-10
widow, 23, 43, 46, 84, 98, 156, 158, 169,
    175-76, 179, 184, 197, 232, 242, 287
Wiersbe, Warren, 246, 260, 274, 296-97,
    301, 317
  God Isn't in a Hurry, 246, 274, 296,
    317
wisdom, 128, 270-71, 300-301, 305-6,
    308

Wolfelt, Alan, 15, 17, 19, 23, 29, 34,
    37-38, 55, 60, 73, 85, 89-90, 116,
    239, 296, 300
  Healing Your Grieving Heart, 73, 85,
    296, 317
  Understanding Grief, 29, 118
World War II, 95, 151
writing. *See* journaling
Writing Down the Bones (Goldberg), 79

Y

Yale School of Medicine, 69
Yancey, Philip, 120, 139, 155
Young, Loretta, 36
young child, loss of a, 196-97
  meanings of, 197-99
  and parental views of death, 209-10
  reactions to, 199-209

Made in the USA
Columbia, SC
13 June 2018